The Politics of Pregnancy:
Policy Dilemmas
in the Maternal-Fetal
Relationship

The Politics of Pregnancy: Policy Dilemmas in the Maternal-Fetal Relationship

Janna C. Merrick
Robert H. Blank
Editors

The Haworth Press, Inc.
New York • London • Norwood (Australia)

The Politics of Pregnancy: Policy Dilemmas in the Maternal-Fetal Relationship has also been published as *Women & Politics*, Volume 13, Numbers 3/4 1993.

The Haworth Press, Inc., 10 Alice Street, Binghamton, NY 13904-1580 USA

Library of Congress-in-Publication Data

The Politics of pregnancy : policy dilemmas in the maternal-fetal relationship / Janna C. Merrick, Robert H. Blank, editors.
     p. cm.
    "Has also been published as Women & politics, volume 13, numbers 3/4, 1993."
    Includes bibliographical references and index.
    ISBN 1-56024-478-X (H : acid-free paper).–ISBN 1-56023-047-9 (HPP : acid-free paper)
    1. Fetus–Legal status, laws, etc.–United States. 2. Pregnant women–Legal status, laws, etc.– United States. I. Merrick, Janna C. II. Blank, Robert H.
KF481.A75P65 1993
346.73′04192–dc20
[347.3064192]
                                     93-5723
                                     CIP

FOR CHRISTOPHER MERRICK

with love, Mom

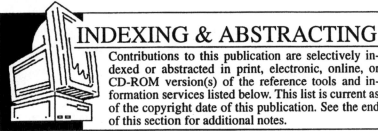

INDEXING & ABSTRACTING

Contributions to this publication are selectively indexed or abstracted in print, electronic, online, or CD-ROM version(s) of the reference tools and information services listed below. This list is current as of the copyright date of this publication. See the end of this section for additional notes.

- *ABC POL SCI: A BIBLIOGRAPHY*, ABC-CLIO, Inc., 130 Cremona Drive, Santa Barbara, CA 93117

- *Academic Abstracts/CD-ROM*, EBSCO Publishing, P.O. Box 2250, Peabody, MA 01960-7250

- *Academic Index (on-line)*, Information Access Company, 362 Lakeside Drive, Foster City, CA 94404

- *America: History and Life*, ABC-CLIO, Inc., 130 Cremona Drive, Santa Barbara, CA 93117

- *Current Contents/Social & Behavioral Sciences*, Institute for Scientific Information, 3501 Market Street, Philadelphia, PA 19104-3302

- *Current Legal Sociology*, International Institute for the Sociology of Law, Ap. 28, 20560 ONATI, GIPUZKOA, Spain

- *Feminist Periodicals: A Current Listing of Contents*, Women's Studies Librarian-at-Large, 728 State Street, 430 Memorial Library, Madison, WI 53706

- *Historical Abstracts*, ABC-CLIO Library, 130 Cremona Drive, Santa Barbara, CA 93117

- *Index to Periodical Articles Related to Law*, University of Texas, 727 East 26th Street, Austin, TX 78705

- *International Political Science Abstracts*, 27 Rue Saint-Guillaume, F-75337 Paris, Cedex 07, France

(continued)

- *Inventory of Marriage and Family Literature (online and hard copy)*, National Council on Family Relations, 3989 Central Avenue NE, Suite 550, Minneapolis, MN 55421

- *Periodical Abstracts, Research I*, UMI Data Courier, P.O. Box 32770, Louisville, KY 40232-2770

- *Periodical Abstracts, Research II*, UMI Data Courier, P.O. Box 32770, Louisville, KY 40232-2770

- *Political Science Abstracts*, IFI/Plenum Data Company, 3202 Kirkwood Highway, Wilmington, DE 19808

- *Public Affairs Information Bulletin (PAIS)*, Public Affairs Information Service, Inc., 521 West 43rd Street, New York, NY 10036-4396

- *Social Planning/Policy & Development Abstracts (SOPODA)*, Sociological Abstracts, Inc., P.O. Box 22206, San Diego, CA 92192-0206

- *Social Sciences Citation Index*, Institute for Scientific Information, 3501 Market Street, Philadelphia, PA 19104

- *Social Work Research & Abstracts*, National Association of Social Workers, 750 First Street NW, 8th Floor, Washington, DC 20002

- *Sociological Abstracts (SA)*, Sociological Abstracts, Inc., P.O. Box 22206, San Diego, CA 92192-0206

- *Studies on Women Abstracts*, Carfax Publishing Company, P.O. Box 25, Abingdon, Oxfordshire OX14 3UE, United Kingdom

- *Urban Affairs Abstracts*, National League of Cities, 1301 Pennsylvania Avenue NW, Washington, DC 20004

- *Women Studies Abstracts*, Rush Publishing Company, P.O. Box 1, Rush, NY 14543

- *Women's Studies Index (indexed comprehensively)*, G.K. Hall & Co., 866 Third Avenue, New York, NY 10022

(continued)

SPECIAL BIBLIOGRAPHIC NOTES

related to special journal issues (separates) and indexing/abstracting

☐ indexing/abstracting services in this list will also cover material in the "separate" that is co-published simultaneously with Haworth's special thematic journal issue or DocuSerial. Indexing/abstracting usually covers material at the article/chapter level.

☐ monographic co-editions are intended for either non-subscribers or libraries which intend to purchase a second copy for their circulating collections.

☐ monographic co-editions are reported to all jobbers/wholesalers/approval plans. The source journal is listed as the "series" to assist the prevention of duplicate purchasing in the same manner utilized for books-in-series.

☐ to facilitate user/access services all indexing/abstracting services are encouraged to utilize the co-indexing entry note indicated at the bottom of the first page of each article/chapter/contribution.

☐ this is intended to assist a library user of any reference tool (whether print, electronic, online, or CD-ROM) to locate the monographic version if the library has purchased this version but not a subscription to the source journal.

☐ individual articles/chapters in any Haworth publication are also available through the Haworth Document Delivery Services (HDDS).

ABOUT THE EDITORS

Janna C. Merrick is Associate Dean for Academic Affairs, University of South Florida at Sarasota and Visiting Scholar, Center for Biomedical Ethics, University of Minnesota School of Medicine. She is a former Visiting Scholar at the Hastings Center. She collaborated with Arthur L. Caplan and Robert H. Blank, in editing *Compelled Compassion: Government Intervention in the Treatment of Critically Ill Newborns* (Humana, 1992). She is currently writing a co-authored book on reproductive rights.

Robert H. Blank is Professor of Political Science at the University of Canterbury in Christchurch, New Zealand. He is the author of numerous books and articles on human reproduction, including *Regulating Reproduction, Mother and Fetus,* and *Fetal Protection in the Workplace*.

The Politics of Pregnancy: Policy Dilemmas in the Maternal-Fetal Relationship

CONTENTS

Acknowledgements

This book is the result of a symposium published by *Women and Politics*. Its purpose is to illustrate the extreme complexity of ethical and policy issues in the maternal-fetal relationship in a time of changing technology and changing values. A number of people have provided much needed input. Michele Hudson and Janet Conwell provided loving care for Janna's son so that she would have the time and energy to devote to this and other projects. Parks Walker provided assistance in too many ways to list here. David Schenck provided substantial professional support so that Janna could complete her work on this project while making transitions from Minnesota to Florida, and from the faculty to administration. Kathy Rutz shepherded the project through The Haworth Press, Inc., and Sidney Walter handled many administrative and editorial tasks for the journal. Our greatest debt, however, is to Janet Clark, whose support and hard work were fundamental in seeing this project through to publication.

Reproductive Technology:
Pregnant Women, the Fetus,
and the Courts

Robert H. Blank

SUMMARY. The maternal-fetal relationship continues to be re-shaped by the changing technological context of prenatal medicine and our expanding knowledge of fetal development. Among other factors, advances in prenatal diagnosis, genetic screening, collaborative conception, and fetal surgery increase empathy for the fetus and heighten concern for the well-being of the fetus. These changes in technology and the courts' responses to them are redefining the notion of responsibility of the pregnant woman for the health of the fetus she decides to carry to term. These trends threaten to further medicalize pregnancy, commodify children, and compromise the autonomy and even the physical integrity of pregnant women.

INTRODUCTION

Many observers who study patterns in tort law have concluded that continued expansion of tort recovery for prenatal injury is leading to the recognition of the fetus as a person (Annas 1982, 17; Lenow 1983, 1). The trend toward abrogating the parental immunity rule and efforts to surmount the practical difficulties of a parent-child suit clearly presage the

Robert H. Blank is affiliated with the Political Science Department at the University of Canterbury, Christchurch, New Zealand.

[Haworth co-indexing entry note]: "Reproductive Technology: Pregnant Women, the Fetus, and the Courts." Blank, Robert H. Co-published simultaneously in *Women & Politics* (The Haworth Press, Inc.) Vol. 13, No. 3/4, 1993, pp. 1-17; and: *The Politics of Pregnancy: Policy Dilemmas in the Maternal-Fetal Relationship* (ed: Janna C. Merrick, and Robert H. Blank) The Haworth Press, Inc., 1993, pp. 1-17. Multiple copies of this article/chapter may be purchased from The Haworth Document Delivery Center [1-800-3-HAWORTH; 9:00 a.m. - 5:00 p.m. (EST)].

1

day when a cause of action by a child against its mother for prenatal injury might be upheld. Furthermore, criminal law has increasingly been used to constrain the choices of pregnant women (Field 1989) or to punish them for their actions which harm the fetuses they are carrying (Balisy 1987; Losco 1989; McNulty 1988). Although these trends are incompatible with a woman's constitutional right to abortion and threaten to contradict her procreative autonomy and bodily integrity, they demonstrate a growing legal concern for the welfare of the unborn and for a right of all children to be born with a sound mind and body.

A major influence on the way the courts, as well as the public, view the maternal-fetal relationship is technology. In fact, one issue that frames all other issues surrounding the potential conflict between the pregnant woman and the fetus centers on societal perceptions of the status of the fetus. Whether dealing with workplace hazards, coerced treatment of pregnant women, or attempts to constrain maternal behavior, the way we view the fetus is critical to our position. It is argued here that rapid advances in biomedical science, as reflected in prenatal diagnosis and therapy, reproduction-aiding techniques such as in vitro fertilization, and a growing array of evermore precise genetic tests are inalterably changing our perceptions of the fetus. In combination with a heightened understanding of fetal development and of the potentially deleterious impact of a broad range of actions of the pregnant woman, these technologies are forcing a reevaluation of maternal responsibility for fetal health. Furthermore, in a culture dominated by a fascination with technology and its ability to "fix" problems, both the public and the courts are often predisposed toward acceptance of a technology without a clear understanding of the broader implications for all the parties. This paper describes recent developments in reproductive technology and explicates the policy issues raised by this current redefinition of the maternal-fetal relationship.

SOCIAL RECOGNITION OF FETUS AS A PERSON

As fetal development proceeds, it brings with it a heightened identification as a human form. In turn, this recognition of humanness inevitably generates a degree of empathy, a perception of possible sharing of experience. According to Grobstein:

> The psychological effect on observers cannot be ignored in discussing status, not only because of the empathy engendered but because it is a forerunner of social recognition and interaction between the developing offspring and others. (1988, 98-99)

Even Baron (1983, 122), who suggests that we are perfectly capable of refusing to grant personhood on the basis of empathy where that status would exact a result we are unwilling to accept, agrees that in close cases the force of empathy may carry the day. Social recognition, in addition to behavioral manifestations and evidence of functional capabilities, is a critical sign that rudiments of personhood might be present.

Until recently, the fetus could not take on social recognition of a human except conceptually. Hidden in the womb, the first evidence of life was the movement detectable to the mother at quickening around the eighteenth week of pregnancy. Even at that stage, however, the evidence was only of some life, not of recognition as a human form. Since the late 1960s, a number of biomedical innovations have significantly altered the perception of the fetus. In combination, these innovations are leading to recognition of human qualities at progressively earlier stages in fetal development. The most obvious dimension of recognition is visualization. Only recently has it become possible to visualize the fetus in utero through sophisticated electronic equipment. As ultrasound technology has advanced to produce more explicit real time images of the fetal limbs and movement, it is not surprising that there has been a tendency to perceive the fetus as a small baby instead of an unseen organism residing in the womb. This tendency is magnified by the "fascination with the fetus" which for some people in our society has become a "status of a veritable object of devotion" (Gallagher 1989, 191).

Ultrasound technology gives evidence of spontaneous fetal movements as early as nine weeks, at least two months before quickening. The most discernible impact of ultrasound on one's perception of the fetus, however, occurs as early as 12 weeks when the fetal image presents miniature yet unmistakable human features. It is not uncommon for women undergoing ultrasound monitoring to refer to their "baby" when discussing the fetus, particularly after they obtain their videotape of the imaging procedure to take home. Some women talk of having "bonded" with the fetus through viewing the image on the screen (Rothman 1986, 113). Petchesky notes that women often express a sense of elation and participation in the ultrasound process, claiming that it "makes the baby more real" and "more our baby."

Visualization of the fetus appears to "create a feeling of intimacy and belonging, as well as a reassuring sense of predictability and control" (1987, 71). Petchesky concludes that rather than be surprised that some women experience this bonding with the fetus after viewing its image, it should be understood as a "culturally embedded component of desire" (1987, 75).

Gallagher sees real dangers in this symbolic development of the fetus as "a token of people's reverence for nature, for natural processes, and for creation itself," that comes from these new means of visualizing the fetus.

> This view of the fetus can foster development of a bizarre and punitive attitude toward pregnant women; whatever their choices. The individual women themselves become invisible or viewed only as vessels–carriers of the infinite more valuable being. (Gallagher 1989, 192)

Moreover, Whitbeck (1988, 50) sees these same problems in the extensive use of electronic fetal monitoring and with magnetic resonance imaging (MRI) as it becomes more commonly used in pregnancy. The very high fixed costs of MRIs increase the pressure on hospitals to use them in pregnancy which represents a "huge potential market" (Whitbeck 1988, 55).

In addition to these diagnostic and monitoring techniques, the capability to determine the sex and other characteristics of a fetus through amniocentesis, and more recently, through chorionic villus sampling as early as the eighth week (Rose 1987, 162), introduces yet another set of human attributes to the fetal identity. The unborn "baby" now takes on the identity of "he" or "she," frequently accompanied by the naming process and preparation for the birth six or seven months in the future.

Fetoscopy, an application of fiber optics that allows direct observation of the fetus, promises even greater potency to "humanize" the fetus. Although fetoscopy is now limited by technical restrictions which enable visualization of only sections of the fetus at a time, observers are able to see minute details of the fetus. Without doubt, this capability accentuates social or at least parental recognition of the fetus as an individual human entity. Although it is questionable at what precise stage the gradual emergence of consciousness and awareness of the fetus will confer on it human status, the appearance of minimal sentience and the possibility of experience of pain and suffering as evidenced by diagnostic technology is critical (Grobstein 1988, 40-41).

Perhaps the most consequential challenges to conventional impressions of the fetus as something "pre-human" are the result of recent successes in fetal surgery. Although corrective prenatal surgery promises some hope for fetuses which otherwise would have been born with severe handicaps or not born at all, it is likely to produce conflict between the right of the woman to her privacy and the right of the fetus to whatever society deems to be proper medical care. King (1980, 190) suggests that "recent research has garnered so much knowledge about the fetus and its environment that we can view the fetus as a 'second patient.'" Should this perception intensify, it would represent a dramatic reversal of the notion that the

woman is the only patient. Petchesky points out, however, that this transformation has already taken place through ultrasound in which the fetus
"is being treated as a patient . . . is being given an ordinary checkup"
(1981: 61). As a 'patient' in its own right, the fetus adopts characteristics
that before were impossible and further diminishes the perceived role and
status of the pregnant woman.

Despite the uncertainties as to whose interests are predominant, the
rapidly evolving advances in a variety of in utero treatments, including
fetal surgery, accentuate a subtle and incremental, but real, shift toward a
recognition of the fetus as an independent self. Although it is not feasible
to speak of the fetus as a fully autonomous person, these technologies
give the fetus broader human characteristics that might lead to a redefinition of parental responsibility to the "unborn" patient. One result of this
progression is to treat the pregnant woman as "clinical material," thus,
"robbing her of her agency and her opportunity to act on behalf of her
baby" (Whitbeck 1988, 51). Another is that the "new technologies help
to establish that gynecologists and obstetricians 'know more' about pregnancy and about women's bodies than do women themselves" (Stanworth 1987, 13).

AN EMERGING MATERNAL DUTY
TO UTILIZE PRENATAL TECHNOLOGIES?

Despite many inconsistencies, recent case law clearly demonstrates a
cause of action against third parties for negligence in informing the parents
about available prenatal diagnostic technologies. Physicians have been
held liable to substantial damage claims for wrongful birth of children
born with defects that would have been identifiable if proper techniques
had been recommended to the parents by the physician. Also, various legal
trends demonstrate that parents are likely to be held liable for prenatal
injury or wrongful death torts in the near future (Blank 1992, 19-123).
Furthermore, as prenatal technologies move from primarily diagnostic in
scope to therapeutic, the courts are even more likely to extend their notions of prenatal injury to include acts of omission as well as acts of
commission. This may well place increased pressure on parents to exercise
responsibility to the unborn child by availing themselves of the rapidly
expanding selection of prenatal diagnostic and treatment technologies. If
they choose not to use technologies recommended by their physician, their
decision is likely to be viewed in the least as "irresponsible," and at the
extreme as criminal. Although both the mother and father might be seen as

having a responsibility, however, it is critical that the risks and constraints will fall exclusively on the woman. The treatments are conducted through her body and thus carry heavy privacy and personal autonomy issues for her alone.

Prenatal Diagnosis

Over the last two decades there has been a continual expansion of the prenatal diagnostic techniques available to women to identify fetal anomalies. Amniocentesis, chorionic villus sampling, and ultrasound have become standard clinical procedures, in some cases before their safety and efficacy have been fully evaluated (Oakley 1987). Although these technologies can enhance a woman's reproductive freedom by providing information that helps her decide how to manage the pregnancy, as with all reproductive technologies, anything that can be done voluntarily can also be coerced. Moreover, coercion can take many forms, from subtle "pressures" to conform to accepted medical practice and the technological imperative, to legally defined duties. For instance, even though a 1984 NIH/FDA report found no clear benefit from routine use of ultrasound, at least one-third of all pregnant women in the U.S. undergo that procedure, with some evidence of substantially higher figures (Petchesky 1987, 66). Even in the absence of legal coercion, then, the culturally imposed sanctions favoring medicalized pregnancies appear strong.

One dilemma surrounding current use of these techniques is that while they give us the ability to reduce the incidence of genetic disease, they do so primarily by eliminating the affected fetus through selective abortion, not by treating the disease. Future developments in gene therapy might shift emphasis toward treatment, but prenatal diagnosis will continue largely to expand maternal choice only to the extent it allows the pregnant woman to terminate the pregnancy of an affected fetus. Thus, it will continue to be a policy issue congruent with abortion.

The dilemma becomes more immediate, however, if therapy is available in conjunction with the diagnosis, for instance in the case of Rh incompatibility. In *Grodin v. Grodin* (301 N.W.2d 869, 1983) a Michigan appellate court recognized the right of a child to sue his or her mother for failure to obtain a pregnancy test. The logic of this ruling implies that a child would also have legal recourse to sue his or her mother for failing to monitor the pregnancy and identify and correct threats to his or her health during gestation. Robertson (1983, 448) points out that, "the issue in such a case would be whether the mother's failure to seek a test was negligent in light of the risks that the test posed to her and the fetus and the probability that the test would uncover a correctable defect." Technically, prenatal diagnosis could be directly mandated by state statute with criminal sanctions for women who fail to comply with the law.

Although Robertson (1983, 449) argues that state authorities could justify such a statute on public health grounds, this seems most unlikely given the absence of any national health insurance which would guarantee access of all pregnant women to such technologies. It would be most unfair and illogical to hold a pregnant woman liable for failing to utilize a medical procedure that she was unable to afford. In addition, other observers argue that the state should never intervene to override the decision of the pregnant woman (see Johnson 1986; McNulty 1988). Field contends that controlling the woman to protect the fetus is both "unwise and unconstitutionally burdens the woman's right to reproduce" (1989, 124). Similarly, Gallagher contends that fetal rights advocates such as Robertson ignore the fact that women possess fundamental rights that preclude the kind and degree of government intervention they propose (1987, 12).

Carrier Screening

Even more problematic is the duty of prospective parents in high-risk groups to be screened for carrier status prior to having children. This involves screening for carriers of particular recessive genetic diseases. Unlike prenatal diagnosis, carrier screening would affect both males and females equally. The primary clinical objective of this type of screening is to identify those individuals who, if mated with another person with that same particular genetic trait, have a 25% chance of having offspring with the disease. Once identified, couples with carrier status can be offered prenatal diagnosis if it is available for that disease or at least be educated as to the risk that they take in having children.

Carrier screening programs have been in effect in many states and localities for Tay-Sachs disease and sickle cell anemia since the early 1970s. The sickle cell programs have been especially controversial because the trait is concentrated in the black population and, unlike Tay-Sachs screening which has always been voluntary, sickle cell screening started out as mandatory in many states. Carrier screening tests for many recessive genetic diseases and even more precise genetic trait markings will be available in the near future. The most rapid developments have been in the area of DNA probes to identify polymorphisms (genetic variations) that mark a particular trait. Following the discovery of such a molecular probe for the Huntington's Disease gene in 1983, efforts have been initiated to identify genetic markers for Alzheimer's Disease, manic depression, malignant melanoma, and a host of other conditions. Out of this research, a gene for cystic fibrosis was found in 1989 (Mark 1989). In addition, considerable attention is being directed to the genetic bases of alcoholism and drug addiction (Holden 1991). The high national priority placed on the Human Genome Initiative ensures that knowledge in this area will heighten demand for even more inclusive testing programs (Blank 1992a).

Ironically, these new capabilities accentuate rather than reduce the policy issues of genetic counseling and screening. When screening leads to aversion or treatment of genetic disease, the issues, though often controversial, are reasonably straightforward. However, when screening involves identifying heightened risk or susceptibility for particular conditions, it is considerably more problematic. As new diagnostic tests and genetic probes emerge, public expectations will intensify and the demand for accessibility to information derived from such efforts will increase. Even though there is considerable phenotypic variance in the expression of genes, in the U.S. culture many persons are likely to perceive a positive gene probe test as an indication of a person's biological destiny (Nelkin and Tancredi 1989). Once the tests become accepted as legitimate by policy makers, it is likely that legislatures and courts will recognize professional standards of care that incorporate them. Legislation in California that requires physicians inform pregnant patients of the availability of alpha-fetoprotein tests (Steinbrook 1986) and similar court pressure involving a variety of prenatal tests attests to the public policy dimensions inherent in these applications.

Collaborative Conception

The new knowledge concerning the transmission of genetic disease, along with the capability to identify carriers of a growing number of deleterious traits, raises another question. Is there a duty of carriers of genetic disease or genes that make their children more susceptible to ill health to either refrain from procreating or utilize collaborative conception technologies such as artificial insemination or ova donation so that these deleterious genes are not transmitted to their offspring? If there is such a duty, where are the lines to be drawn: a genetic disease like Huntington's or sickle cell anemia; a heightened risk for manic depression or alcoholism; or susceptibility to early heart disease?

With current techniques in artificial insemination, cryopreservation, and ova donation, no longer need these individuals necessarily refrain from conception in order to protect their offspring. Now, for instance, if a husband is suspected of carrying a dominant gene for Huntington's Disease, he can use the services of a sperm bank or donor. Although this process eliminates his biological contribution to the child, it also eliminates the 50% risk of transmitting the disease to his progeny. Similarly, if both persons in a couple are identified as carriers of a recessive disease they can: (1) take a 25% chance that a child will have the disease and live with it; (2) undergo prenatal diagnosis if available for that disease and abort the one-in-four fetus that is identified as having the disease; or, (3) use reproductive technology and be content with a healthy child, albeit one which is not genetically both of theirs.

The Fetus as a Patient: In Utero Surgery

Technologies in prenatal diagnostics have given us the capacity to discern an array of fetal defects in utero. The newer generation of prenatal technologies, however, is shifting emphasis to treatment prior to birth. Fetal therapy and surgery, although still in the formative stages, promise to aggrandize concern for the fetus significantly. As we rapidly move from the choice between aborting and carrying to term an identified affected fetus toward surgical treatment of the defect, situations will arise where the benefits to the fetus may outweigh the risks to the mother. Although the interests of the mother in having a healthy child and the fetus are likely to be congruent, in some cases their interests may conflict.

One of the most difficult legal issues to be faced in the near future will be how to balance the rights of the mother and the medical needs of the fetus when they are contradictory. The basic issue here is whether the fetus is a patient separate from its mother in cases where the fetus can be treated either medically or surgically. Prior to recent developments in fetal surgery, the fetus was considered at most a medical patient and certain problems were treated with medicines administered to the mother or directly into the amniotic fluid. Although these procedures required the cooperation of the pregnant woman, they were not as physically intrusive or potentially risky as surgery. The difficulty with fetal surgery is that any treatment of the fetus can be accomplished only by invading the physical integrity and privacy of the woman. She must consent to surgery, not only on her unborn child, but also on herself.

Although many obstetricians prefer to view the mother and fetus as a single biological entity sharing interests which are furthered by proper maternal care during pregnancy, this perception is being altered in light of advances in fetal care which clearly contrast the fetus from its mother for treatment purposes (Harrison et al. 1990). Although medical practitioners often identify the fear of malpractice suits as the prime motivation behind expanded use of these technologies, critics often point to the profit motive and market interests as critical factors driving the expanding use and dissemination of these technologies. Petchesky, for instance, argues that the timing of the proliferation of these techniques in obstetrical practice corresponds to the end of the baby boom and rapid drop in fertility and represents the interests of the profession in developing a new "patient population" to "look at and treat" (1987, 65). Whatever the causes of this expansion, the rapid advances being made in fetal surgery are certain to accentuate potential conflict between maternal interests and the fetus as a patient.

Pressures on the pregnant woman to use available fetal therapies will increase as the techniques are transformed from experimental status to routine therapeutic procedures. Although fetal surgery is now at a primitive stage, and immediate concern focuses on possible harm to the fetus and the mother, rapid advances in instrumentation, technique, and skills will soon lower the risk to fetus and mother and expand substantially the options available for intervening in utero to surgically correct fetal defects. Fletcher (1983) feels that "improvements in fetal therapy will establish a stronger ground to protect the affected fetus' right to life" and that this will collide with the established ground for the woman's right to choice concerning abortion. Ruddick and Wilcox (1982, 11) agree that "fetal therapy, especially lifesaving surgery, would seem to make it easier to respect" the fetal claim to the right to life. While Elias and Annas view forcible medical treatment as "brutish and horrible," they concede:

> (w)hen fetal surgery becomes accepted medical practice, and if the procedure can be done with minimal invasiveness and risk to the mother and significant benefit to the fetus, there is an argument to be made that the woman should not be permitted to reject it. Such rejection of therapy could be considered "fetal abuse" and, at a late stage in pregnancy, "child abuse," and an appropriate court order sought to force treatment. (1983, 811)

One problem with this argument is the danger in our medicalized society that new technologies might be offered to, or even forced upon, pregnant women without adequate proof of benefit. Our dependence on technological fixes, reinforced by a medical community trained in the technological imperative, often gives us a false degree of security as to what medicine can accomplish. Many therapies come into widespread use without adequate assessment as to their risks and benefits. Increasingly, as demand for medical fixes escalates, the line between experimentation and therapy becomes a tenuous one. Arguments that a pregnant woman has a legal duty to use "established" medical procedures, therefore, must be approached critically. We cannot assume that because a procedure is accepted as routine, that the benefit to the fetus warrants state intervention under force of law.

The unique feature of fetal surgery is that it requires violation of the mother's rights of personal autonomy if she does not consent to have the surgery. No new legal problems arise unless the mother refuses to consent, in which case the legal dilemma is agonizing, especially if she desires to carry the fetus to term. Of course, "consent" is a subjective term. Although in theory it requires a free, informed choice, in practice women might legally consent not out of free choice, but instead under powerful cultural expectations of what constitutes a responsible decision. Although her "consent" obviates the legal problem, it raises severe ethical issues. In our society, the status of patient usually carries with it the notion of autonomy. But in these cases, whose rights take precedence, those of the fetus or those of the mother whose body must be "invaded" in order to facilitate the surgery?

Although case law is still emerging in this area, some precedents exist in which the courts have ordered surgical procedures over the objections of the mother solely to provide medical care for her unborn child (see *Jefferson v. Griffin Spaulding Mem. Hosp.*, 274 S.E. 2d 457, Ga.1981; Taft v. Taft, 146 N.E.2d 395, Mass. 1983; *In re: A.C.*, 539 A.2d, 1988, en banc, D.C. Ct.App., April 26, 1990, reversed). Kolder and associates uncovered such a pattern of court-ordered treatment of pregnant women (1987). In a survey of obstetricians in 45 states, the authors found that court orders for Cesarian sections had been obtained in 11 states. Among the 21 cases in which court orders were sought, orders were obtained in 86%. Significantly, the data indicate a greater likelihood of hospitals to seek court orders for minority women. Eighty percent of the women were black, Asian, or Hispanic, and 24% did not speak English as their primary language (Kolder et al. 1987, 1193).

THE TECHNOLOGICAL IMPERATIVE AND PREGNANT WOMEN

The issue of maternal responsibility for fetal health is framed by the broader social value system in the United States. Our great faith in technology and medical knowledge and over-dependence on the technological fix has not only medicalized pregnancy, but created a perfect-child mentality. This is clearly reflected in many courts' acceptance of medical "fact" in cases of forced Cesarean sections, even when "fact" is uncertain and probabilistic. Woliver contends that reproductive technologies often contain hidden policy implications–"they increase medical intervention in women's lives, diminishing women's power over their bodies and babies" (1989, 43). Significantly, the public's view of responsible maternal behavior is shaped by the rapidly changing technological context.

As a result of society's reliance on medical technology, when new "choices" become available to women they rapidly become obligations to make the "right" choice by "choosing" the socially-approved alternative (Hubbard 1990, 156).

> The "right to choose" means very little when women are powerless ... women make their own reproductive choices, but they do not make them just as they please; they do not make them under conditions which they themselves create but under social conditions and constraints which they, as mere individuals, are powerless to change. (Petchesky 1980, 685)

Furthermore, these technologies contribute to the medicalization of reproduction which threatens the freedom and dignity of women in general. By requiring third-party involvement and dependence on medical expertise, new technologies force the woman to surrender her control over procreation. Hubbard (1985, 567) decries the practice of making every pregnancy a medical event and sees it as a result of the economic incentives for physicians to stimulate a new need for their services during pregnancy in light of declining birth rates and increasing interest in midwifery and home birth. Rothman (1986, 114) adds that the new images of the fetus resulting from prenatal technologies are making us aware of the "unborn" as people, "but they do so at the cost of making transparent the mother." Furthermore, diagnostic technologies that pronounce judgments halfway through the pregnancy make extraordinary demands on women to separate themselves from the fetus within.

> The medical status of the fetus as distinct from the woman who is pregnant is becoming a star criterion to judge a woman's behavior before, during, and after pregnancy. It is no longer only our sexuality or marital status which defines us as good woman-mothers; now, we must not smoke or drink or deny medical intervention when we are pregnant, or else we are not acting in the "best interests of the fetus." Meanwhile, obstetricians have authorized themselves to act against the wishes of the pregnant woman if necessary to "protect" the interests of the fetus. (Spallone 1989, 40)

Some feminists rightly argue that women bear most of the risks of any reproductive research and technological application (Corea 1985). The history of human reproduction has been, in large measure, a story of control of women, their fertility, and fecundity by society. This control, whether self-imposed or inflicted by others in a given society, has resulted in a significant loss of freedom to women and their exclusion from many activities including intellectual creativity, waged work, and training for self support (Oakley 1984, 84). Women, it is alleged, have been held hostage to the reproductive needs of society throughout history. The new prenatal technologies in many ways reinforce this condition. As persons whose self-identity and social role have been defined historically in relation to their procreative capacities, then, women have a great deal at stake in questions of reproductive freedom (Ryan 1990, 6).

There is little doubt that the status of women is intimately related to prenatal technologies. Technology is never neutral–it both reflects and shapes social values. Because of women's critical biological role as the bearers of children, any technologies that deal with reproduction affect their social role directly. Moreover, because these technologies focus on the role of women as mothers, they could lead to diminution of other roles. Some feminists argue that too much emphasis is already placed on women as only mothers in this society. Rowland (1985, 39) insists that women must reevaluate this social overstatement of the role of motherhood. "The catchcry 'but women want it' has been sounded over and over again by the medical profession to justify continuing medical advances in this field. Women need to reevaluate just what it is they want and question this justification for turning women into living laboratories."

As Hubbard (1985, 567) cogently states, "The point is that once such a test is available and a woman decides not to use it, if her baby is born with a disability that could have been diagnosed, it is no longer an act of fate but has become her fault." Mies (1987, 334) adds that the emphasis on quality control means for most women a loss of confidence in their own bodies and their childbearing competence. She argues that the social pressure on women to produce perfect children is already enormous today.

CONCLUSIONS: SHAPING REPRODUCTIVE TECHNOLOGIES

Despite the developing patterns in the medical and legal context of the technologies described here, it is important to understand that we can, indeed, shape the boundaries and future directions of reproductive technologies. There is a tendency upon examining the rapidity and scope of technological change to assume that its very momentum is so powerful that it denies society the capacity to manage and direct its development. Although history shows that the ability to control technology is difficult, if society so desires, significant control is possible.

Although technologies transform values and the way we think about things, the relationship between values and technology is reciprocal–values also shape the boundaries of technology. For example, surrogate motherhood became an issue in the 1980s, not because of some dramatic breakthrough in technology, but rather because of an underlying change in the way we think about reproduction. The technique for effectuating surrogate contracts as largely practiced today, donor insemination, has been in existence for over a century, but surrogacy contracts became common only in the last decade after childless couples found adoption difficult. Also contributing to the demand was a reemergence in the last decade of the importance of genetic roots and the attainment of sufficient wealth by young professionals to afford these expensive fertility interventions. Likewise, the acceptance of, or demand for, prenatal diagnosis, genetic screening, and in utero surgery is heightened by the trend toward one- or two-children families. While the "perfect child" mentality has been encouraged by advances in technology, it has also been a powerful force behind the diffusion of the technologies. This quest for the perfect child can be traced to smaller families which, in turn, reflect the changing image of the family brought on by the economic realities of raising children, a concern for population control, and drastically altered lifestyles.

It is also critical to understand that medical advances can be used for many different ends and will affect different persons differently. As Stanworth notes, these technologies are controversial because they "crystallize issues at the heart of contemporary controversies over sexuality, parenthood, reproduction, and the family. . . ." (1987, 18). The ongoing debate over these innovations should rightly focus not on whether they will continue to be developed, but rather on distinguishing acceptable from non-acceptable uses. "The technology is underway, but how we as a species choose to use it, where we allow it to be used, and when we draw limits, are critical issues for all of us, but especially for women" (Harrison 1987, 2).

Although the technologies that allow for the conscious design of children do not necessarily result in the denigration of the role of women or the mandatory invasion of their reproductive privacy, within the context of a social value system sympathetic to that end and without a conscious shaping process, the danger clearly exists. A full policy assessment of these technologies, therefore, requires close attention to their cumulative impact on women as well as to women's actual experiences as reproductive beings (Overall 1987). Given the trends discussed here, however, those persons who firmly reject any notions of fetal interests and, thus, any constraints on pregnant women, are facing a very difficult battle against these advances in medical technology.

Moreover, growing medical evidence demonstrates that many actions by the pregnant woman can be devastating to the developing fetus. Although the U.S. Supreme Court invalidated fetal protection policies in *Automotive Workers v. Johnson Controls* (No. 89-1215, 1991), the issue of harm to the fetus through exposure to workplace hazards by either the mother or father will continue to be debated as will issues of maternal (or paternal) substance abuse and other actions that might be harmful to the fetus. These data become increasingly convincing evidence of proximate cause in prenatal injury or wrongful death torts and of negligence or even abuse in criminal cases. Unless legislatures act to protect women from liability or prosecution for alleged injury to the fetus, case law with its emphasis on the facts presented by the parties to each particular case is likely to further constrain or punish high-risk actions of pregnant women. To date, legislatures have been hesitant to take such policy initiatives, thus abdicating this responsibility to the courts.

Through efforts to protect the interests of the unborn child and to deter harmful parental behavior, there is an increasing danger of compromising the autonomy and even the physical integrity of pregnant women. The rapid diffusion of these technologies and their acceptance by society is creating an environment in which the courts might be tempted to adopt very stringent standards of care for pregnant women–standards that not only dictate life-style choice during pregnancy, but also mandate use of prenatal diagnostic tests, genetic screening, and any other appropriate medical innovations. Although counteraction of these potent legal and medical developments in order to reshape and direct the use of these technologies is yet possible, political action must be effectively taken before these initial patterns become entrenched in the value system and legal policy.

REFERENCES

Annas, George J. 1982. "Forced Cesarians: The Most Unkindest Cut of All." *Hastings Center Report* 12(3): 16-17, 45.

Arditti, Rita. 1985. "Review Essay: Reducing Women to Matter." *Women's Studies International Forum* 8(6): 577-582.

Baron, Charles H. 1983. "The Concept of Person in the Law." In A. Edward Doudera and Margery W. Shaw, eds., *Defining Human Life.* Ann Arbor: Health Administration Press.

Blank, Robert H. 1992. *Mother and Fetus: Changing Notions of Maternal Responsibility.* Westport, Conn.: Greenwood Press.

_____ 1992b. "Politics and Genetic Engineering." *Politics and the Life Sciences* 10(2): 81-85.

Corea, Gena. 1985. *The Hidden Malpractice: How American Medicine Mistreats Women*. 2nd ed. New York: Harper & Row.

Elias, Sherman and George J. Annas. 1983. "Perspectives on Fetal Surgery." *American Journal of Obstetrics and Gynecology* 145: 807-812.

Field, Martha A. 1989. "Controlling the Woman to Protect the Fetus." *Law, Medicine and Health Care* 17(2): 114-129.

Fletcher, John C. 1983. "Emerging Ethical Issues in Fetal Therapy." In Kare Berg and Knut E. Tranoy, eds., *Research Ethics*. New York: Alan R. Liss, Inc.

Gallagher, Janet. 1987. "Prenatal Invasions and Interventions: What's Wrong with Fetal Rights?" *Harvard Women's Law Journal* 10: 9-58.

_____ 1989. "Fetus as Patient." In Sherrill Cohen and Nadine Taub, eds., *Reproductive Laws for the 1990s*. Clifton, NJ: Humana Press.

Grobstein, Clifford. 1988. *Science and the Unborn: Choosing Human Futures*. New York: Basic Books.

Harrison, Michelle. 1987. "Women as Breeders: Ethical and Racial Issues." *News for Women in Psychiatry* 5(4): 1-2.

Harrison, Michael R., N. Scott Adzick, Michael Longaker et al. 1990. "Successful Repair In Utero of a Fetal Diaphragmatic Hernia After Removal of Herniated Viscera from the Left Thorax." *The New England Journal of Medicine* 322(22): 1582-1584.

Holden, Constance. 1991. "Probing the Complex Genetics of Alcoholism." *Science* 251: 336-337.

Hubbard, Ruth. 1985. "Prenatal Diagnosis and Eugenic Ideology." *Women's Studies International Forum* 8(6): 567-576.

_____ 1990. *The Politics of Women's Biology*. New Brunswick: Rutgers University Press.

Johnsen, Dawn. 1986. "The Creation of Fetal Rights: Conflicts with Women's Constitutional Rights to Liberty, Privacy, and Equal Protection." *Yale Law Journal* 95: 599-625.

King, Patricia A. 1980. "The Juridical Status of the Fetus: A Proposal for the Protection of the Unborn." In C.E. Schneider and M.A. Vinovskis, eds., *The Law and Politics of Abortion*. Lexington, Mass.: Lexington Books.

Kolder, V.E.B., Janet Gallagher, and M.T. Parsons. 1987. "Court-Ordered Obstetrical Interventions." *New England Journal of Medicine* 316 (19): 1192-1196.

Lenow, Jeffrey L. 1983. "The Fetus as a Patient: Emerging Rights as a Person?" American Journal of Law and Medicine 9(1): 1-29.

Losco, Joseph. 1989. "Fetal Abuse: An Exploration of Emerging Philosophic, Legal, and Policy Issues." *Western Political Quarterly* 42(2): 265-286.

Marx, Jean L. 1989. "The Cystic Fibrosis Gene is Found." *Science* 245: 923-925.

McNulty, Molly. 1988. "Pregnancy Police: The Health Policy and Legal Implications of Punishing Pregnant Women for Harm to their Fetuses." *Review of Law and Social Change* 16: 277-319.

Mies, Maria. 1987. "Sexist and Racist Implications of New Reproductive Technologies." *Alternatives* 12: 323-342.

Nelkin, Dorothy, and L. Tancredi. 1989. *Dangerous Diagnostics: The Social Power of Biological Information.* New York: Basic Books.

Oakley, Ann. 1984. *The Captured Womb: A History of Medical Care of Pregnant Women.* Oxford: Oxford University Press.

———. 1987. "From Walking Wombs to Test-Tube Babies." In Michelle Stanworth, ed., *Reproductive Technologies: Gender, Motherhood, and Medicine.* Minneapolis: University of Minnesota Press.

Overall, Christine. 1987. *Ethics and Human Reproduction: A Feminist Analysis.* Boston: Allen and Unwin.

Petchesky, Rosiland. 1980. "Reproductive Freedom: Beyond a Woman's Right to Choose." *Signs: Journal of Women in Culture and Society.* 5: 661-685.

———. 1987. "Foetal Images: The Power of Visual Culture in the Politics of Reproduction." In Michelle Stanworth, ed., *Reproductive Technologies: Gender, Motherhood, and Medicine.* Minneapolis: University of Minnesota Press.

Robertson, John, A. 1983. "Procreative Liberty and the Control of Conception, Pregnancy, and Childbirth." *Virginia Law Review* 69(3): 405-464.

Rose, Hilary. 1987. "Victorian Values in the Test-Tube: The Politics of Reproductive Science and Technology." In Michelle Stanworth, ed., *Reproductive Technologies: Gender, Motherhood, and Medicine.* Minneapolis: University of Minnesota Press.

Rothman, Barbara Katz. 1986. *The Tentative Pregnancy: Prenatal Diagnosis and the Future of Motherhood.* New York: Viking.

Rowland, Robin. 1985. Quoted *New Birth Technologies.* Wellington, New Zealand: Law Reform Commission, Department of Justice.

Ruddick, W., and W. Wilcox. 1982. "Operating on the Fetus." *Hastings Center Report* 12(5): 10-14.

Ryan, Maura A. 1990. "The Argument for Unlimited Procreative Liberty: A Feminist Critique." *Hastings Center Report* 20(4): 6-12.

Spallone, Patricia. 1989. *Beyond Conception: The Politics of Reproduction.* Granby, MA: Bergin and Garvey Pubs.

Stanworth, Michelle. 1987. "Reproductive Technologies and the Deconstruction of Motherhood." In Michelle Stanworth, ed., *Reproductive Technologies: Gender, Motherhood, and Medicine.* Minneapolis: University of Minnesota Press.

Steinbrook, R. 1986. "In California, Voluntary Mass Prenatal Screening." *Hastings Center Report* 16 (5): 5-7.

Whitbeck, Caroline. 1988. "Fetal Imaging and Fetal Monitoring: Finding the Ethical Issues." In Elaine Hoffman Baruch, Amadeo F. D'Amano, Jr., and Joni Seager, eds., *Embryos, Ethics, and Women's Rights: Exploring New Reproductive Technologies.* New York: The Haworth Press, Inc.

Woliver, Laura R. 1989. "New Reproductive Technologies: Challenges to Women's Control of Gestation and Birth." In Robert H. Blank and Miriam K. Mills, eds., *Biomedical Technology and Public Policy.* Westport, CT: Greenwood Press.

The Moral Permissibility
of *In Utero* Experimentation

Bambi E. S. Robinson

SUMMARY. In this paper the argument is made that *in utero* experimentation which results in abortion is permissible. The discussion then turns to some troubling questions raised by this sort of research. Chief among these are questions concerning limitations placed on the autonomy of the women involved. The argument is made that women ought not change their minds regarding abortion once research has begun. Other issues discussed include objecting to this sort of research on the grounds that it presents a harm to the fetus and whether programs of *in utero* research condone the practice of abortion.

INTRODUCTION

Much attention has been focused in recent years on the question of the moral permissibility of fetal tissue research, i.e., research done on the tissue of aborted fetuses. Much has been said in favor of this practice which may produce such benefits as a cure for Parkinson's Disease or diabetes. Such research is done *ex utero,* i.e., after the fetus has been removed from the uterus.

An area of research which has received less attention is that of *in utero* fetal research, i.e., research done on the fetus in the womb prior to an

---

Bambi E. S. Robinson is affiliated with the Department of Philosophy at Southeast Missouri State University.

[Haworth co-indexing entry note]: "The Moral Permissibility of *In Utero* Experimentation." Robinson, Bambi E. S. Co-published simultaneously in *Women & Politics* (The Haworth Press, Inc.) Vol. 13, No. 3/4, 1993, pp. 19-30; and: *The Politics of Pregnancy: Policy Dilemmas in the Maternal-Fetal Relationship* (ed: Janna C. Merrick, and Robert H. Blank) The Haworth Press, Inc., 1993, pp. 19-30. Multiple copies of this article/chapter may be purchased from The Haworth Document Delivery Center [1-800-3-HAWORTH; 9:00 a.m. - 5:00 p.m. (EST)].

abortion. This sort of research allows researchers to perfect and practice diagnostic techniques such as fetoscopy, chorionic villus biopsy and amniocentesis without risking injury or death to a wanted fetus. Another type of *in utero* research involves injecting substances, such as a rubella vaccine, into a woman prior to an abortion, then examining the aborted fetus to determine if this substance is able to cross the placenta and enter the fetus.

Richard Wasserstrom (Wasserstrom 1975) is one of a very few authors who have turned their attention from the question of fetal tissue research to that of *in utero* research. He objects to it on the grounds that it limits the autonomy of the women involved. This objection will be addressed below.

This paper will address the question of *in utero* experimentation. It will be argued that such research is morally permissible[1] and that once the research has begun, the woman involved may not change her mind regarding the intended abortion.

RUBELLA EXPERIMENT

The placenta normally acts as a barrier to keep substances in the woman's body from entering the fetus and possibly causing it damage. The placenta is not a perfect barrier; sometimes substances harmful to the fetus cross it with devastating results. One such substance is the rubella, or German Measles, virus. If a woman contracts rubella within the first two months of pregnancy, the resulting baby is likely to suffer from a number of defects, including cataracts, congestive heart failure, low birth weight, feeding difficulty, deafness and/or retardation (Cooper et al. 1969, 18).

One way to prevent these defects from occurring would be to vaccinate all women of child bearing age with a rubella vaccine. Once vaccinated, the women would not contract rubella and any developing fetuses or future fetuses would be safe from the devastation of rubella.

Or would they? The rubella vaccine is a live, attenuated virus, i.e., it consists of live viruses which are treated so as to be less virulent than the normal rubella virus. We know that the rubella virus can cross the placental barrier and infect the fetus. Studies vary in the percent of exposed fetuses which are harmed by exposure to rubella. The percentage of abnormality ranges from 10% to 100%. All studies showed that the earlier in the pregnancy the fetus is exposed, the greater the amount of harm that is caused (Cooper et al. 1969, 18). Could the same thing occur with the less virulent form of the virus found in the vaccine?

Faced with such a question, physicians have several options. First, they could restrict the vaccine to males, pre-pubescent girls and post-menopausal women on the grounds that they are ignorant of the possible effects of the virus and thus will not risk the possibility of deliberate harm to a fetus. It would be better that the mother and fetus take their chances with the disease. Second, they could inject newly pregnant women with the vaccine and study the resulting babies for signs of harm. This has the disadvantage of producing children with defects should the virus in the vaccine cross the placenta. Third, physicians could use *in utero* experimentation. They could inject women scheduled for abortions with the vaccine, wait a day or so to give the virus time to cross the placenta, perform the abortions, then study the fetal remains for signs of the rubella virus. This has the advantage of erasing medicine's ignorance as to whether or not the virus in the vaccine can cross the placenta without the risk of doing harm to a fetus that will be brought to term.

This latter approach was the approach taken by a number of researchers (Alford et al. 1964; Bolognese et al. 1971; Chin et al. 1971; Larson et al. 1971; Vaheri et al. 1969; Vaheri et al. 1972). They discovered that the virus in the rubella vaccine infects the placenta approximately 25% of the time. In some cases, the fetus is infected. Thus physicians were able to recommend that any woman of childbearing years should not be pregnant when vaccinated and should follow a reliable program of birth control for two months following vaccination.[2]

BENEFITS OF IN UTERO EXPERIMENTATION

What reasons can be given for proceeding with this type of research? The main arguments for supporting *in utero* experimentation cite the benefits it brings women and developing fetuses.

As discussed earlier, it was this sort of research that showed physicians that the virus of the rubella vaccine can infect the developing fetus. Some would argue that in cases such as this, we should rely on animal experimentation for answers. However, what is true of animals is not necessarily true of humans. This experiment was done on monkeys prior to being done on humans, and in those experiments there was no evidence that the virus crossed the placenta. In humans, however, the virus has been found to cross the placental barrier. In all areas of medical research, there comes a point at which the drugs or techniques which are to be used on humans must be tried on humans. It is advantageous to fetuses which will be brought to term for us to know which drugs, both harmful and helpful, can cross the placental barrier.

The *in utero* research which has been done has reaped enormous benefits for pregnant women. *In utero* testing was key in the development and perfection of amniocentesis. This diagnostic technique allows physicians to sample the amniotic fluid surrounding the fetus for various defects such as Down's Syndrome. This is routinely done to pregnant women in their thirties: a group at risk for "defective" babies and a rapidly growing segment of the population of mothers. Developing and testing diagnostic techniques such as this have allowed women to choose an abortion should they wish. It also reassures countless women that their babies are "normal."

In utero research was also used to test the efficacy and safety of chorionic villus sampling (CVS). With CVS, the physician removes part of the chorion frondosum, a villous part of the embryonic membrane that enters the developing placenta. As these cells are genetically identical to the fetal cells, they can be tested to determine whether or not the fetus has certain genetic disorders. CVS is usually done between nine and eleven weeks of gestation, which is earlier than amniocentesis is performed (Fletcher and Schulman 1985, 9).

The development of this procedure, like amniocentesis, has reassured countless women that their babies will be "normal." It also allows those whose fetuses are discovered to have a genetic defect to choose abortions if they wish. Those who do not choose to abort are given time to come to terms with raising a child with disabilities.

Additionally, some conditions may be correctable *in utero,* but only if they are discovered. Erythromycin can cure syphilis, but there were questions as to whether it would cross the placenta in sufficient concentrations to prevent congenital syphilis. *In utero* research was done which determined that not only erythromycin, but also clindamycin, both of which are alternatives to penicillin, can cross the placenta and enter the fetus. Thus congenital syphilis can be prevented in fetuses (Philipson et al. 1973).

The benefits of this research are enormous and affect women everywhere, which is good reason to proceed with it. Yet not everyone believes this sort of research is permissible. The next sections will discuss possible problems for the practice of *in utero* experimentation.

PROBLEM OF AUTONOMY

In utero experimentation such as that done with the rubella vaccine raises some troubling questions. Chief among these are questions concerning moral limitations placed on the autonomy of the women involved (Wasserstrom 1975, 22).

When women have abortions, a small percentage of them change their minds regarding the abortion just before the abortion procedure begins. If the woman changes her mind after an experiment on her fetus has begun, the chances are increased that the resulting child will be harmed. It seems unfair to the child, as well as to its parents and society on whom it may be a burden, to bring into the world a child whose disabilities or defects could have been prevented just by the mother not receiving a drug. After all, if she had not participated in the experiment, the developing fetus would not have been exposed to the harmful substance.[3]

The question to be asked, then, is: "Should the woman be permitted to change her mind regarding the abortion after the experiment has begun?" If we answer "yes," then we preserve the woman's autonomy at the cost of the possibility of severe harm to her child. If we answer "no," then we place limitations on the woman's autonomy in order to prevent a possible harm to her child. Thus the question is part of a larger issue: Should personal autonomy be limited when there is a very real possibility of harm to another person? The answer is that it should.

It is generally accepted that personal autonomy is not limitless. Even people who place high values on things such as freedom of speech will admit that limits must be placed on what can be said, e.g., it is wrong to yell "Fire!" in a crowded theater. Autonomy is generally limited when complete autonomy threatens the well being of others. In such cases, autonomy is limited just to the extent necessary to prevent harm to others.

In addition, it should be recognized that in the case of *in utero* experimentation, the woman is freely choosing to limit her own autonomy. Self-imposed limitations on autonomy are less problematic than those imposed either by others or by the constraints of morality. In limiting her own autonomy, the woman is, in effect, saying: "I am currently an autonomous being and I am freely choosing a course of action which I understand will limit my options in the future. I understand that I am now freely making a morally irrevocable decision."

This is, after all, not so different from what happens during any abortion. In any abortion, there is a point of no return, generally once the procedure has begun, after which the woman cannot change her mind. In cases of *in utero* experimentation, the point just comes sooner. In both cases, even if the fetus were to survive, it would likely have suffered great harm needlessly, and so the decision should be irrevocable.

Thus the simple answer to the question of limitations on a woman's autonomy is that it must be limited since to do otherwise will harm a potential being. She is not morally permitted to change her mind regarding the abortion once she has begun participation in the experiment.

Yet some people might see the simple answer as unsatisfactory. This solution can be viewed as an affront to the notion of informed consent.

One part of informed consent is that a research subject, who has been apprised of the nature of the study and the risks it entails, may withdraw from the experiment at any time. A woman who must have an abortion during the research to prevent harm to the fetus is not given this option.

Yet *in utero* research is different from most medical experiments. In most medical experiments, the participants freely take on the risks *for themselves* and since they are the ones who may be harmed, they may choose to stay or withdraw as they wish. With *in utero* experimentation, the woman is not assuming a great risk for herself: the being which is subject to harm is the fetus which will likely develop into a child with deformities. Thus the woman may not be permitted to withdraw since this may result in a baby who was needlessly deformed. In order to uphold the spirit of informed consent as much as possible, the woman must be told of the nature of the experiment, and a special emphasis should be placed on the risks to the fetus so that she enters the experiment with the understanding that withdrawal is not permitted once the experiment has begun.

HARM TO FETUS

Other people may object to the entire idea of *in utero* experimentation on the grounds that the experiment itself is a harm to the fetus. If the experiment is a harm to the fetus and we ought not allow harm to occur to a being, then it follows that we ought not allow this sort of experiment to occur.

The reasoning that might be used to show that an experiment such as a rubella experiment is a harm is as follows. If an action is done to a person now that will cause harm to that person in the future, then we can claim that the harm is done *now*. Thus if an evil and malicious person infects someone with the AIDS virus, he harms her now even though she will not manifest the problems associated with AIDS for several years to come. Analogously, if an act harms an infant and that act was done at 8 weeks or so of pregnancy, then that act harms the fetus at the time the act was done.

This reasoning, however, is incorrect in one crucial respect: it rests on a bad analogy. The analogy should not be made to someone who will face unfortunate consequences down the road, but to someone with a terminal condition who agrees to undergo medical experimentation (e.g., the testing of new drugs or treatments) that will not benefit him. Such experimentation cannot be done to a normal healthy person because of the possible adverse consequences of the experiment. The experiment can be done to someone with a terminal condition, however, because it will make no difference to the quality of life.

If someone is given the AIDS virus now, she can only really call it harm because of its eventual effects. If she gets it, knowing she will die tomorrow of some other unfortunate condition, it is annoying, but not the harm it would be to one who has the expectation of a happy life. The only real sense in which it is a harm to her now, given her certain death, is the brief pain of the injection and possible feelings of invasion of privacy.

Similar reasoning applies to a fetus which will be aborted. It is true that researchers found evidence of the rubella virus in the fetus after the woman was injected with the vaccine; however, the effects of rubella do not manifest themselves until late in pregnancy and after birth. Until then, the virus is merely a time-bomb, ticking quietly away. When an abortion is performed, the deformities which accompany rubella have not occurred, so there is no real harm to the fetus. There is only the potential for harm which is kept from becoming actual by the abortion.

Is there another sense in which the fetus is harmed? Is it aware of the virus entering its body? Can it reflect on any pain associated with the experiment? It seems quite doubtful. The best guess of when a fetus becomes a thinking, conscious being (although of what, no one knows) is between 19 and 30 weeks of gestation when the most rapid physical and electrical development of the fetal brain occurs (Martyn 1989, 237). Experimentation is done on fetuses typically between 8 and 12 weeks of gestation. Thus the fetus is most likely unaware of any pain that happens, if indeed it feels pain. This is especially true as it is the woman who receives the injection; the fetus gets the rubella virus mixed in with the material that naturally crosses the placenta. Also, the fetus certainly cannot reflect on what is happening as the virus enters its body.[4]

The fetus will be aborted prior to the manifestation of rubella complications and is unaware of what has happened, so it cannot dread the possibilities of future harm. In what sense, then, is it actually harmed? None that this author can make sense of.

It might seem strange to worry about the research harming a fetus when its ultimate fate is abortion. After all, it would seem that being killed is a terrible harm to befall a person. Thus, the above argument would seem to show that abortion is morally impermissible.

This line of reasoning, however, assumes that the fetus is a person, i.e., a being possessing the full complement of moral rights.[5] While a discussion of the moral status of the fetus is beyond the scope of this paper, the philosophical literature is replete with arguments showing that fetuses of the ages of those involved in the experiments are not persons.[6]

To harm something by killing it, its right to life must be violated or it must suffer. As shown above, fetuses of the age involved in the research do not yet possess a right to life and do not suffer other types of harm. Thus abortion is not a harm to the fetus. Without the occurrence of actual harm to the fetus, one cannot object to *in utero* research on those grounds. The fetus is only actually harmed if it is carried to term and, as argued above, once the experiment has begun, the abortion must be done.

APPEARS TO CONDONE ABORTION

Another problem facing programs of *in utero* research is that this type of research may appear to condone abortion. After all, abortions are an integral part of this type of research.

There is confusion, however, underlying this general objection. Two issues are being conflated. The first is the permissibility of research done from abortions performed for the purpose of family planning. The second is the permissibility of research done from abortions performed solely for the purpose of participating in the research. The latter is more problematic than the former, but is not the issue. If *in utero* research involved persuading women to have abortions purely for the sake of the research, then it would seem to condone abortion.

However, roughly 1 1/2 million abortions are performed annually in the United States for the purposes of ending an unwanted pregnancy. With this large number of abortions, there is no need to persuade women to have abortions purely for the sake of the experiment. There is only the problem of finding those women who, in addition to wanting an abortion, would also be willing to participate in a medical experiment.

With regards to research done from family planning abortions, however, the accusation is made not just that the researcher condones the abortion, but that she is complicit in the abortion. In discussing the issue of fetal tissue research, James Burtchaell argues that the researcher is an accomplice to the act of abortion because she enters into a supportive alliance with the evil lying behind the benefit of her research (Burtchaell 1988, 7-11).

While it is true that the researcher derives benefit from the abortion–her whole program depends on the abortion being carried out–she does not have to support it. She may, instead, view all abortion as morally wrong, yet try to get some good out of it. The research she is doing has the potential to help many future fetuses who will be brought to term that might otherwise be harmed without knowledge derived from this research.

The researcher is not soliciting women to have abortions for the purpose of her research. She is finding–most likely through a proxy who works in a hospital or abortion clinic–women who will have abortions for personal reasons and then using them in her research. But the abortion will occur regardless of her research.

Burtchaell's approach to complicity assumes that researchers necessarily applaud the underlying act of abortion. But the researcher can benefit from what the abortionist does without approving of what he does. Thus the researcher is not complicit in the act of abortion; she is merely deriving a benefit from it, and this is not morally impermissible.

Analogous events occur in other facets of our lives fairly frequently. For example, Beth may see that her boss is about to be fired without just cause: a wrongful act is about to occur. It is not wrong for Beth to work to excel in the eyes of those who will fire her boss so that when a replacement is sought, it's she. Here, Beth is deriving a benefit from an act that would occur regardless of her actions or benefits to her. She does not have to approve of her boss getting fired, but she is not complicit in it if she derives a benefit from it.

Furthermore, as John Robertson notes in discussing fetal tissue research, even if the researcher were an accomplice, complicity is not a great problem when the act making the benefit possible–abortion–is legal and when it is far from clear that the act is morally wrong (Robertson 1985, 6).

NAZI EXPERIMENTATION

There is yet another objection that could be raised to the use of fetuses in research: it seems akin to the research carried out by the Nazi doctors in concentration camps during World War II. On this line of argumentation, both Nazi doctors and present day doctors involved in fetal research have used living humans in their experiments. The Nazi experiments are universally condemned, in part because of the hideous nature of the suffering and deaths inflicted on people who did not consent to the experiment but who were slated to die. Thus, it can be argued, *in utero* experiments on fetuses which are to be aborted should be universally condemned.

There are, however, significant differences between the subjects of the Nazi experiments and the subjects of *in utero* experiments. The people involved in the Nazi experiments were fully conscious and aware children and adults. Due to the sadistic nature of the experiments and experimenters, little, if any, anesthesia was used and subjects were frequently told of the experiments and of their eventual demise. Thus, not only did the people involved experience great physical pain, they were also made to experience great psychological pain.

Fetuses, however, are quite different from children and adults. As discussed above, even if the experiments were painful (which they generally are not), as best as can be determined, fetuses in the early stages of development are unable to feel pain. Even if there were to be pain during the experiment, the fetus is unable to dread it, and thus cannot be harmed psychologically.

Morally, fetuses are in a different category than children and adults. While a discussion of the moral status of the fetus is beyond the scope of this paper, as indicated above, the philosophical literature is replete with arguments showing that fetuses of the ages of those involved in the experiments lack full moral status, i.e., do not possess the moral rights of children and adults.

Present day experimenters are not committing atrocities as did Nazi researchers. The women who are involved are willing volunteers and are willing to accept any pain which may be involved. The fetuses rarely, if ever, experience pain and cannot anticipate or dread anything which might befall them. Finally, fetuses do not have the same moral status as the subjects of the Nazi experiments. Thus there are no grounds on which to argue that *in utero* experimentation is an atrocity in the manner of the Nazi experiments.

ENFORCING THE OBLIGATION TO ABORT

There remains one last problem to confront–this time a practical one. How are the doctors to enforce the moral policy that women may not change their minds? There seems to be something wrong with the picture of a doctor strapping his patient kicking and screaming to the table and performing an abortion. (Not only would this be morally wrong, but it would also be a clear case of assault and thus legally wrong.)

Two things can be done to prevent this sort of situation from occurring. First, restrict participation to women who have already had an abortion. One reason women may back out of a scheduled abortion is that they do not realize until just before the procedure begins what it would be like. They do not realize until then that they cannot go through with the abortion. A woman who already has undergone an abortion knows what she is getting into. Secondly, a counselor should talk with the woman at great length about the nature of the experiment and discuss that, because of the risk involved, she is not morally permitted to change her mind regarding the abortion. If the woman is forced to "sleep on it" for a day or so, she has time to think through her decision to participate in the experiment.

Another factor to consider is that the percentage of women who change their minds regarding abortion is small. Planned Parenthood of Des

Moines, Iowa, estimates that while one in five women who schedules an appointment for abortion fails to show up, of those who do show up, the group from which research subjects are drawn, only one in 500 women changes her mind just prior to the abortion. The experiments which have been done typically have used only a few women–between 3 and 35–so it is unlikely that the women volunteering for the experiment will be some of the reluctant few I discussed above even if they were having abortions for the first time.

Given that there are women who are willing to participate in medical research to benefit others, and that this research has already proven to be of enormous value, the practice of *in utero* research should continue.

NOTES

1. Throughout this paper, "permissible" is always to be understood to mean 'morally permissible' and "obligation" is always to be understood as 'moral obligation.' The author is a philosopher working in ethics and makes no claims about legal permissibility or legal obligation. Unless explicitly stated otherwise, this paper is only about moral concerns.

2. Such research was quite legal in the days before *Roe v. Wade*. Abortion was legal in some sates, such as New York, prior to the passage of *Roe v. Wade*. Other states permitted therapeutic abortions. The research was also done in other countries.

3. None of this should be taken to mean that I advocate the killing of disabled persons after they are born. I am merely arguing that it is wrong to take actions which we know will cause people to be born with disabilities.

4. Although researchers and physicians do not know exactly when the brain is sufficiently developed to feel pain, it follows from this argument that experiments should be limited to the first 18 weeks of gestation so that the fetus is not subjected to unnecessary pain.

5. It should be noted that the word "person" is being used in its philosophical sense. "Person" is not being equated with "human" as is mistakenly done by members of the right to life movement.

6. Those who are interested in a survey of the philosophical literature and arguments on abortion might start with Michael Tooley. 1983. *Abortion and Infanticide.* Oxford and New York: Oxford University Press.

REFERENCES

Alford, Charles A. et al. 1964 "Virologic and Serologic Studies on Human Products of Conception after Maternal Rubella." *The New England Journal of Medicine* 271:1275-81

Bolognese, Ronald J. et al. 1972 "Rubella Vaccination During Pregnancy." *American Journal of Obstetrics and Gynecology* 11:903-7

Burtchaell, James. 1988 "Case Study: University Policy on Experimental Use of Aborted Fetal Tissue." *IRB: A Review of Human Subjects Research* 10:7-11

Chin, James et al. 1971 "Avoidance of Rubella Immunization of Women During or Shortly After Pregnancy." *JAMA* 215:632-34

Cooper, Louis Z. et al. 1969 "Rubella Clinical Manifestations and Management." *American Journal of Diseases in Children* 118:18-29

Fletcher, John C. and Joseph D. Schulman. 1985 "Fetal Research: The State of the Question." *Hastings Center Report,* 28:6-12

Larson, H. Elliot et al. 1971 "Transmission of Attenuated Rubella Vaccines to the Human Fetus." *The New England Journal of Medicine* 284:870-3

Martyn, Ken. 1989 "Technological Advances and Roe v Wade: The Need to Rethink Abortion Law." in Tom Beauchamp and LeRoy Walters, eds. *Contemporary Issues in Bioethics* Wadsworth, Belmont CA

Philipson, Agneta, L.D. Sabath, and David Charles. 1973 "Transplacental Passage of Erythromycin and Clindamycin." *New England Journal of Medicine* 288:1219-1221

Robertson, John A. 1988 "Rights, Symbolism, and Public Policy in Fetal Tissue Transplants." *Hastings Center Report* 28:5-12

Tooley, Michael. 1983. *Abortion and Infanticide* Oxford and New York: Oxford University Press.

Vaheri, Antti et al. 1972 "Isolation of Attenuated Rubella-Vaccine Virus from the Human Products of Conception and Uterine Cervix." *The New England Journal of Medicine* 286:1071-74

Vaheri, Antti et al. 1969 "Transmission of Attenuated Rubella Vaccines to the Human Fetus." *American Journal of Diseases in Children* 118:243-46

Wasserstrom, Richard. 1975 "The Status of the Fetus." *Hastings Center Report* 18-22

Good, Bad, and Captive Samaritans: Adding-In Pregnancy and Consent to the Abortion Debate

Eileen L. McDonagh

SUMMARY. This paper adds-in pregnancy and consent to the abortion debate in the context of good samaritan arguments initiated by Judith Jarvis Thomson. Drawing upon legal and medical definitions, the abortion issue is reframed as the right of a woman to consent to what will be done to her body by the fetus rather than her right merely to choose what to do with her own body. This argument shifts abortion rights from the right to decisional autonomy established in *Roe* to the right to bodily integrity affirmed by samaritan case law. As a result, we see why women who are pregnant without their consent, in effect, are captive samaritans, a status unsubstantiated by either legislative statutes or legal precedents. Recasting abortion as a response to nonconsensual pregnancy opens new grounds guaranteeing women's reproductive rights.

INTRODUCTION

Over 20 years ago Judith Jarvis Thomson published her provocative argument claiming abortion rights were analogous to good samaritan cases.[1] In her abstract scenario, a person woke up one morning and found

Eileen L. McDonagh is affiliated with the Murray Research Center at Radcliffe College and Northeastern University.

[Haworth co-indexing entry note]: "Good, Bad, and Captive Samaritans: Adding-In Pregnancy and Consent to the Abortion Debate." McDonagh, Eileen L. Co-published simultaneously in *Women & Politics* (The Haworth Press, Inc.) Vol. 13, No. 3/4, 1993, pp. 31-49; and: *The Politics of Pregnancy: Policy Dilemmas in the Maternal-Fetal Relationship* (ed: Janna C. Merrick, and Robert H. Blank) The Haworth Press, Inc., 1993, pp. 31-49. Multiple copies of this article/chapter may be purchased from The Haworth Document Delivery Center [1-800-3-HAWORTH; 9:00 a.m. - 5:00 p.m. (EST)].

31

her/himself physically linked up to a world-renowned violinist. Should this tie be broken, the violinist would die (Thomson 1986, 2-3). Thomson asserted, however, that morally the donor need not continue samaritan life-support of the violinist. Though the need of the violinist is great, it is not this criterion that determines the parameters of good and bad samaritan behavior. To the contrary, the moral obligation of all samaritan behavior is set by the degree of intrusion it imposes on the donor.[2]

The analogy with abortion lies in the evaluation of the pregnant woman as a potential donor, and the fetus as the recipient whose life depends upon that donation. The burdens imposed upon a woman by pregnancy are too great, according to Thomson, to demand automatically that she act as a good samaritan to the fetus. Rather, according to her, because of the extent of the donations required in pregnancy, a pregnant woman has the moral right to be a bad samaritan.

Legal precedents and public opinion support Thomson's analysis of good and bad samaritan behavior. While five states impose limited duties to aid someone whose life is in danger, this legal imposition only applies when the aid can be offered safely and easily (McIntyre 1992). In the case of bodily donations, rather than bodily actions, however, legally coerced good samaritan behavior is virtually nonexistent.[3] Even minimal bodily intrusion, such as a blood test, for example, requires the consent of the donor, even if the life of the recipient hangs in the balance.[4]

What is more, legally, consent is required for both good samaritan behavior when making the donation and bad samaritan behavior when refusing the donation. Even when a donor agrees to be a good samaritan, therefore, legal reasoning and public opinion concentrate on the necessity for such an agreement to rest on the explicit consent of the donor, rather than the need of the recipient.

While Thomson's path-breaking article is oft-cited and oft-anthologized in the academic community, samaritan reasoning is notably absent from Supreme Court cases considering the abortion issue. This research argues that it is time to correct this omission, not only by adding-in more information about pregnancy, but also, by reformulating women's reproductive rights in terms of the right to consent to pregnancy, rather than merely the right to choose an abortion.

Switching from a focus on abortion to a focus on pregnancy, and from a focus on choice to a focus on consent, has profound legal implications by reframing the samaritan status of the pregnant woman. Rather than being caught in the nexus between good and bad samaritan behavior, she is more accurately seen to be a captive samaritan.

Recognizing the captive condition of a pregnant woman who does not consent to pregnancy promises new avenues for advancing women's legal rights. First, it shifts the type of privacy claimed by a woman seeking an abortion from the right to choose what to do with her own body (without interference from the state) to the right to be let alone from nonconsensual intrusion by another entity (the fetus). The right to be let alone is a more narrow judicial principle carrying less controversial baggage than the right to decisional autonomy. Invoking the right to be let alone as the privacy referenced by consent, therefore, grounds abortion rights on a more secure legal foundation.

Second, while the privacy of choice entails the right to be free of government interference, the privacy to be let alone implies the assistance of the state, should one's physical integrity be violated by another entity. Recovering the captive samaritan status of a woman in a nonconsensual pregnancy relationship with a fetus, therefore, opens the door for demands for state aid to assist the woman to end that relationship. Put simply, this means public funding for abortion as the means for ending a woman's captive samaritan status.

PREGNANCY

The definition of abortion provided by the American Bar Association and adopted by the Supreme Court is that abortion is the "termination of human pregnancy with an intention other than to produce a live birth or to remove a dead fetus" (*Roe* v. *Wade* 1973, 146). While the burdens of pregnancy, the potential health risks of abnormal pregnancies, and the life style changes of bearing and caring for children often are cited, the nature of pregnancy itself remains virtually invisible.

Pregnancy legally is defined as the "condition (in a woman's body) resulting from a fertilized ovum . . . beginning at the moment of conception and terminating with the delivery of the child" (Black 1990, 1179). The key to this definition is that pregnancy is an asymmetric condition produced in the woman by the fertilized ovum. That is, the fertilized ovum causes the condition, pregnancy, to result in the woman's body.

Even ardent pro-life advocates recognize the asymmetric causal nature of pregnancy. Representative Henry J. Hyde (R-IL), for example, contends that people should not refer to a pregnant woman as "going to have a baby," because she "already has a baby *implanted in her womb*" (quoted in Pilpel 1982, 1112, emphasis added). This is exactly correct. The fertilized ovum, fetus, baby, or "whatever" is the implanter who implants itself upon the woman in contrast to the woman who is the recipient of that implantation, or the implantee.

While it is most usual for analyses of abortion to focus on the status of the fetus, particularly its viability and/or personhood status, the obvious reality is that it is the woman who is pregnant, not the fertilized ovum, fetus, or even baby. It is the condition of pregnancy in a woman, therefore, in her position as the recipient of action initiated by another, therefore, that is the key issue, not the personhood or viability status of the fetus.

The key question to determine, therefore, is what does a fertilized ovum do to a woman to make her pregnant? Turning to the medical profession for the answer yields language telling a story of massive physical intrusion upon the body of the woman, all as a part of normal pregnancy. It is not merely that pregnancy is a burden or a condition that may involve physical discomfort, if not risk. Rather, normal pregnancy is a profound alteration of a woman's entire body from its base line state. Medical language, in fact, portrays pregnancy as an aggressive, even violent, intrusion of the fertilized ovum upon the woman's body.

For example, when the fertilized ovum implants itself in the lining of the woman's uterus, it causes her "endometrium (to) *degenerate*," allowing the trophoblast or fertilized ovum to come "*into contact* with the (woman's) endometrial stroma." Subsequently, the trophoblast is able to grow only as a result of its "*engulfment*" of the woman's "endometrial capillaries" (Fox 1990, 31-35, emphasis added). During the early weeks of gestation, cytorophoblastic cells of the fertilized ovum:

> *stream out* from the tips of the anchoring villi, *penetrate* the trophoblastic shell and *extensively colonize* the decidua and adjacent myometrium of the placental bed . . . endovascular trophoblastic cells *destroy and replace the endothelium of the maternal vessels* and then *invade the media [of the woman] with resulting destruction of the [woman's] medial elastic and muscular tissue. . . .* The end result of this trophoblastic *invasion of, and attack on, the [woman's] vessels* is that the thick-walled muscular spiral arteries [of the woman] are *converted* into flaccid, sac-like uteroplacental vessels . . . which can *passively dilate* in order *to accommodate* the greatly augmented blood flow through this vascular system *which is required as pregnancy progresses.* (Fox 1990, 35-36, emphasis added)

Tissues in the woman's uterus are destroyed and altered as the fertilized ovum implants itself and grows. The woman's entire blood circulation system is rerouted so that all of her blood is available to the fertilized ovum. Discussions of the process consume entire chapters in medical texts on pregnancy, because of the complexity and depth of the physiological and biological transformations of the woman's body (Fox 1990, 38-41; McParland and Pearce 1990, 89-126). In addition, as a result of the fertilized ovum acting upon the woman's body, hormonal levels in her body reach elevations 400 times their normal level. It is this change, in fact, that often is used medically as the most accurate diagnosis of whether a woman is pregnant.

Furthermore, physical alterations caused by the fertilized ovum in a woman's body which define the condition of pregnancy, though physically necessary for the survival and growth of the fertilized ovum, are unnecessary for the woman's own physical survival. Of course, many women actively seek to be pregnant, which is essential for the survival of human society, as the Supreme Court noted in *Roe* (1973, 125).

What is more, pregnancy, like all else, can be socially constructed to have a wide range of meanings.[5] Yet, however one might alter the metaphors used to depict the relationship between the woman and the fetus, the asymmetric effect of the parasitic fertilized ovum causing pregnancy in the body of a woman is a reality that remains as a common denominator. Depicting this condition in altruistic terms, for example, would not change the asymmetric nature of the relationship between the parasitic fertilized ovum and the woman. Reconstructing the language to say that the fertilized ovum "bestows" itself upon the woman's body, "gives" its cells to her, or "activates" her capacity to be pregnant, for example, does not alter the reality that the pregnant condition produced in the woman's body results from the fertilized ovum. As such, it is the fertilized ovum's transformation of the woman's body in producing pregnancy that is key to the legal relationship between the fertilized ovum and the woman, not the exact metaphorical content of that relationship.

The deep value attached to women's willingness, if not desire, to make their bodies available to enable the survival of the human species, therefore, must not obscure the reality of what pregnancy involves: namely, the massive intrusion and use of a human body by a fertilized ovum to serve its own survival and developmental needs. For some women, pregnancy entails far greater health risks and physical dangers than abortion ever could. Furthermore, the labor and work of childbirth itself is the necessary final stage of pregnancy, one requiring a woman's complete involvement to the exclusion of all else, sometimes even entailing the physical intrusion and complications of a Caesarian section.

Despite pro-life attempts to equate abortion with slavery, therefore, the more accurate analogy is that between nonconsensual pregnancy and slavery. Noted legal scholars, for example, view state coerced pregnancy and childbirth as a violation of the Thirteenth Amendment which deemed slavery and involuntary servitude to be unconstitutional (Koppelman 1990). This perspective can be expanded, however, by recognizing that prior to any state coercion, the fetus, in effect, is an agent of coercion, should a woman fail to consent to the pregnancy it induces in her body.

While there are profound reasons to applaud, of course, both women's willingness and desire to exercise their unique capacity to be pregnant, there also must be ways to protect women from the coercion to be pregnant, defined not merely in relation to the state, but in relation to the agent legally designated as responsible for pregnancy in the first place: the fertilized ovum throughout its developmental stages.

CONSENT

The key to making pregnancy an ethically and legally acceptable experience, though yet to be explored, is the principle of consent.[6] Legally, consent is a "concurrence of wills" or "voluntarily yielding the will to the proposition of another." It means "voluntary agreement by a person in the possession and exercise of sufficient mental capacity to make an intelligent choice to do something proposed by another. . . . It is an act unclouded by fraud, duress, or sometimes even mistake." Consent is the "willingness in fact that an act or an invasion of interest shall take place. . . . submission under the influence of fear or terror cannot amount to real consent. There must be an exercise of intelligence based on knowledge of its significance and moral quality and there must be a choice between resistance and assent" (Black 1990, 305).

It is the asymmetric principle defining pregnancy, therefore, that necessitates a woman's consent. Rather than a choice about what to do with her own body, pregnancy involves the woman's consent to how her body may be acted upon by another entity. Furthermore, in order for consent to be operating, a woman must have the choice to resist or to assent to the invasion of her body, and this choice must be free of fear, duress, force or violence.

Introducing consent into the abortion debate, therefore, reframes the language used to depict women's rights. Rather than focusing on women's choice to terminate pregnancy, or even women's choice to be pregnant, the major question becomes women's choice to consent to be pregnant or not. A woman must have the right to consent or not to the invasion and use of her body by the fertilized ovum which initiates and sustains the condition of pregnancy.

Adding-in consent and pregnancy to the abortion debate, therefore, reframes samaritan analogies. Rather than viewing a pregnant woman seeking an abortion as a bad samaritan who refuses to donate her body to a fertilized ovum, a pregnant woman seeking an abortion has the status of a captive samaritan whose body already is being used by a fertilized ovum without her consent. It is the right of a pregnant woman to have her body let alone from another entity–be it a fertilized ovum, fetus, baby, person, or potential person–therefore, that is the key samaritan issue. As a consequence, the focus turns to the woman's right to state aid in freeing herself from the captive status caused by the fertilized ovum, rather than merely her choice about whether to be a good or bad samaritan in the first place.

GOOD SAMARITAN CASES

The primacy of one's bodily integrity and consent are evident in cases involving good samaritan behavior, particularly when the good samaritan is a person under the age of consent or who is legally incompetent to give consent for herself/himself.

One of the most well known cases is that of *Strunk* v. *Strunk* (1969) involving a kidney donation from a 27-year-old, who had the mental capacity of a six-year-old, to his 28-year-old brother, whose life depended on the donation.[7] The donor's mother and the Department of Mental Health both recommended that the transplant take place. They based their claims not on the need of the recipient, but on the best interests of the donor, claiming that the donor was "greatly dependent upon [his brother], emotionally and psychologically," and that the donor's "well-being would be jeopardized more severely by the loss of his brother than by the removal of a kidney" (quoted in *Curran* v. *Bosze* 1990, 8), a position affirmed by the donor's psychiatrist.

Yet, before such good samaritan behavior could take place, the case was sent to the Kentucky Court of Appeals, which in a close 4 to 3 decision, eventually upheld the lower court's decision to approve the transplant. The key to this affirmation lay in the Court of Appeals upholding that "the operative procedures in this instance are to the best interest of (the ward)," based on the substitute judgement of his guardian (cited in *Curran* v. *Bosze* 1990, 9).

As was stated later in another samaritan case relying on the *Strunk* decision, "It is clear . . . that courts . . . will consider the benefits to the donor as a basis for permitting an incompetent to donate an organ . . . the conclusion of the majority there (the court in *Strunk*) was based on the benefits that the incompetent donor would derive, rather than on the theory that the incompetent would have consented to the transplant if he were competent" (quoted in *Curran* v. *Bosze* 1990, 11).

More recently, the centrality of consent and bodily integrity rights for good samaritan behavior was evident in the case of Marissa Ayala, a baby conceived and born with the intention to use her bone marrow, if genetically suitable, to save the life of an older sibling. When this did prove feasible, Marissa Ayala at the age of 14 months served as a life-saving bone marrow donor to her 19-year-old sister.

Marissa's health was never an issue. Bone marrow transplants, in fact, pose little risk to the donor, and afterward, Marissa suffered no more than an ache in her hip where the one inch long needle had been inserted for the operation. The major question raised, however, centered on the baby's consent and whether the transplant had been in her best interest, as she would have posed it, had she been able to make her own choice about her donation (*Time* June 17, 1991, 54).

The American public is decidedly in favor of explicit consent in samaritan situations. As reported by *Time,* 42% think it is unethical even to ask a child under the age of 18 to give up a kidney for a transplant to a relative. Only 15% say that they would apply emotional pressure to a relative to get him or her to donate a transplant, even to a family member. And what is most interesting, only a minuscule 6% respond that they would take legal action to force a relative to donate a transplant against his or her will (*Time* 1991, 57).

Good samaritan behavior involving bodily integrity rights, therefore, is firmly based on the principle of consent, focusing on the rights of the donor in contrast to the needs of the recipient.

BAD SAMARITAN CASES

Though Judith Jarvis Thomson posed the right to be a bad samaritan on the basis of an abstract moral scenario, this right is backed-up by law. The primacy of bodily integrity and consent is evident, for example, in legal cases involving a person's right to be a bad samaritan, that is, to withhold life-saving bodily parts from a recipient who will die without them.

A recent case demonstrating the legal right to be a bad samaritan is the *Curran* v. *Bosze* case in Illinois (1990). This case involved two twin boys who were nearly four years old who were asked by their father to undergo blood tests to determine if they would be suitable blood marrow donors for their half sibling who had leukemia and would die without such a transplant, since it had already been determined that no other family members were genetically suitable as donors.

The mother of the twins, as their legal guardian, said "no" to the blood tests on their behalf. This decision was upheld in court and upheld on an appeal from the twins' father, even though the effect would be to let the twin's half sibling die, which, in fact, did happen (*Time* June 17, 1991, 58). Although there are reasons to question the bad samaritan behavior of the mother of the twins on ethical grounds, the law clearly protects donors' legal right to say "no."

THE PREGNANT WOMAN AS CAPTIVE SAMARITAN

As Laurence Tribe puts it, "There can be no doubt that forcing a woman into continued pregnancy does entail using her body" (Tribe 1990, 102). My point is that all pregnancy entails using a woman's body, not merely "forced" pregnancy. What makes pregnancy legally acceptable, therefore, is a woman's consent to have her body used by the fetus for pregnancy.

As Tribe continues, "To say that the fetus might have rights of its own does not demonstrate that it is somehow a being separate and distinct from its mother, at least in the beginning. It is not a lodger or prisoner or guest, nor is its mother a mere home or incubator" (Tribe 1990, 102). Quite true, the fetus is more like a *trespasser* on the woman's body, should it be present and acting upon her body without her consent.

Legally, a trespasser is "[o]ne who has committed trespass" where trespass legally is defined as "[a]ny unauthorized intrusion or invasion of private premises or land of another . . . [which] comprehends any misfeasance, transgression or offense which damages another person's health, reputation or property" (Black 1990, 1502-1503). A trespasser, therefore, is one "who enters upon property of another without any right, lawful authority, or express or implied invitation, permission, or license, not in performance of any duties to owner, but merely for his own purpose, pleasure or convenience" (Black 1990, 1504).

The physical location of the fetus inside the woman and the degree of its physical attachment and use of the woman's body, far from negating the integrity of the distinctly separate identities of the fetus and the woman, should highlight this distinction, casting the fetus as a trespasser upon the body of the woman.[8]

In sum, the fetus as trespasser upon the woman's body making use of her flesh and blood to sustain and develop its own physical flesh and blood casts the woman not as a good or bad samaritan, but rather as a captive samaritan. It is the captive status of the pregnant woman that needs to be retrieved in the abortion debate. Introducing the definition of nonconsensual pregnancy as a captive samaritan status focuses on the primacy of the woman as a victim of pregnancy, rather than merely the fetus as the victim of abortion.

SEX AND THE PREGNANT WOMAN

Before successfully laying claim to state protection against nonconsensual physical intrusion by a fertilized ovum, predictably women will be called upon to answer the following question: Does not a woman's consent to engage in sexual intercourse entail her consent to be pregnant, should this condition occur? The attachment of sex with pregnancy is of long standing. The common cultural view, also reflected in Supreme Court language, is that a woman, by agreeing to sexual intercourse, in effect not only has participated in the creation of a fertilized ovum, but has implicitly agreed to maintain and support its physical dependence upon her.

This view, however, is not medically or legally correct. No woman, however much she might try, can make the fertilized ovum act upon her. All she can do is control the degree of risk that the fertilized ovum might act upon her. Much like walking down a dark street at night exposes a person to the probability or risk of being mugged, still, it takes a mugger as an initiating agent to do the job. Sexual intercourse for fertile women always involves an element of risk that a fertilized ovum not only may be conceived, but may subsequently act upon the body of the woman to produce the condition of pregnancy. Some women, seeking to be pregnant, maximize this risk. Others, seeking to avoid pregnancy, minimize this risk. Yet, no woman can control what the fertilized ovum actually does. Pregnancy as a condition, therefore, is not directly controlled by any woman. All a woman can control is her consent to be pregnant or not, should the fertilized ovum actually act upon her to produce that condition.

The case of a woman who does not consent to be pregnant is analogous, therefore, to the person who is mugged. Even a person assuming a high risk that a mugging will occur, nevertheless, does not lose her/his right to refuse to be mugged. Not only that, but it is an assumed function of the police power of the state to protect all victims of mugging, even those who exposed themselves to unusually high risks that such an event would occur in the first place.

All samaritan cases share a common denominator based on the bodily integrity rights of the donor in relation to a recipient. How much more so if the consent of the donor has been overridden by the recipient. It was exactly this coercive, captive status, in fact, that so troubled people in the Marissa Ayala case. It was as if a child had been born to donate, and many were disturbed.

WOMEN: BORN TO BE PREGNANT?

Some, of course, may see women's identities so attached to biological and social motherhood that it is as if women are born to be pregnant. Yet, there is no constitutional support for such a view. Most women for some part of their lives have a capacity to be pregnant and bear a child, and many women eagerly seek at one or more points in their lives to exercise this capacity. Yet, the Constitution does not require women to be pregnant, nor do any congressional or state legislative statutes directly mandate that women must exercise a capacity to be pregnant. It is not a political or legal obligation, therefore, for any woman to be pregnant.

Pregnancy, far from being the legal purpose or political obligation of a woman in relation to the state, by contrast is merely a life option held by most women for some part of their lives. And, while it is the deepest wish of many women to exercise this option, politically and legally, it remains just that: an option, not a proactive legal mandate.

Yet, as many point out, pregnancy is "symbolic of the continuation of the human race" (Mariner and Glantz 1990, 32). When pregnant women say "no" to their pregnant condition, therefore, this can transform them in the eyes of some from a reified status as idealized nurturers to symbols of evil and death. This problem results when a culture attributes to all women at all times the role of natural nurturer, as if women are born to give and to serve.

Rather, women's right to be "consensual nurturers" needs to be culturally and legally established. Consensual nurturing means that women have a right to consent to whether or not they will nurture others. And, if they say "no" to their pregnant condition, then a fetus maintaining the pregnant condition in a woman's body without her consent, casts the woman as the victim of its nonconsensual physical intrusion upon her. While the fetus correctly may be depicted as "dependent" upon the woman, its responsibility as the causal agent of a pregnancy which serves its own interest problematizes any representation of the fetus as "innocent."

An analogy might be the following. A man donates a pint of blood to a hospital.[9] Then, he decides not to nurture, and refuses to consent to donate any more blood. The hospital is in desperate need of blood, and kidnaps him in order to take a pint of his blood. Who, in such a case, would be designated as the victim? It seems reasonable to assume that police arriving on the scene would protect the man who is kidnapped, not the hospital personnel taking his blood without his consent.

While recognizing the value associated with women's nurturing, as well as women's disproportionate contributions to society as nurturers, it nevertheless remains paramount to protect women's right to say "no" to nurturing. Further, women trapped in a condition where they are coerced to nurture, as captive samaritans, must be seen as the victims in such a context, not the entities, such as fetuses that do the trapping.

THE QUESTION OF PRIVACY

The abortion debate has for too long been represented by pro-choice advocates both on and off the Court as an issue affording women "the right to make intimate decisions about abortion free of governmental interference" (Kolbert 1989, 154). This misrepresents abortion as invoking a privacy of choice about what to do with your own body rather than privacy defined by the right to be let alone from nonconsensual bodily intrusion by others. The consequences have been serious, and threaten to grow even greater in the times lying ahead.

In the first place, invoking the privacy of choice, rather than consent, grounds abortion rights on the Due Process clause of the Fourteenth Amendment. The legal basis for the use of this principle is that the state may not interfere in one's private life without procedural and substantive due process regulations in place. Many precedents establish this constitutional right, and in a variety of legal contexts. Perhaps the most often cited in relation to abortion, however, is the constitutional right to use contraceptives (*Griswold* v. *Connecticut* (1965)).

Using the Due Process clause to protect a constitutional right to choose abortion in the context of the privacy of choice, however, renders abortion rights very vulnerable, indeed. The main reason is that the privacy of choice has been restricted by the Court in some very significant ways. It does not cover, for example, such fundamental personal decisions as the right to engage in consensual homosexual sodomy, as was shown in *Bowers* v. *Hardwick* (1986).[10]

If the Constitution does not guarantee individuals the right to make personal decisions about their own sexual orientation, then on what basis can it be assumed that the Constitution guarantees the right to make a personal decision to have an abortion? It is precisely this question, of course, that currently divides the Supreme Court into a very fragile majority. Five justices currently say the Constitution does guarantee abortion as a private choice (before viability). The all but equal conservative minority, however, say it does not, as became clear in the recent *Casey et al* v. *Planned Parenthood of Southeastern Pennsylvania et al* (1992). Soon-to-retire Justice Blackmun, casting himself as the swing vote on this issue, warns that darkness lies ahead (*Casey* 1992, 52).

As if this were not enough, however, there is another lethal problem attached to basing abortion rights on the privacy of choice, rather than the privacy of consent. This is the absolute requirement of the pro-choice position that the fetus be a nonperson. This follows from the privacy of choice position, because even if individuals do have the right to make private choices about how to use their own bodies, and even if this privacy of choice includes abortion, no one has the right to exercise such a choice if it should involve killing another person. Hence the pro-choice-all-but-sacred precept: the entity killed in abortion is not a person.

The politics of personhood, of course, have become the name of the game in the ensuing public opinion, legislative, and legal battles waged over abortion. Pro-life advocates predictably direct considerable efforts toward undermining the nonpersonhood status of the fetus. And, modern technology has aided them in this mission considerably. As Rosalind Petchesky points out, in our visually oriented culture, pro-life advocates can make fetal personhood an experienced reality for many by playing upon the illusions and fantasies associated with ultrasound images of fetuses and their translation into video and television filming (Petchesky 1992). Others seek to destroy the choice option by equating it with such nauseous choices as euthanasia, eugenics, and Naziism (Leuchter 1991). No matter how deplorable and misconceived these distortions surely are, they nonetheless succeed in setting the agenda and defining the terms which pro-choice advocates must contradict.

OF PRINCIPLES AND POLITICS

Perhaps there is no reason to worry. Congress may pass the Freedom of Choice Act, thereby short-circuiting the possible loss of a constitutional right of privacy to make personal decisions about abortion resulting from a membership replacement on the Court. Further, the argument that the fetus is a person, while emotionally laden and a strong pull for some, creates its own countervailing forces, as pro-choice advocates battle the war of public opinion as well.

Yet, the Freedom of Choice Act has not yet been debated in Congress, much less passed. And, although the new presidential leadership of Bill

Clinton promises assurances to pro-choice advocates, there is still reason to be concerned about the long-term composition of the Supreme Court. If only for these reasons, therefore, it is worth asking, what would happen, legally and legislatively, if women's reproductive rights were framed as the right to consent to pregnancy relationships with fetuses rather than merely the right to make private choices about their own bodies inclusive of abortion?

Many positive consequences could result from opening up new avenues guaranteeing women's reproductive rights on the basis of consent. First, switching from privacy defined as the right to choose what to do with your own body to privacy defined as the right to be let alone from nonconsensual intrusion by another entity grounds abortion rights on the more secure principle of consent compared to choice. As reviewed above, there are exceptions to how people have been allowed to exercise private choices, such as restrictions on the right of homosexuals to engage in consensual sodomy. The right of people to consent to physical intrusion upon their bodies by another private person, however, is all but absolute.[11]

Second, switching from choice to consent removes the issue of the personhood status of the fetus. If the fertilized ovum is socially constructed merely as physiological mass of cells, of course, the notion of consent is superfluous and unnecessary. To the extent, however, that the fetus acquires any of the attributes of a person, basing abortion rights on a woman's consent to be pregnant requires that the fetus acquire the restrictions of a personhood status as well. The most absolute of all restrictions is that no person may intrude upon the body of another person without her/his consent. Promoting the fetus to a personhood status, therefore, in no way jeopardizes women's abortion rights when they are based upon a principle of consent.

Third, introducing the right to consent to be pregnant provides a way to apply the Court's recent affirmation in *Casey* (1992, 24-30) of the constitutionality of informed consent, established in the context of an abortion, to pregnancy itself. Legally, consent requires that an individual be informed about alternatives. When pregnancy is framed as a woman's consent to the intrusion of the fertilized ovum upon her body, it means a woman must be knowledgeable about alternatives to this intrusion. Put simply, the state must inform pregnant women that abortion is an option to pregnancy, in order for their pregnancy to be consensual.

Instead of lamenting the Court's affirmation of informed consent for abortion as a set-back for women's reproductive rights, substituting the consent to be pregnant for the choice to have an abortion opens new doors protecting women's options. Specifically, the consent to be pregnant becomes a basis for applying this recent Supreme Court ruling to pregnancy itself. When pregnancy is framed as a woman's consent to the intrusion of the fertilized ovum upon body, she must be knowledgeable about the alternatives to this intrusion in order for her consent to be informed. She must be informed of abortion, therefore, as an alternative to pregnancy.

Fourth, switching to the consent to be pregnant opens the door for public funding of abortion. It does so, as discussed above, because privacy defined as the right to make personal decisions without state interference invokes the Due Process clause of the Fourteenth Amendment. The right to consent to pregnancy, however, invokes the Equal Protection clause of the Fourteenth Amendment, should a woman refuse to consent to her pregnant condition. Pregnant women, whose bodies are intruded upon without their consent, would have the right to call upon the aid of the police power of the state to rid them of the intruder on the same basis as would any other person call upon the state for aid in defense of violations of her/his bodily integrity. In plain language, women could make claims upon the state to fund abortion as the means necessary for protecting them from the effects of pregnancy defined as nonconsensual intrusion.

FROM "PRO-CHOICE" TO "PRO-CONSENT"

"Consent" promises a potent counter-punch–legally, legislatively, and culturally–to what has been the almost intractable appeal of the powerful slogan, "right to life." How can anyone, after all, be "against" the "right to life." And to the extent that "choice" implies "abortion," advocates of "choice" are burdened with the task of deflecting the claim that they "favor abortion." For these, and other reasons, "choice" has long been lamented by many of its advocates as a weak parallel to "life," having less emotional, if not less legal, appeal in the intense debates ensuing.

Conservatives, suspicious in general about the value of choice in comparison to the value of what is chosen, have held the labeling offensive far too long. The right to choose, as is well proven, provides no guarantees on what might be chosen. Women might choose abortion, individuals might choose to create art objectionable to the tastes of some, and people might choose to establish homosexual relationships, all "choices" that have been targets of vehement conservative attacks.

"Consent," in contrast to "choice," is a principle much more resistant to conservative attack. Who, among conservatives, would support the right of one person to take things from another without the consent of the owner? Would Jesse Helms support legislation legally guaranteeing the right of a person, much less potential person, to "take" a pint of blood from him without his consent? Would Justice Scalia? Would Robert Bork? Probably, they would not. Similarly, would conservatives support legislation or judicial rulings that permit the state to take over the property of a person without his/her consent, due process, or compensation, much less the body of a person? Not likely.[12]

Shifting from "pro-choice" to "pro-consent" as the legal parallel to "pro-life," puts conservatives on the defensive. It forces them to find the legal grounds to justify the physical "taking" of a person's body without her/his consent by either a person, potential person, or the state. As such, it is the legal grounds for coercing pregnancy that must be produced, not the legal grounds for terminating it.

George Bush, for example, when launching his 1992 presidential campaign,

> The most compelling legacy of this nation is Jefferson's concept that all are created equal . . . It doesn't say 'born.' . . . He (Jefferson) says 'created.' From the moment the miracle of life occurs, human beings must cherish that life, must hold it in awe, must *preserve,* protect, and *defend it.*[13]

Missing, of course, from Bush's statement is "how" the miracle of life occurs. As legal and medical depictions affirm, it occurs only on the basis of the "use" of another person's body. Using another person's body to preserve, protect, and defend your own, of course, requires the consent of the other person involved, a principle it seems reasonable to assume would be upheld by any reading of Thomas Jefferson's thoughts. Though a long road lies ahead to make effective use of this reframing of women's abortion rights, as briefly outlined here,[14] it promises not only new empowerment to women, but an empowerment consonant with the very writings of the Founders and their judicial descendants so often relied upon by the opposition.

NOTES

1. This is a revision of a paper presented at Princeton University, Women's History Month, March 1992, and incorporates revised material presented at the 1991 annual meetings of the New England Political Science Association and the Social Science History Association. The author thanks Benjamin Alpers, Marcia Angell, Barbara Craig, Robert Cord, Cynthia Daniels, Robert Davoli, Laura Frader, Mary Katzanstein, W. D. Kay, Andrew Koppelman, Elizabeth Lunbeck, Barbara Machtinger, Stephen Nathanson, Lynn Paltrow, John Przybylski, David Roche-

fort and Michael Tolley for their advice and critiques; Susan Lee for research assistance; and Lisa Ginsberg and Christina Kulich for their association on papers presented at the 1991 annual meetings of the New England Political Science Association and the Social Science History Association.

2. Thomson contends, of course, that there might be Minimally Decent Samaritan behavior which could be legally coerced. In the famous Kitty Genovese case, for example, 38 people in New York stood by while she was murdered before their very eyes. Though Thomson thinks it is unreasonable legally or morally to compel bystanders to directly intervene as good samaritans in such a case, she does think it reasonable to demand that they legally or morally be required at least to pick up a phone and call the police (Thomson, 1986:16-17).

3. Regan (1979) makes the telling point, of course, that a variety of behavioral obligations may be legally required, given contexts established by tort law. Not only is it questionable whether the situations involving behavioral obligations apply to a pregnant woman, but there are no precedents requiring obligations for one person to donate the use or parts of his/her body to another person, save the telling exception of reproductive contexts involving women as donors (Daniels, forthcoming).

4. Regan makes the point that in the absence of legislative statutes requiring good samaritan bodily donations, there is no way to know if such statutes would withstand constitutional tests (1979). At this point, the strongest evidence, therefore, is simply the absence of such statutes along with common law precedents used to establish the right of a person to refuse bodily donations, as in *Union Pacific Ry. Co. v. Botsford* (1891), 141 U.S. 250, 251.

5. Many scholars, in fact, point to how the use of metaphors reflect the values and world's views of those telling the stories constituting "reality." Since the most dominant stories told often are those constructed by individuals experiencing the world from the standpoint of men, there is the danger that reality becomes defined with metaphors capturing masculine and male, rather than feminine and female, perspectives. As Emily Martin has demonstrated, metaphors used to describe and explain the biological process of conception for much too long have recapitulated stereotypical views of how men generally relate to women, including men's active pursuit, competition, dominance, and possession of women (Martin, 1991).

6. See author's forthcoming book, *From 'Pro-Choice' to 'Pro-Consent' in the Abortion Debate* for a more complete explication of this thesis.

7. *Strunk v. Strunk* (Ky. 1969), 445 S.W. 2d 145, cited in *Curran v. Bosze* (1990) WL 209554 (Ill.), pg 8.

8. The point is that viewing the fetus and pregnant woman as "one" simply offers one more example of the severity with which the fetus intrudes upon the pregnant woman's body, an intrusion so massive that it even calls into question, for some, whether a distinction between the intruder (fetus) and woman remains.

9. The example focuses on a man to disentangle it from cultural associations with women automatically assuming normatively that they should be nurturers.

10. Technically, *Bowers* involved the right to engage in consensual sodomy,

not the right to be a homosexual. The Court recognized the issue of consensual sodomy, however, only in relation to homosexuality (*Bowers* 1986, 188, 215). Its decision was that there was no constitutional right to engage in consensual sodomy, and that restrictions on consensual sodomy did not violate fundamental rights of homosexuals (*Bowers* 1986, 189-191).

11. The state may intrude upon a person's body in some limited contexts, but not a private person, such as the fetus might be, were it to be attributed some form of personhood status.

12. In legal terms, the right not to have your body controlled by others is a much more narrow right than is the right to choose what to do with your own body. Koppelman, *supra* note 5, at 494.

13. Quoted in *New York Times,* A1 (January 23, 1992), (emphasis added).

14. See forthcoming book by author, *From "Pro-choice" to "Pro-consent" in the Abortion Debate.*

REFERENCES

Black, Henry Campbell. 1990. *Black's Law Dictionary.* St. Paul, MN: West Publishing Co.

Bowers v. *Hardwick*, 478 U. S. 186 (1986).

Casey et al v. *Planned parenthood of Southeastern Pennsylvania et al,* 1922 WL 142546 (U.S.).

Curran v. *Bosze*. WL 209554 Ill. (1990).

Daniels, Cynthia. (forthcoming). *Fetal Rights/State Power.* Cambridge, MA: Harvard University Press.

Fox, Harold. 1990. "Placental Structure in Health and Disease," in *Modern Antenatal Care of the Fetus,* edited by Geoffrey Chamberlain. Oxford: Blackwell Scientific Publications.

Griswold v. *Connecticut*, 381 U. S. 479 (1965).

Kolbert, Kathryn. 1989. "Introduction: Did the Amici Effort Make a Difference?" *American Journal of Law & Medicine.* 15:1-2, 153-168.

Koppelman, Andrew. 1990. "Forced Labor: A Thirteenth Amendment Defense of Abortion," *Northwestern University Law Review,* 84:2, 480-535.

Leuchter, Janet. 1991. "Abortion and the Holocaust: Responding to a False Equation," *Anti-Defamation League of B'nai b'rith,* New York, NY.

Mariner, Wendy K., Leonard H. Glantz, George J. Annas. 1990. "Pregnancy, Drugs, and the Perils of Prosecution," *Criminal Justice Ethics.* 9:7, 30-40.

McIntyre, Alison. 1992. "Guilty Bystanders? Reflections on Good Samaritan Laws," paper presented at the Bunting Institute Colloquium Series, Radcliffe College, April.

McParland, Peter J. and J. Malcolm Pearce. 1990. "Uteroplacental and Fetal Blood Flow," in *Modern Antenatal Care of the Fetus,* edited by Geoffrey Chamberlain. Oxford: Blackwell Scientific Publications.

Petchesky, Rosalind Pollack. 1992. "The Power of Visual Culture in the Politics of Reproduction," in Mary Joe Frug, *Women and the Law.* Westbury, NY: The Foundation Press.

Pilpel, Harriet F. 1982. "Hyde and Go Seek: A Response to Representative Hyde," *New York Law School Law Review,* 27:4, 1101-1123.

Regan, Donald H. 1979. "Rewriting *Roe v. Wade,*" *Michigan Law Review,* 77:1569-1646.

Roe v. *Wade.* 410 U.S. 113 (1973).

Strunk v. *Strunk* (Ky. 1969), 445 S.W. 2d 145, cited in Curran v. Bosze (1990) WL 209554 (Ill.).

Thomson, Judith Jarvis. 1986. "A Defense of Abortion," in *Rights, Restitution, and Risk: Essays in Moral Theory,* edited by William Parent. Cambridge, MA: Harvard University Press.

Time, June 17, 1991.

Tribe, Laurence H. 1991. *Abortion: The Clash of Absolutes.* New York: W.W. Norton & Co.

Union Pacific Ry. Co. v. *Botsford* (1891), 141 U.S. 250, 251, 35 L.Ed. 734, 737, 11 S.Ct. 1000, 1010; as cited in *Curran* v. *Botsford* (1990) WL 209554 (Ill.).

Webster and the Rights to Life

Jay E. Kantor

SUMMARY. The Supreme Court's refusal to recognize the existence of a basic affirmative right to health care may entail that women must retain a legal right to expel unwanted fetuses, even if *Roe v. Wade* is reversed and states are permitted to give fetuses legal standing as persons. Further, recognition of a basic affirmative right to health care would not entail that a woman is obliged to carry her fetus, even if a failure to do so would result in fetus' death. Duties correlative to basic affirmative rights are distributed among the members of society, not solely vested in single individuals.

INTRODUCTION

In upholding Missouri's refusal to publicly fund abortions in *Webster v. Reproductive Services* (1989), the Supreme Court depended on earlier rulings such as *DeShaney v. Winnebago County Department of Social Services* (1989) in which it held that a State has no fundamental obligation to provide health care to its citizens: "The Due Process Clauses generally confer no affirmative right to governmental aid, even when such aid may be necessary to secure life, liberty, or property interests of which the government may not provide the individual." That denial of the existence of a basic Constitutional affirmative right to health care was part of the

Jay E. Kantor is affiliated with the Department of Psychiatry (Bellevue 19W13), New York University School of Medicine, 550 First Avenue, New York, NY 10016.

[Haworth co-indexing entry note]: "Webster and the Rights to Life." Kantor, Jay E. Co-published simultaneously in *Women & Politics* (The Haworth Press, Inc.) Vol. 13, No. 3/4, 1993, pp. 51-61; and: *The Politics of Pregnancy: Policy Dilemmas in the Maternal-Fetal Relationship* (ed: Janna C. Merrick, and Robert H. Blank) The Haworth Press, Inc., 1993, pp. 51-61. Multiple copies of this article/chapter may be purchased from The Haworth Document Delivery Center [1-800-3-HAWORTH; 9:00 a.m. - 5:00 p.m. (EST)].

51

Court's rationale for deciding that Missouri could choose not to fund abortions with public monies. The Court agreed with Missouri's argument that it had no obligation to fund or provide abortions.

The author will argue here that an acceptance of the claim that there is no basic affirmative right to health care may entail acceptance of the claim that a woman must retain a legal right to expel an unwanted fetus,[1] even if *Roe v. Wade* (1973) is eventually overturned.

THE RIGHT TO LIFE

Let us assume that the Supreme Court was correct in its claims that the state has an interest in protecting fetuses because of their potential for personhood (*Roe v. Wade,* 163-164), and that the state may favor childbirth over abortion (*Maher v. Roe* (1989)). We can even further assume a stronger and even more controversial claim that the fetus, regardless of its gestational age, has a right to life. What about the continued legality of abortions really follows from those claims? That may depend in part on what is meant by a "right to life."

Imagine three hypothetical cases:

Alice, pregnant, decides to terminate her pregnancy by injecting her fetus with a lethal saline solution. The fetus is killed by the injection.

Betty, pregnant, decides that she wants to terminate her pregnancy and injects herself with prostaglandin which causes the expulsion of her living fetus. The expelled fetus subsequently dies.

Carla, not wishing to have children, obtains an intrauterine birth control device (I.U.D.). As a result, a fertilized ovum is prevented from implanting in her uterus and subsequently dies.

On the assumption that a fetus has a right to life, have Alice, Betty, and Carla each violated that right?

The Right to Life As a Negative Right

Roughly, if Delia has a negative right in regard to X, Delia: (1) Has a right to pursue X free from direct interference by others and, (2) If Delia already possesses X, Delia has a right to hold on to X free from direct interference by others. For example, Delia's negative right in regard to food is her right to try to get food. If she owns land, she may grow food; if she is employed, she may use her earnings to buy food. If Delia possesses food, she has a right not to have the food taken away.

If Delia has a negative right to life, she has a right not to be killed. That is, having possession of life, Delia has a right that life not be taken from her.

If the putative fetal "right to life" is solely a negative right–a right not to be killed, then Alice has clearly violated a fetus' right to life by directly killing the fetus. However, neither Betty, who expelled a living fetus, nor Carla, who prevented the implantation of a fertilized ovum, have necessarily violated a fetus' negative right to life. Betty and Carla have not killed fetuses, they have only refused to provide fetuses with those things the fetuses need in order to stay alive.[2]

The Right to Life As a Positive Right

To have a positive ("welfare" or "affirmative") right in regard to X is to have a right to be given X if one needs X.[3] For example, if Elizabeth has a positive right to food, she has a right to be given food if she is hungry. Positive rights are additive to their related negative rights. Thus, a person who has a positive right to (be given) food still retains a negative right to try to get food.

A positive right to life would almost certainly have to include a derivative right to basic health care at least sufficient to keep one alive if one were dying of a treatable illness or trauma. It is difficult to imagine a meaningful sense of a positive "right to life" that did not include a right to at least some health care. To be meaningful, a positive right to life would also have to include derivative rights to be given sufficient food, water, and air to keep one alive if one were starving, dying of thirst, or suffocating.[4]

If a fetus' right to life is looked upon as including a positive right to be kept alive, it may seem that Betty and Carla have violated fetuses' right to life by not providing them[5] with the basics they need in order to stay alive. However, even if this strong reading of a fetal "right to life" is accepted, it still may be argued that neither Betty nor Carla have violated a fetus' positive right to life.[6] That is because the duties correlative to positive rights differ from the duties correlative to negative rights.

THE DUTIES CORRELATIVE TO RIGHTS

The concept of a basic positive right to life presents some problems. First, many of those who are willing to recognize basic negative rights find problems about the existence or force of basic positive rights. For example, as noted above, the Supreme Court majorities in *Webster,* and in *DeShaney* in affirming that a state has no fundamental Constitutional obligation to provide even basic health care to its citizens, seems to be claiming by implication that there is no basic positive right to life held by anyone or anything, either fetus or adult person. The Court did claim that a state could *choose* to provide the needs sufficient to preserve the life of its citizens. Thus, if a state wrote a provision into its constitution which guaranteed that it would provide those needs, or enacted legislation that guaranteed the provision of these needs, then it would establish some positive right to life for its citizens. Too, Congress can legislate nationally recognized positive rights into existence. (For example, rights to Medicaid and Medicare.) However, rights of that sort, whose existence, strength, and limits are decided by simple majority vote, are clearly not as basic and "unalienable" as the basic rights delineated in the Constitution.

Second, regardless of the source or strength of generally-held positive rights, they differ from negative rights in regard to their respective correlative duties. Having a right implies that others have duties to honor that right. In the case of basic and generally-held negative rights, all persons owe these correlative duties directly to the holder of the right. Thus, if Elizabeth has a right not to be killed (a negative right to life), each and every other person has a direct duty to Elizabeth not to kill her (i.e., she has a right against each and every person that they not kill her). On the other hand, the duties correlative to generally-held positive rights are distributed among the population rather than totally vested in individual persons. An individual's duties in regard to others' positive rights are usually fulfilled by paying a share of taxes. The tax revenues are used by the government to provide the needs to claimants of positive rights. Thus, if Delia has a basic positive right to life, the burden of providing her with the necessary food, shelter, and health care is not placed on any individual member of society, but is shared by all taxpayers. In general, an individual has no legal duty to directly provide Elizabeth with food, even if she is starving.

Thus, even if Betty's or Carla's fetuses have a positive right to life, Betty and Carla may claim that it would be unfair to require them to take on the whole burden of upholding that right. Both may argue that to impose that duty on them would be inconsistent with the way duties correlative to general positive rights are usually ascribed.

It might be argued that Betty and Carla do have that total obligation to the fetuses because they happen to be the only persons who can guarantee the fetuses' positive right to life. That is, it might be claimed that they do have to bear the entire burden because the burden cannot be shared with society since the fetus needs *their* particular help in order to survive. This sort of claim is problematic for at least two reasons: first, in the earlier stages of development, the fetus could be transplanted to another uterus, or frozen for later implant. Thus, the burden of providing for the fetus could be taken on by others during at least some stages of pregnancy. Second, forcing such a duty upon Betty or Carla might be inconsistent with the law's refusal to impose similar Good Samaritan duties upon individuals in similar circumstances. If Andrew needs blood, and Ben is the only available source of his blood type, Ben cannot be forced to donate blood to Andrew even if it is needed to save Andrew's life. The courts' attitudes towards forcing affirmative duties upon women to undergo medical procedures for the sake of their fetuses has been mixed (Obade 1990). However, in the recent case of *In re: AC,* an Appeals Court overturned a prior court decision that had forced a pregnant woman to undergo a Caesarian section to save a fetus. The Appeals Court argued that "courts do not compel one person to permit a significant intrusion upon his or her bodily integrity for the benefit of another person's health . . ." (*In re: A.C.,* 1990). The Appeals Court found that questions about the personhood of the fetus and its unique dependency upon the pregnant woman were not relevant factors, holding that ". . . a fetus cannot have rights in this respect superior to those of a person who has already been born." The *AC* court spoke only of the right of women to refuse to submit to "significant intrusions" even if they were necessary to save a fetus. But the decision makes it clear that while inviting fetuses into the class of rights holders may make it illegal to directly kill them, that invitation alone should not guarantee that there is an absolute legal duty to keep them alive. While the Supreme Court may allow states to prohibit the direct killing of fetuses, further argument would be needed to establish that pregnant women have legal duties not to allow their fetuses to die.

At first glance, it appears that not even a reversal of *Roe v. Wade* should automatically interfere with a woman's right to expel or remove a living fetus, or with her right to prevent the implantation of a fetus in her uterus, or with her concomitant right to refuse to take up the whole burden of trying to keep an expelled fetus alive.

AFFIRMATIVE DUTIES ARISING OUT OF SPECIAL RELATIONSHIPS

Things are really more complicated than that, however. First, sometimes the duties correlative to a positive right *are* entirely vested in one individual. That may happen when there is an agreement formed between individuals or between an individual and an institution which includes a contractual rights-duties relationship. For example, if Frank contracts with George that he sell Frank his car for an agreed upon sum, it may be said that once Frank has paid George the money, Frank has a positive right that George give him the title to the car. Or, if a lifeguard has been hired by a hotel or municipality to watch over a beach, the swimmers on that beach have a positive right to the lifeguard's help if they are drowning.

An individual may even gain positive rights against another individual or against an institution without voluntarily entering into an agreement with them if the other individual or institution limits the individual's freedom by taking him into custody and control. Thus, for example, prisoners and involuntarily committed mental patients may have a positive right to health care (*Wyatt v. Aderholt,* 1974); (*Buffington v. Baltimore County,* 1990) against the institutions that have limited their freedom and thus limited their negative right to try to secure their own health care.

Some might argue that a woman who becomes pregnant has taken the fetus into her custody and control, and thus has affirmative duties to it that are analogous to a state's duty to care for its prisoners and involuntary mental patients. Whatever the merits of this argument, it does not establish that all pregnant women always have affirmative duties towards their fetuses. It does not establish that a woman who became pregnant involuntarily could be said to have created such a binding special relationship with a fetus. Even if we speak of instances in which the onset of a pregnancy could be categorized as voluntary (e.g., intended or foreseeable), and thus incurring of affirmative duties of care upon the woman, there are still problems about the extent of those duties. There are limits to what can be required of the parties in any "special relationships." For instance, we cannot demand that lifeguards try to save swimmers if they have good reason to believe that to attempt to do so would probably cost them their own lives.

A similar line of "care and custody" argument that might be offered to support a claim that a woman has strict affirmative obligations towards the fetus analyzes the woman's duties towards her fetus as simply an instance of a parent's legal duties to care for her child while it is in her custody. A woman has those duties whether or not the pregnancy producing the child was voluntary. The law does not permit parents to abuse, or neglect, or abandon their children to die. It might be argued that abortion by live fetal expulsion, or a refusal to permit uterine implantation of fertilized eggs, would be seen as instances of abandoning children to die if *Roe v. Wade* is reversed and states give fetuses the legal status of children.

However, even under this analysis, we must bear in mind that a mother's legal duties of care towards her child have limits. First, the law allows women the option of giving up their born children to the state for adoption. Of course, while permitting parents to give up their children to the care of the state, the law requires them to care for the children until a safe transfer of custody is made. Applied to fetuses, such laws would seemingly require the woman to care for the fetus until she can transplant it, or until it is viable and thus transferable to state custody. However, we have already seen that there are limits to what the law requires a parent to do in order to preserve the life or well-being of his child. Thus, even if it is established that a fetus may have a legal claim to a positive right to life against the pregnant woman, that claim may be overridden if continuation of the pregnancy will place an undue risk or burden on the woman. Answers to the question of how much risk and burden the state can justifiably impose on a woman in order to protect a fetus will be crucial if the Supreme Court reverses *Roe v. Wade* and allows states to declare that fetuses are persons from the moment of conception. For example, the number of concepti that never implant is estimated at over 50% and the number of spontaneous miscarriages after implantation is estimated at 22-28% (Grobstein 1988, p. 9). Would a woman be obliged to take measures to facilitate implantation of all fertilized eggs? Would she be obligated to take measures to try to prevent any spontaneous miscarriages? Under what conditions would such measures be categorizable as "significant intrusions" that she cannot be forced to accept? Moreover, there are instances in which a woman's medical condition, or her lifestyle, or her employment, might be seen as "interfering" with the fetus' putative negative right to life, or seen as conflicting with her affirmative duty to support the fetus' putative positive right to life. It is by no means clear that the fetus' putative negative or positive right to life entails that a woman always has an absolute obligation to do whatever is necessary to correct or change any medical condition, lifestyle, or employment that is fetus-endangering. For example, will the woman with malaria who refuses to stop taking quinine (a possible abortifacient) be guilty of violating or endangering a fetus' negative or positive right to life? Or the woman who refuses to correct a progesterone imbalance, prior to or during pregnancy? Or the woman who refuses to have an IUD removed prior to having intercourse?

Some may argue that the burden of bringing a fetus to birth is normally minimal enough to weigh the balance in favor of forcing most women to continue their pregnancies. However, that claim is based on some questionable assumptions about the "actualizing" of a fetus' potential to exist independently of the woman. Many seem to equate the normal human fetus' potential for independent existence with a turtle egg's potential for existence as a turtle. Left alone, without interference, and given the proper weather, many sorts of turtle eggs will develop into turtles long after their mothers have left the scene. On the other hand, the human fetus will *not* realize its potential if it is simply "left alone." Even in normal pregnancies it needs help from the pregnant woman in order for its potential to be realized. It needs access to *her* blood supply, *her* protective environment, and it requires that *she* limit her behavior during the pregnancy. Even more effort on her part would be needed in order to try to save that large number of concepti that wouldn't normally implant, and the significant number of implanted embryos that would ordinarily spontaneously abort. Certainly her providing the birthing process itself requires both effort and risk on her part.[7] Whether the pregnant woman has an overriding obligation to provide that help to, and undergo that risk and "labor" for, the fetus, is questionable. Whether a woman who rejects these putative obligations by performing actions that eventuate in expulsion and/or death of a fetus (e.g., use of IUDs, prostaglandin, or freezing of live embryos), or by inactions that eventuate in expulsion and/or death (e.g., refusal to take measures to ensure implantation and prevent spontaneous miscarriage) is guilty of violating a fetus' negative or positive right to life, is also questionable.

THE PHYSICIAN'S OBLIGATIONS

It has been argued here that no matter what status or legal standing the state legislatures or the Supreme Court give to the fetus, that status alone may not entail that a woman will be prohibited from expelling a living fetus from her body, or from refusing to take measures necessary to prevent her *in utero* fetus from dying. If that argument has merit, it may safeguard the legality of "morning after" pills and I.U.Ds. However, fetal expulsions in the later stages of pregnancy would probably require the help of health care providers. The intercession of third parties raises other ethical and legal questions: even if such expulsions are legal, could a physician be forbidden from performing such procedures? If such an expulsion is performed, will the provider have a moral or legal obligation to try to keep the fetus alive? Even if physicians are forbidden from directly killing fetuses, could they be prohibited from prescribing drugs or devices, such as IUDs or morning after pills, that cause expulsion?

In saying that states may pick and choose what health care they will fund, the *Webster* Court has already said that states may forbid physicians who work for, or in, publicly funded facilities from performing almost *any* medical procedure. That part of their decision does not hinge on assumptions about the moral status of early-stage fetuses. The *Roe v. Wade* Court ruled in essence that early stage abortions must be treated solely as medical procedures, and the Webster Court was able to use that precedent as a wedge in its ruling. As a result, a state could legally prohibit such abortions in those facilities without depending on a claim that early-stage fetuses have legal standing. Presumably, the Court would also permit states to force physicians who are publicly funded to attempt to save any aborted living fetuses, viable or not. A state can simply require that state-funded institutions write the duty into the physician's job description. As for privately-funded abortions, it would seem that the states could not prohibit willing physicians from expelling live early-stage fetuses unless they either exclude the relevant medical procedures from the class of acceptable medical procedures, or give the fetuses legal standing. If the fetus has standing, then a physician who performed an early-stage fetal expulsion might be held responsible for performing actions that foreseeably caused the death of the fetus.

The option of excluding abortions (either by expelling living fetuses or by killing fetuses) from the procedures permissible within the medical standards of practice raises another set of profound issues. These have to do with the question of whether legislatures have a moral right to decide which procedures are "medically acceptable."

CONCLUSION

The author has argued here that a minimalist view of basic rights may entail that a woman has limited obligations towards her fetus even if the fetus is considered to be a "person" with a right to life. There are many who believe that the conservative minimalist view of basic rights is incorrect, arguing that there are basic positive rights, including rights to health care, that should be recognized in law.

Even if that more liberal view of rights is correct, the author has argued that position may not entail that a woman must take on the total obligation to care for her fetus, even if a failure to do so will result in the death of the fetus. As argued above, the duties correlative to basic positive rights are distributed among the members of society, not solely vested in any one individual.

With all this, this paper has not addressed the fundamental question of the personhood of the fetus, nor addressed the fundamental questions concerning the meaning and moral force of "fetal potentiality." These are the questions that we really must continue to focus on if we are to solve the maze of the abortion issue.

NOTES

1. The word "fetus" will be used here as a catch-all term to include everything from the conceptus to the viable fetus.

2. Of course, it could be argued that the violation of a right to life is not limited to direct killing. Ben may violate Andrew's negative right to life by negligently acting (or not acting) in a way that would foreseeably cause the death of Andrew. This point is obviously crucial to the discussion and will be discussed later.

3. Usually, need must be established by the claimant to a fundamental positive right. What constitutes "need" is a major issue in and of itself. Proof of need is not prerequisite for the validity of a claim to a positive right that has been created as the result of an agreement between persons or persons and institutions.

4. What would count as "minimal" food, water, and health care is a difficult issue related to another difficult issue about the meaning of "life" in both readings of a "right to life." I think few would say that a positive right to life would be meaningful if it guaranteed only enough food, water, oxygen and health care to keep one somatically alive, but left with no brain function or even in a state of reversible and treatable coma.

5. Those who would say "depriving" instead of "not providing" must establish that the fetus had a claim to those basics.

6. The author's arguments in this paper somewhat parallel Judith Jarvis Thomson's argument that a woman's obligation to sustain a fetus to term may be overridden if fulfilling the obligation would be unduly burdensome to her (Thomson 1971). The argument in this paper is set in a fuller analysis of rights and applies directly to the Webster decision.

7. In fact, as claimed in *Roe v. Wade,* the birthing would require more risk to the woman than would an (early stage) abortion.

REFERENCES

Buffington v. Baltimore County, 913 F.2d 113 4th Cir. (1990).

DeShaney v. Winnebago County Department of Social Services, 851 F. 1071 U.S. (1989).

Grobstein, C. 1988. *Science and the Unborn.* New York: Basic Books, Inc.

In re: A.C., D.C. 573 A.2d 1235 (D.C. App. 1990),–*reversing and remanding* 533 A.2d 611 D.C. (1987).

Maher v. Roe, 432 U.S. 474 (1989).

Obade, C.C., Spring, 1990. "Compelling Treatment of the Mother to Protect the Fetus: The Limits of Personal Privacy and Paternalism." *The Journal of Clinical Ethics* 1:85-88.

Roe v. Wade, 410 U.S. 113, 93 S.CT. 705 (1973).

Thomson, J.J. (1971) "A Defense of Abortion," *Philosophy and Public Affairs* vol.1(1).47-66.

Webster v. Reproductive Services, 851 F. 1071 U.S. (1989).

Wyatt v. Aderholt, 503 F.2d 507 5th Cir. (1974).

Caring for the Fetus
to Protect the Born Child?
Ethical and Legal Dilemmas
in Coerced Obstetrical Intervention

Janna C. Merrick

SUMMARY. This article analyzes the circumstances under which physicians have sought court orders to force pregnant women to comply with unwanted obstetrical interventions. It argues that pregnant women have moral obligations to care for their fetuses, not because the fetus has rights, but because the fetus becomes the born child, and children are vulnerable and in need of care. While the overwhelming majority of women are willing to make significant personal sacrifices in the interest of having a healthy baby, sometimes it is difficult for pregnant women to comply with treatment recommendations due to intervening variables beyond their control. Utilization of the court system to coerce unwanted treatment raises serious ethical and legal problems.

INTRODUCTION

Pregnancy is a unique medical condition because there are two patients, with access to one made possible only by invading the body of the

---

Janna C. Merrick is affiliated with the University of South Florida at Sarasota, 5700 Tamiami Trail, Sarasota, FL 34243.

[Haworth co-indexing entry note]: "Caring for the Fetus to Protect the Born Child? Ethical and Legal Dilemmas in Coerced Obstetrical Intervention." Merrick, Janna C. Co-published simultaneously in *Women & Politics* (The Haworth Press, Inc.) Vol. 13, No. 3/4, 1993, pp. 63-81; and: *The Politics of Pregnancy: Policy Dilemmas in the Maternal-Fetal Relationship* (ed: Janna C. Merrick, and Robert H. Blank) The Haworth Press, Inc., 1993, pp. 63-81. Multiple copies of this article/chapter may be purchased from The Haworth Document Delivery Center [1-800-3-HAWORTH; 9:00 a.m. - 5:00 p.m. (EST)].

63

other.[1] Thus potential conflict exists and is exacerbated because generally a single physician treats both the pregnant woman and the fetus. This dilemma is addressed by the American College of Obstetricians and Gynecologists (ACOG) which argues that "the obstetrician should be concerned with the health care of both the pregnant woman and the fetus within her, assessing the attendant risks and benefits to each during the course of care" (1987).

Discussion of potential conflicts between a woman and the fetus is relatively recent and is primarily the result of new technologies such as ultrasound, amniocentesis, and fetal surgery which allow intrauterine diagnosis and treatment of the fetus. The range of such interventions and their levels of invasiveness vary dramatically. An ultrasound, which is used for a variety of prenatal diagnostic purposes, is painless and virtually risk-free for the pregnant woman and the fetus. Intrauterine blood transfusions, commonly recommended to treat RH incompatibility, are of little risk to the pregnant woman, but without the transfusion, there is a high likelihood of a stillborn birth. Medication to prevent pre-term delivery may make the woman feel uncomfortable, but premature delivery can be devastating for the neonate because it may lead to intracranial bleeding, respiratory problems, and/or blindness in the born child. There is also a higher incidence of cerebral palsy among pre-term babies.

Much of the controversy involving unwanted obstetrical intervention centers on delivery by cesarean section, which is highly invasive and carries a number of risks for the pregnant woman, including a higher mortality rate[2] and a longer period of recovery than for vaginal delivery. Since recommendations for cesarean sections are often made in emergency situations, there is little time for the pregnant woman to make a reasoned decision or to request a second opinion. Moreover, the rate of delivery by cesarean section is high in the U.S. compared to other countries, leading some to believe that they are often medically unnecessary.

Medicine is not an exact science, and diagnosis is rarely 100% accurate. Thus conditions such as fetal distress, fetal sepsis, or placenta previa which indicate a need for cesarean delivery cannot be diagnosed with complete accuracy. If in fact these conditions exist, however, the results can be devastating for the infant, and sometimes for the pregnant woman as well. Vaginal delivery when electronic fetal monitoring indicates fetal distress is associated with a high incidence of major compromise in the psychomotor development of the born child. Fetal sepsis can result in brain damage or death of the baby. Vaginal delivery in cases of placenta previa is almost universally fatal for the child, and there is a very high likelihood of maternal mortality as well.

In the vast majority of pregnancies, conflict does not emerge because physicians and pregnant women usually agree on the course of treatment. Most women will go to great lengths to deliver a healthy baby. Conflict may arise, however, when a woman refuses a treatment recommendation. When such conflict occurs, the physician may seek a court order to force the treatment. Such a decision may result from the physician's concern for the well-being of the fetus, the subsequent born child, and/or the pregnant woman. It may also be motivated by a fear of potential malpractice litigation.

The purpose of this article is to analyze the circumstances under which physicians have sought court orders to force pregnant women to comply with interventions. It argues that pregnant women have moral obligations to care for their fetuses, not because the fetus has rights, but because the fetus becomes the born child, and children are vulnerable and in need of care. While both parents incur the obligation to care for the fetus, the burden regarding obstetrical intervention falls on the woman since she is the one who is asked to submit to such intervention.

The article also argues, however, that sometimes it is difficult for a pregnant woman to comply with recommended interventions due to variables beyond her control. It examines reported cases in which physicians have sought court orders and discusses a number of serious flaws in utilizing the judicial system. The conclusion calls for more data to ascertain why some pregnant women refuse recommended treatment. It also calls for a retrospective case study to determine the accuracy of medical diagnoses in previously performed obstetrical interventions.

ETHICAL CONSIDERATIONS DURING THE PRENATAL PERIOD

From both ethical and legal perspectives, physicians must obtain informed consent prior to administering treatment. Treatment without consent constitutes battery (a tort injury) by the physician against the patient. A competent adult can generally refuse such treatment, even if it results in his/her death. A fetus, however, cannot give either informed consent or informed refusal, and thus the woman gives the consent or refusal both for herself and for the fetus. This creates an inherent ethical dilemma because what is beneficial for the fetus may not be beneficial for the pregnant woman, or at least the woman's perception may be that it is not beneficial for her.

Scholars have typically framed discussion of this dilemma in terms of conflict between the pregnant woman and the *fetus*. That approach leads to a debate that in many ways is characteristic of the abortion debate because it focuses on questions involving when human life begins, when the fetus acquires rights, and what rights a woman has to control her body. It would be fruitless to re-analyze those issues in this article. Philosophers, ethicists, and theologians disagree, and in the policy arena, the Supreme Court has specifically avoided establishing a point at which human life begins.

In reality, focusing on maternal-*fetal* conflict begs the most fundamental question, which is: How does this conflict affect the woman and the *born* child? This naturally involves discussion of the fetus because it is the fetus that ultimately becomes the born child. If the woman terminates the pregnancy, the issue of obstetrical intervention is moot. If she continues the pregnancy, the objectives are to deliver a healthy child and to have a healthy recovery for the pregnant woman. Conflict becomes a reality when failure to intervene results in the birth of a child whose health or life is compromised or when intervention is pursued and the pregnant woman's personal values, financial security, health and/or life are compromised. Thus, this article is not devoted to maternal-*fetal* conflict, but to conflict during the prenatal period between the pregnant woman and the fetus that becomes the *born* child.

Ethical issues in the prenatal period are appropriately analyzed in terms of the pregnant woman's autonomy versus her duty to the born child. A number of scholars have written that a woman should be free from government interference in decision-making regarding her pregnancy. Nelson and Milliken argue that while a pregnant woman has an ethical obligation to accept reasonable, nonexperimental medical treatment, that obligation should not be legally enforced through court-ordered obstetrical intervention because it invades the woman's privacy, thrusts her into an adversarial system at a time when she is both psychologically and physically ill-disposed to deal with it, demonstrates the physician's willingness to use physical force against a competent adult, and violates the tradition of bodily integrity. In the end, they conclude:

> society will . . . gain far more by allowing each pregnant woman to live as seems good to her, rather than by compelling each to live as seems good to the rest of us. (1988, 1066)

Johnsen argues that "by creating an adversarial relationship between the woman and her fetus, the state provides itself with a powerful means for controlling women's behavior during pregnancy, thereby threatening women's fundamental rights" (1986, 600). Field takes a similar view, arguing that "controlling women to protect their fetuses is using pregnancy to deprive women of the most basic civil rights" (1989, 16). Annas holds that:

> the use of the judiciary to force women to undergo medical treatments against their will is not only counterproductive, unprincipled, sexist, and repressive, it is also lawless. (1990, 29)

The late Nancy Rhoden analyzed court-ordered cesarean sections in the context of Samaritan law (the law of rescue) and opposed mandated interventions because they impose an unparalleled intrusion on pregnant women, undermine the principles of informed consent, and contain the seeds of widespread and pernicious usurpation of women's choices during obstetrical care (1987, 118). She asserted that in no other situation in America are rescues that risk life and limb mandated by law (1986, 1952).

ACOG also opposes court-ordered intervention:

> Clinicians should be aware of the destructive effect of court orders on the pregnant woman's autonomy and on the physician-patient relationship. Because of the urgency of situations in pregnancy, the courts are often petitioned for a speedy decision, which may have serious limitations and unexpected outcomes. In light of the foregoing considerations, resort to the courts is almost never justified. (1987)

Despite these powerful arguments, claims on behalf of complete maternal autonomy ignore a number of important principles. For example, all people surrender some autonomy by living in an organized social system. The law specifies the rights that individuals have and the obligations each has to others. The law also restricts individuals' control over their own bodies. Federal law prohibits people from selling their bodily organs, federal and state laws prohibit the use of illegal drugs, and most states prohibit a person from attempting suicide or selling his/her body for prostitution. Thus, people do not have complete autonomy regarding their lives or bodies.

Moreover, voluntary relationships also create moral and legal obligations and, therefore, reduce the individual's autonomy even further. This is true of husbands and wives, parents and children. Parents have both moral and legal responsibilities to care for their born children because children are vulnerable. One way in which a parent discharges that duty is by caring for the fetus. The loss of some autonomy is inherent in this relationship. As Blank writes:

> [A]lthough the mother's right to autonomy and privacy in reproduction is fundamental, like all other constitutional rights it is not abso-

lute. Therefore, at times she may be legally restrained from performing some action that under other circumstances would be considered
a personal choice. . . . (1986, 442)

He argues that while it is unreasonable to force a woman to refrain
from all contact that could harm the fetus, it is also unreasonable to
conclude that she has no obligations to it. He takes the position that
the more severe the effect on the fetus and the higher risk of that
effect, the greater should be the standard of care followed. (1986,
444)

Fost argues that "it is morally irresponsible to voluntarily bring an
infant into the world but refuse to make reasonable efforts to allow that
child to be born healthy" (1989, 252). Compelling women to behave in
ways that avoid fetal risk should be confined, he argues, to circumstances
when there is a high probability of live birth, a high probability of serious
physical harm to the "infant to be," a high probability that the harm can be
prevented using standard established treatment, and a low probability of
serious harm to the mother.

Shaw draws an analogy between child abuse and fetal abuse in arguing
that:

> We should not allow children to be victimized by adult behavior either
> before or after birth. They need special safeguards, including legal
> protection. The parent's right to reproduce, even though constitution-
> ally protected, should be subordinated to the needs of the child. (1984,
> 102)

According to Robertson, if the woman chooses to abort, the issue of
obligation is moot. Otherwise, the obligation to care for the fetus exists.
He writes:

> [T]he mother has, if she conceives and chooses not to abort, a legal and
> moral duty to bring the child into the world as healthy as is reasonably
> possible. She has a duty to avoid actions or omissions that will damage
> the fetus and child, just as she has a duty to protect the child's welfare
> once it is born. . . . In terms of fetal rights, a fetus has no right to be
> conceived—or, once conceived, to be carried to viability. But once the
> mother decides not to terminate the pregnancy, the viable fetus ac-
> quires rights to have the mother conduct her life in ways that will not
> injure it. (1983, 438)

One modification seems appropriate to Robertson's analysis, and that is
his reference to viability. A number of treatable conditions which compro-

mise the health and/or life of the born child occur prior to viability. For example, a pregnant woman with diabetes subjects the born child to a higher incidence of abnormal blood sugars, large-for-gestational-age size, increased congenital anomalies, and potential fetal death. Such complications can be minimized through careful monitoring and controlling of blood sugar throughout the pregnancy, including the period prior to viability. Thus, under Robertson's model, it seems more appropriate to argue that the woman incurs the obligation as soon as she knows she is pregnant, and she continues to have the obligation as long as she remains pregnant, including the period prior to viability.

While it is both reasonable and ethically defensible to argue that women have obligations to care for the fetus because the fetus becomes the born child, it is also important to consider why women might refuse recommended interventions. A number of reasons are readily apparent. First, as the cases discussed below will exemplify, a number of women have refused obstetrical interventions on religious or cultural grounds. Jehovah's Witnesses refuse blood transfusions. Hmongs oppose a variety of invasive procedures, including delivery by cesarean section. Moreover, decisions regarding major medical treatment for Hmong women are made by their husbands or other male members of their clan.

A pregnant woman is placed in a very difficult ethical position when she is asked to choose between the recommendations of her physician and the teachings of her church. If she chooses the physician's recommendations, she may believe she has condemned herself and/or her child to eternal life in hell. For a devoutly religious person, having to submit to an unwanted intervention may be emotionally devastating.

Secondly, cost becomes a factor. More than 35 million Americans are uninsured (Reagan 1992, 15). More than one-third of families headed by women live in poverty (Dye 1992, 118). For women in these circumstances, the cost of an expensive intervention such as a cesarean section can create financial disaster. Even interventions which appear to be cost-free may, in reality, be quite expensive. For example, bed rest is typically recommended for the pregnant woman if she has gestational hypertension. Without such bed rest, the child could be growth retarded and could conceivably die. But bed rest is not a viable alternative to the woman who must work full-time to support her family. Bed rest for her may mean the loss of her job, her income, and possibly her employer-paid health insurance. Even if she is not employed outside the home, if she has other young children to care for and no child care assistance and no financial means to secure child care assistance, it will be very difficult for her to comply with a bed rest recommendation.

It is also difficult for women to comply with unwanted interventions if they disagree with the diagnosis or fear that the procedure will harm themselves, their fetuses, or their children once born. This situation is made even more difficult because, for a variety of reasons, abortion may not be a realistic alternative. Many interventions occur too late in pregnancy to obtain a legal abortion in most states. Even when an abortion can be legally obtained, it is not readily accessible to poor women or to women whose religious or other personal views exclude it as an acceptable alternative.

Thus when a woman is asked to submit to an unwanted obstetrical intervention, she faces an extremely complex ethical dilemma. If she ultimately refuses to consent to the intervention, she risks the possibility that the physician may seek a court order forcing her to submit. As the cases discussed below indicate, use of the legal system to resolve these disputes raises a number of serious problems.

IN THE LEGAL ARENA

The Legal Status of the Fetus

Generally speaking, when the courts have addressed issues involving the fetus, they have done so in the context of it becoming–or potentially becoming–the born child. In ruling on abortion in *Roe v. Wade,* the Supreme Court stated that "the word 'person,' as used in the Fourteenth Amendment, does not include the unborn" (1973, 158). However, the Court ruled that the state does have an important and legitimate interest in potential life, and the compelling point at which that interest comes into place is at viability:

> This is so because the fetus then presumably has the capability of meaningful life outside the mother's womb. State regulation protective of fetal life after viability thus has both logical and biological justifications. (1973, 163)

The Supreme Court again addressed the issue of potential life in *Webster v. Reproductive Health Services,* when it upheld a Missouri abortion statute that required physicians to perform viability tests when they had reason to believe that a woman seeking an abortion was 20 or more weeks pregnant:

The tests that [the statute] requires . . . are designed to determine viability. The State here has chosen viability as the point at which its interest in potential human life must be safeguarded. . . . [W]e are satisfied that the requirement of these tests permissibly furthers the State's interest in protecting potential human life. . . . (1989, 3057)

The rights of the born child during the fetal stage have been addressed in a number of lower court decisions. Generally speaking, the fetus has inheritance rights, but only exercisable after live birth. Born children have civil claims for prenatal injuries, sometimes against parents. For example, a 1980 Michigan appellate decision upheld the right of a child to be compensated for damages (stained teeth) resulting from the mother's use of tetracycline during pregnancy (*Grodin v. Grodin*). According to Blank, a majority of jurisdictions allow for causes of action for the death of an unborn child (1992, 61), thus leading to potential litigation based on maternal liability:

Although few cases to date have dealt with civil and criminal liability of mothers for their actions during pregnancy, the abrogation of intrafamily immunity and the heightened awareness and evidence of the deleterious effects on the fetus of certain maternal behavior make it likely that such suits will proliferate. Furthermore, the heightened acceptance of causes of action against third parties for prenatal injuries or fetal death is bound logically to extend to causes where prenatal injury resulted from parental negligence . . . the manifestation of these trends is likely to alter substantially notions of responsible maternal behavior and in some cases pit the rights of privacy and autonomy of the mother against the rights of a child to be born with a sound mind and body. (1992, 89)

Court-Ordered Interventions

The courts have also moved to protect the fetus during the prenatal period through court-ordered intervention. For example, in 1964 a New Jersey court ordered a Jehovah's Witness to submit to blood transfusions to save her life and that of her unborn child (*Raleigh Fitkin-Paul Morgan Memorial Hospital v. Anderson*), however, the woman left the hospital and the transfusion never took place (Annas 1982, 17). The pregnancy outcome is unknown. In another Jehovah's Witness case, a New York court ordered a blood transfusion for the benefit of a pre-viable (18 week) fetus based on a finding that the state's interest in the fetus outweighed the patient's interest (*In re Jamaica Hospital* 1985). Also in New York, hospital officials were made *guardian ad litem* for a pregnant woman and her fetus with authority to consent to diagnostic and therapeutic procedures necessary to preserve the health of the fetus (*North Central Bronx v. Headley* 1986, cited in Rhoden 1986, 2026).

In a case reported in 1981, a court order was also granted requiring an unidentified Colorado woman to submit to a cesarean section. She had received no prenatal care and had a lifelong history of morbid obesity. Physicians recommended delivery by cesarean section because her membranes had ruptured prior to admission, the amniotic fluid was meconium stained, and fetal monitors indicated fetal distress. She was advised of the need for the cesarean section, but refused, citing her fear of surgery. Her family attempted unsuccessfully to persuade her, as did medical staff. The hospital then obtained a court order requiring the woman to submit to the surgery. The finding of the juvenile court was that the "baby" was a dependent and neglected child.

Once the order was issued, the woman became more cooperative and a female infant was delivered by cesarean. Clinical and laboratory findings confirmed that the baby had been oxygen deprived. Several months later, the juvenile court placed the infant and two older siblings in foster care due to maternal neglect (Bowes and Selgestad 1981). Long-term follow-up for the child was not conducted because the physicians lost contact with her.

While some courts have been willing to order such interventions, others have not. Bringing such cases to court raises a host of ethical and policy dilemmas. Several themes are readily apparent when such cases are analyzed. First, equal protection, as provided in the Fourteenth Amendment, becomes an issue because only women are affected by court-ordered obstetrical interventions (Johnsen 1986, 620), and additionally because racial and socioeconomic discrimination are apparent. A 1986 survey of obstetricians in 45 states conducted by Kolder et al., reported that 21 court orders for obstetrical intervention including cesarean sections, hospital detentions, and intrauterine transfusions were sought at the respondents' institutions during a five year period. The data showed a greater likelihood to seek orders for minority women than for white women. Seventeen of the women (81%) were black, Asian, or Hispanic, and five (24%) did not speak English as their primary language (1987, 1193).

An additional problem is that the American legal system is adversarial in nature, and adversarial relations between the pregnant woman and her physician may develop if the court system is utilized to coerce treatment.

Some women may avoid prenatal care as a result. Court-ordered intervention may also create adversarial relations between the woman and the fetus–and subsequently the born child–if she feels her own health and welfare are being sacrificed. Both potentially adversarial situations should be avoided. Moreover, utilization of the courts places the decision in the hands of judges who are untrained in medicine and therefore ill-equipped to make such judgments.

But perhaps the two most prominent problems in reported cases of court-ordered obstetrical interventions are that the courts have rushed to judgement, and the diagnoses have often been inaccurate. Due to the emergency nature of some obstetrical interventions, court hearings are typically scheduled with little notice and thus women lack sufficient opportunity to retain legal counsel and once retained, legal counsel lack sufficient opportunity to prepare their cases. The Kolder data indicate that in 14 of 20 cases (70%), hospital administrators and lawyers were aware of the situation for a day or less before the order was pursued. In 14 of 16 cases (88%), it took six hours or less to obtain the orders, in three cases (19%) the orders were issued in one hour or less, and at least one order was granted by telephone. Moreover, medicine is not an exact science, and diagnosis is rarely 100% accurate. The Kolder data indicate that 16 orders were sought for cesarean delivery, and in six cases the prediction of harm to the fetus was inaccurate (1987, 1195). In nearly all of the court cases analyzed below, the judicial time clock became a high speed stopwatch, and in most of these cases, the medical diagnoses and prognoses were incorrect.

For example, in 1981, Griffin Spaulding County Hospital sought an order requiring that Jessie May Jefferson undergo delivery by cesarean section in the event she admitted herself to the hospital because she had been diagnosed with complete placenta previa (a condition where the placenta is located between the fetus and the birth canal). While she had diligently sought prenatal care, she refused to consent to surgery or blood transfusions on religious grounds. The following day, the Georgia Department of Human Resources (DHR) petitioned the court for temporary custody of the unborn child, alleging that it was deprived of proper parental care. The court granted custody to the DHR and ordered Jefferson to submit to an ultrasound with the provision that if the ultrasound showed the placenta blocking the child's passage, Jefferson would be ordered to submit to a cesarean section and related procedures (including blood transfusions). The Superior Court found that:

> it is virtually impossible that this condition will correct itself prior to delivery; and that it is a 99% certainty that the child cannot survive

natural childbirth (vaginal delivery). The chances of [the] defendant surviving vaginal delivery are no better than 50%. The examining physician is of the opinion that a delivery by cesarean section prior to labor beginning would have an almost 100% chance of preserving the life of the child, along with that of the defendant. (*Jefferson v. Griffin Spaulding County Hospital* 1981, 458)

Jefferson appealed to the Georgia Supreme Court for a stay of the Superior Court order, but her motion was denied. Despite the statistics cited by the court, the condition either corrected itself or was misdiagnosed because Jefferson subsequently had a successful vaginal delivery.

A similar situation occurred the following year in Jackson County, Michigan. A woman named Jeffries also was diagnosed with placenta previa and also refused consent for a cesarean section on religious grounds. While information on the Jeffries case is limited, it is reported that the fetus was found by the court to be a dependent and neglected child, and surgery was ordered (Rhoden 1986, 1951 and 1962). Jeffries went into hiding, and police were authorized to bring her to the hospital against her will. Their search, however, was unsuccessful, and newspapers reported that she subsequently had a successful vaginal delivery at another hospital. In the North Central Bronx case cited earlier, the woman left the hospital and had a successful vaginal delivery at home in order to avoid a cesarean section (Rhoden 1986, 2009).

In *Taft v. Taft* (1983) a Massachusetts man sought to force his wife, who was four months pregnant, to have her cervix sutured to prevent premature labor. She refused on religious grounds, although the operation had been performed in previous pregnancies.[3] The trial court appointed counsel for both the husband and wife, and in the hearing accepted the physician's written report without cross examination (Murray 1992). The court found for the husband, but the appellate court stayed the order pending an appeal. The Massachusetts Supreme Court vacated the trial court's order because the wife was competent, and there were no trial court findings describing the operation or stating the nature of the risks to the wife or unborn child. The procedure was not performed, and the woman had an uneventful full-term vaginal delivery.

In 1986, Georgetown University Hospital obtained a court order to perform a cesarean section on 19-year-old Ayesha Madyun. Her membrane had ruptured 48 hours before her arrival at the hospital. After an additional 18 hours of labor, doctors decided she needed a cesarean section because labor was not progressing, and there was a risk of fetal infection. Madyun attended the hearing even though her contractions were coming at five minute intervals.

The physician testified that the risk of fetal sepsis was 50% to 75% and that the risk of the cesarean section to Madyun was 0.25%. While the only symptom Madyun exhibited was a slightly elevated temperature, the physician testified that evidence of sepsis may not become apparent until the baby is already septic. Madyun and her husband opposed the surgery because they did not feel that it was warranted. She testified that a Muslim woman has the right to decide whether or not to risk her own health in order to eliminate a possible risk to the life of her undelivered fetus. The Superior Court of the District of Columbia ordered the cesarean section, stating that "the parents may not make a martyr of their unborn infant" (*In re Madyun* 1986). The trial court decision was upheld by a late night conference call to two appellate justices. Madyun's son was born by cesarean section without complication. He was healthy and showed no signs of sepsis. Madyun also recovered without complication.

Another case developed in December 1990 in LaCrosse, Wisconsin. Chao Lee was a 37-year-old Hmong immigrant. She had lived in the U.S. for less than a year and spoke no English. Her previous six children were all born at home. She was diagnosed with placenta previa late in pregnancy, and when she refused to consent to a cesarean delivery, her physician requested a court order. The physician testified that she and her husband would have agreed to the surgery, but that they were pressured not to by other members of their clan (Perlich 1992). Chao Lee did not attend the hearing. It is not known whether she was ever informed about the hearing or even understood the American judicial process.

Shortly before the hearing, a public defender was appointed to represent her. Due to the emergency nature of the hearing, he was not given adequate time to prepare a defense, he had never met or even talked with his client, he did not know the facts of the case, and the issues were outside of his normal practice of law. Despite this, the hearing was conducted, and the judge issued an order requiring the cesarean section in the event that Chao Lee arrived voluntarily at the hospital, and the procedure was necessary to save her life (Perlich 1992). The judge also scheduled a second hearing for the following week. By then, Chao Lee had consulted another physician who believed that the child could be delivered vaginally. This physician testified at the second hearing, and the judge rescinded his order. The defendant subsequently delivered a healthy child by vaginal birth (Passell 1992).

But the most poignant example of court-ordered intervention gone wrong is that of 27-year-old Angela Carder, who had been diagnosed with cancer at age 13. During the ensuing years, she had radiation, chemotherapy, and several major operations, including a leg amputation. Her cancer had been in remission for a period of three years when she married and shortly thereafter became pregnant. On June 15, 1987, at 26 1/2 weeks gestation, physicians at George Washington University Medical Center (GWUMC) advised her that she had terminal cancer and was close to death. She agreed to palliative treatment in order to extend the life of the fetus to 28 weeks in the event it became necessary to perform a cesarean section (*In Re: A.C., Appellant* 1990, 1110). At this point, she was equivocal about wanting to have the baby.

The following morning the trial court convened at the hospital, but without Carder present because she was heavily sedated. The court appointed counsel for both Carder and the fetus, and the District of Columbia was permitted to intervene as *parens patriae*. The trial was convened so quickly that Carder's attorney did not have the opportunity to meet with her, nor was her personal physician, who had been treating her for years, even advised of the hearing or the intent to perform surgery. Her husband did not testify at the hearing; however, her mother testified in opposition to the surgery. Her personal physician later indicated that he would have opposed the surgery had he known about it. However, hearing testimony from other physicians, the court ordered that a cesarean section be performed.

When Carder was informed of the court order by a physician, she initially agreed, but shortly thereafter indicated she had changed her mind and did not want the cesarean section after all. The court was advised of her objection, yet again ordered the surgery claiming it was unclear about her intent (*In Re: A.C., Appellant* 1990, 1117). Her counsel immediately sought a stay from the District of Columbia Court of Appeals, which was denied by a hastily assembled panel of three judges. The surgery was performed, the infant daughter died about two hours later as a result of extreme prematurity and maternal respiratory failure, and Carder died two days later.

Several months later, the District of Columbia Court of Appeals reversed its denial on the motion to stay the surgery despite the fact that it had already been performed and both mother and daughter were dead. Subsequently, the American Civil Liberties Union requested a review of the case, and in 1990, the District of Columbia Court of Appeals issued an en banc decision, *In Re: A.C., Appellant,* reversing the trial court's order to perform the cesarean and simultaneously making a clear and strong statement on behalf of the rights of all patients to make informed decisions regarding their medical treatment. Regarding cesarean deliveries, it found that "in virtually all cases the question of what is to be done is to be decided by the patient–the pregnant woman–on behalf of herself and the fetus" (*In Re: A.C., Appellant* 1990, 1110). The notion of maternal obligation to "rescue" the fetus was clearly ruled out:

> (The) courts do not compel one person to permit a significant intrusion upon his or her bodily integrity for the benefit of another person's health. . . . Surely . . . a fetus cannot have rights in this respect superior to those of a person who has already been born. (1990, 1123)

The court also found that the patient's quality of life cannot affect decision-making:

> It matters not what the quality of the patient's life may be; the right of bodily integrity is not extinguished simply because someone is ill, or even at death's door. To protect that right against intrusion by others– family members, doctors, hospitals, or anyone else, however well-intentioned–we hold that a court must determine the patient's wishes by any means available, and must abide by those wishes unless there are truly extraordinary or compelling reasons to override them. (1990, 1130)

If the patient is incompetent and cannot give informed consent, the court must become a surrogate to determine what choice she would have made if she were competent. Since a pregnant patient may be concerned with the welfare of the fetus:

> it is proper for the court in a case such as this, to weigh (along with all the other factors) the mother's prognosis, the viability of the fetus, and the probable result of treatment or nontreatment for both mother and fetus, and the mother's likely interest in avoiding impairment for her child together with her own instincts for survival. (1990, 1140)

The court concluded that its decision did not preclude the notion that the state's interest could prevail over the interests of the pregnant patient. However:

> it would be an extraordinary case indeed in which a court might ever be justified in overriding the patient's wishes and authorizing a major surgical procedure such as a cesarean section. (1990, 1142)

The Angela Carder case is a tragic example of obstetrical intervention gone wrong. The legal process moved with great speed, but the diagnosis indicating a reasonable likelihood of a successful birth was inaccurate. Great harm came to both the mother and child. Invasive surgery was performed, Carder's life was shortened, and she died with the knowledge that her daughter had preceded her in death. Angela Carder became a maternal martyr.

CONCLUSION

Conflict regarding decision-making during the prenatal period raises important ethical and legal issues because there are two patients, one inescapably within the other. Scholars have typically framed discussions regarding this conflict in terms of maternal-*fetal* conflict, however, this approach ignores the most fundamental issue, which is how the conflict affects the pregnant woman and the *born* child. While the latter involves discussion of the fetus, such discussion is framed in the context of optimizing the pregnancy outcome in order to deliver a healthy child along with providing a healthy recovery for the pregnant woman.

The essential question becomes one of maternal obligations to care for the born child. Infants and young children cannot care for themselves, and thus parents have an obligation to provide this care. One way in which that duty is discharged is by caring for and protecting the fetus during the prenatal period because injury to the fetus may result in injury or death to the born child. However, there are intervening circumstances which may make it difficult for a woman to discharge these duties to the fetus. As previously noted, a woman sometimes refuses treatment which her physician feels is in the best interest of the fetus. She may do this, for example, for religious reasons, or because she disagrees with the physician's diagnosis or recommendations, or feels the intervention presents an unreasonable risk to her life or health or to the life or health of the fetus. It is likely that such conflicts will continue–and possibly increase–as prenatal care becomes increasingly sophisticated, and physicians learn more about the treatment needs of the fetus.

While some physicians have turned to the courts in order to force pregnant women to comply with treatment recommendations, the use of the judicial system creates additional problems. Equal protection surfaces as an issue because only women are affected, and also because there is greater likelihood that such orders will be sought for minority women than for white women. The American legal system is adversarial in nature, and using it during the prenatal period creates a strong likelihood of adversarial relations between the physician and the pregnant patient, and also between her, the fetus, and later, the born child. The judicial system is ill-equipped to make such choices because judges are not trained in medicine. Moreover, due to the emergency nature of some interventions, "speedy justice" is sought, but "justice" in these cases may be elusive because litigants lack the opportunity to retain legal counsel, and the courts lack the time for reasoned deliberation.

The cases discussed earlier in this article provide evidence that sometimes—we do not know how often—patients are misdiagnosed and unnecessary procedures pursued. Other than the Kolder survey of obstetricians, data on the number and types of court orders pursued are unavailable. More data would be extremely helpful in sorting out these complex issues. For example, a retrospective analysis of completed interventions would help determine how often the diagnoses and recommended interventions were incorrect. Also, data are needed on the number of times physicians recommend procedures, the pregnant woman refuses, no court order is sought, and a baby is delivered with a serious harm that could have been prevented. Such data would shed enormous light on this very complex and clouded issue.

NOTES

1. This research was funded by the American Political Science Association and the American Philosophical Society. I would like to thank Carolyn Braun, Dana Johnson, Norman Fost, and the staff of the Hastings Center for their contributions.

2. Reports of maternal mortality in cesarean deliveries vary from study to study. A 1983 study showed a rate of one maternal death per 1,635 cesarean operations. Only about one-half of these deaths, however, were directly attributable to the cesarean section itself. A 1988 study showed 27 maternal deaths associated with 121,000 cesarean deliveries, but only seven were directly caused by the operation (Cunningham, MacDonald, and Gant 1989, 443).

3. At the time of the litigation, Susan and Lawrence Taft had four children. In three of those pregnancies, Ms. Taft's cervix was sutured to prevent pre-term delivery. A fourth pregnancy was successfully carried full term without the procedure, and a fifth pregnancy miscarried in the seventh month resulting in the death of the fetus.

REFERENCES

American College of Obstetricians and Gynecologists. October 1987. "Patient Choice: Maternal-Fetal Conflict." Number 55.

Annas, George. 1982. "Forced Cesareans: The Most Unkindest Cut of All." *Hastings Center Report.* 12, 3:16-7 & 45.

Blank, Robert H. 1986. "Emerging Notions of Women's Rights and Responsibilities During Gestation." *The Journal of Legal Medicine.* 7, 4:441-469.

Blank, Robert H. 1992. *Mother and Fetus: Changing Notions of Maternal Responsibility.* New York: Greenwood.

Bowes, Watson A., Selgestad, Brad. 1981. "Fetal Versus Maternal Rights: Medical and Legal Perspectives." *Obstetrics and Gynecology.* 58, 2:209-214.

Cunningham, F. Gary, Paul C. MacDonald, Norman F. Gant. 1989. *Williams Obstetrics.* Norwalk, Conn.: Appleton and Lange.

Dye, Thomas R. 1992. *Understanding Public Policy.* Englewood Cliffs, N.J.: Prentice-Hall.

Field, Martha A. 1989. "Controlling the Woman to Protect the Fetus." *Law Medicine and Health Care.* 17, 2:114-129.

Fost, Norman. 1989. "Maternal-Fetal Conflicts: Ethical and Legal Considerations." *Annals New York Academy of Sciences.* 562:248-254.

Grodin v. Grodin, 102 Mich. App. 396, 301 N.W. 2d 869 (1980).

In re: A.C., D.C. Ct. App., April 26, 1990 (en banc, slip op.).

In re Jamaica Hospital, 128 Misc. 2d 1006, 491 N.Y.S.2d 898 (Sup. Ct. 1985).

In re Madyun. 114 Daily Wash. L. Rptr. 2233 (D.C. Super. Ct. July 26, 1986).

Jefferson v. Griffin Spaulding County Hospital, 247 Ga. 86, 274 S.E.2d 457 (1981).

Johnsen, Dawn. 1986. "Creation of Fetal Rights: Conflicts with Women's Constitutional Rights to Liberty, Privacy, and Equal Protection." *The Yale Law Journal.* 95:599-625.

Kolder, Veronika, Janet Gallagher, and Michael T. Parsons. 1987. "Court-Ordered Obstetrical Interventions." *The New England Journal of Medicine.* 316:1192-1196.

Murray, William A., attorney for Lawrence Taft. Telephone interview September 16, 1992.

Nelson, Lawrence J. and Nancy Milliken. 1988. "Compelled Medical Treatment of Pregnant Women: Life, Liberty, and Law in Conflict." *Journal of the American Medical Association.* 259, 7:1060-1066.

Passell, Dale. Attorney for Chao Lee, *Unborn Child of Chao Lee.* Case number: 90 JV 210, LaCrosse County, Wisconsin. Telephone interview September 17, 1992.

Perlich, John J. Circuit Judge, Branch 4, LaCrosse, Wisconsin. Presiding judge in *Unborn Child of Chao Lee.* Case number: 90 JV 210, LaCrosse County, Wisconsin. Personal correspondence to the author, September 22, 1992.

Raleigh Fitkin-Paul Morgan Memorial Hospital v. Anderson, 42 N.J. 421, 201 A.2d 537 cert denied, 377 U.S. 985 (1964).

Reagan, Michael D. 1992. *Curing the Crisis: Options for America's Health Care.* Boulder, Colo.: Westview Press.

Rhoden, Nancy. 1986. "The Judge in the Delivery Room: The Emergence of Court Ordered Cesareans." *California Law Review.* 74, 6:951-2030.

Rhoden, Nancy. 1987. "Cesareans and Samaritans." *Law, Medicine and Health Care.* 15, 3:118-125.

Robertson, John. 1983. "Procreative Liberty and the Control of Conception, Pregnancy, and Childbirth." *Virginia Law Review.* 69, 3:405-464.

Roe v. Wade, 410 U.S. 113 (1973).

Shaw, Margery W. 1984. "Conditional Prospective Rights of the Fetus." *The Journal of Legal Medicine.* 5, 1:63-116.

Taft v. Taft. 388 Mass. 331, 146 N.E. 2d 395 (1983).

Webster v. Reproductive Health Services. 109 S.Ct. 3040 (1989).

What Is the Purpose
of Neonatal Drug Testing?
Towards a Rational Social Policy

Robert M. Nelson

SUMMARY. Controversy over neonatal drug testing may be due to a lack of agreement on the purposes for such testing. This article examines six issues: (1) the purpose of neonatal testing; (2) the selection of infants for testing; (3) the requirement for parental consent; (4) the concept of prenatal harm; (5) the standard of conduct required of a pregnant woman; and (6) the practical application of such a standard in designing a testing policy. It is argued that maternal consent does not need to be required for testing provided that: (1) adequate drug treatment services are available for the mother and infant; and (2) test results are excluded from use in legal proceedings. If prevention, therapy and research (rather than punishment) guides a neonatal testing policy, the sporadic testing of an infant's urine for the presence of illicit substances clearly falls short of the desired goals.

INTRODUCTION

Prenatal substance abuse and the subsequent birth of drug-affected infants have increasingly become the focus of criminal prosecution and

Robert M. Nelson is Assistant Professor of Pediatrics and Bioethics, at the Department of Pediatrics and the Center for the Study of Bioethics, Medical College of Wisconsin, Milwaukee, WI 53226.

The author can be reached at Children's Hospital of Wisconsin, 9000 West Wisconsin Avenue, MS #9, Milwaukee, WI 53226.

[Haworth co-indexing entry note]: "What Is the Purpose of Neonatal Drug Testing? Towards a Rational Social Policy." Nelson, Robert M. Co-published simultaneously in *Women & Politics* (The Haworth Press, Inc.) Vol. 13, No. 3/4, 1993, pp. 83-97; and: *The Politics of Pregnancy: Policy Dilemmas in the Maternal-Fetal Relationship* (ed: Janna C. Merrick, and Robert H. Blank) The Haworth Press, Inc., 1993, pp. 83-97. Multiple copies of this article/chapter may be purchased from The Haworth Document Delivery Center [1-800-3-HAWORTH; 9:00 a.m. - 5:00 p.m. (EST)].

state legislation. Approaches range from the incarceration of drug-addicted pregnant women in order to eliminate fetal exposure, through criminal prosecution for child abuse and neglect or the delivery of controlled substances to a minor, to expanding the availability of treatment services for drug addicted pregnant women (King 1991; Larson 1991). Such attention is partly the result of the increasing prevalence of fetal exposure to illicit drugs combined with a better understanding of the impact of substances such as cocaine on the developing fetus (Volpe 1992). Using an estimate of a 10% incidence of illicit drug use by pregnant women, in the State of Wisconsin there are over 7,000 newborn infants each year who are exposed to the potentially detrimental effects of illicit drugs (WAPC 1992).

Central to the determination of whether an infant has been exposed to an illicit substance is testing of either the mother or infant. As discussed below, there are at least four purposes for neonatal drug testing: research, punishment, prevention or therapy. The type and timing of testing will depend on the purpose of performing the test. For example, if the purpose is to prosecute the mother for delivering a controlled substance to her infant prior to cutting the umbilical cord, only blood or urine testing of the infant immediately after birth will provide the needed evidence. If the purpose is to study the impact of in utero drug exposure on infant development, perhaps the testing of an infant's hair will be the best way to determine the timing and extent of exposure (Volpe 1992). If the purpose is to prevent the birth of a drug-affected infant, perhaps the emphasis should be on screening and testing pregnant women. The controversy over neonatal drug testing may be due in part to a lack of clarity and agreement on the purposes for such testing.

THE WISCONSIN LAW ON NEONATAL DRUG TESTING

Wisconsin Statute, section 146.0255, states that when a physician suspects that a mother has ingested a controlled substance while pregnant, the infant's parent or guardian must give consent in order for the physician to test the infant's urine for the presence of controlled substances. Passed without amendment in October of 1989, the law went into effect on January 1, 1990. As originally drafted, the statute allowed for testing an infant without parental consent and amended the definition of medical neglect to include illicit drug use during pregnancy (Roe 1991). The draft and subsequent legislation was altered by the sponsoring committee to require parental consent and remove the extended definition of neglect in order to protect the mother from prosecution (WAPC 1992). As a result, a law which would have allowed for the liberal identification of drug-affected newborns without parental consent became a more restrictive bill designed to protect the mother from potential prosecution for her illicit drug use while pregnant.

The law as it stands has come under considerable criticism from the Wisconsin medical community. Pediatricians are concerned that the law favors a woman's interest in protection from civil or criminal liability at the expense of the infant's interest in receiving necessary services aimed at preventing further morbidity from prenatal drug exposure. In addition, some obstetricians have objected to any restrictions on physician discretion in obtaining a maternal or neonatal drug screen given the fact that a positive drug screen may protect the obstetrician from liability for an infant's potentially poor outcome. Finally, the law ignores any community or state interest in identifying a drug-addicted woman so as to prevent potential harm to future infants through treating the drug-addicted woman prior to her next pregnancy (WAPC 1992).

Discussions at a statewide meeting of Wisconsin health care providers revealed diverse interpretations of the Wisconsin Statute, reflecting the divergent balancing of the infant's (and mother's) interest in treatment, the mother's right to privacy and the physician's interest in protection from malpractice liability. On the one hand, some hospitals and physicians believe that the blanket consent form signed on admission to the hospital allows for obtaining maternal and neonatal drug screens without additional consent; on the other hand, the majority of hospitals and physicians recognize that the law requires specific parental consent for the sending of a neonatal drug screen, documented with either a separate signed consent form or a written note in the chart. Obtaining a maternal or neonatal drug screen based on a blanket consent form amounts to testing without consent. Finally, though the statute requires that test results be disclosed to the infant's parent or guardian, it does not specify whether the requirement for mandatory reporting of positive results to the county social services needs to be disclosed as part of the consent process. Some physicians report almost universal consent to the sending of a drug screen, although this may reflect the variability in information provided as part of the consent process as well as the fact that women are often under the impression that they do not have a choice (WAPC 1992).

There is almost universal agreement that the Wisconsin law does little to improve the access of drug-affected infants and mothers to necessary medical and social services (WAPC 1992). Though the law will expire in June of 1993, the issue of the appropriate design of a neonatal testing policy will remain given the increase in drug-affected pregnant women and newborns (Chasnoff 1990; Frank 1988; George 1991; Gillogley 1990; Matera 1990; McCalla 1991; Ney 1990; Schutzman 1991) and further knowledge of the effect of in utero drug exposure on fetal and subsequent infant development (Chasnoff 1992; Frank 1990; Mayes 1992; Parker 1990; Volpe 1992; Zuckerman 1989). In developing a defensible policy on the drug testing of newborn infants, this article will briefly examine six areas: (1) the purpose of neonatal testing; (2) the selection of infants for testing; (3) the requirement for parental consent; (4) the concept of prenatal harm; (5) the standard of conduct required of a pregnant woman towards her fetus; and (6) the practical application of such a standard towards the design of a testing policy. It will be argued that maternal consent need not be required for either prenatal or neonatal testing provided that: (1) adequate drug treatment and rehabilitative services are available for both the mother and her infant; and (2) the test results are excluded from use in civil or criminal proceedings.

THE PURPOSE OF NEONATAL TESTING

Why test an infant for the presence of maternally ingested substances? There are at least four purposes which can be identified: research, punishment, prevention, and therapy. Lacking accepted criteria for the objective selection of an "at risk" population (see below), any research project involving drug-affected newborns should involve universal testing of a broadly defined population. For example, although numerous studies have determined the incidence of drug-affected infants using universal testing (George 1991; Gillogley 1990; Matera 1990; McCalla 1991; Schutzman 1991), only a few of the published studies to date have linked in utero cocaine exposure with the long-term outcome of a specific neonate (Chasnoff 1991; Schneider 1992). This is understandable given the concern to protect maternal and neonatal confidentiality; however, it is impossible to assess the variable effect of cocaine on a newborn without accurately determining the timing and extent of a particular infant's exposure (Mayes 1992; Volpe 1992). A research-based testing program would allow for therapeutic studies on drug-affected newborns to establish whether early intervention programs are effective in preventing morbidity. More importantly, a prospective population-based study would determine the impact of prenatal drug exposure on an infant (Mayes 1992). It remains possible, even probable, that a number of infants who have been exposed prenatally to maternally ingested substances such as cocaine or marijuana do not suffer any significant or measurable harm (Zuckerman 1992).

The second purpose of testing is to attempt to punish the woman for ingesting an illicit substance during pregnancy. Grounds for prosecution may include child abuse, medical neglect, illicit drug use, and delivery of a controlled substance to a minor (AMA 1990; Larson 1991; Nolan 1990, 18-20; Roberts 1991, 1428-32). Testing an infant's urine thus allows access to the mother. Performed without maternal consent, testing may violate a woman's right not to be subject to an unconsented search and seizure. Drug testing without consent has been justified on the grounds of protecting public safety, for example, in the case of airline pilots. However, neonatal testing without maternal consent cannot be justified simply on the grounds of protecting the infant from harm for the drug exposure has already occurred. If the rationale for unconsented testing and criminal prosecution is to prevent harm to the fetus, there is no principled way to limit criminal prosecution to illicit drug use as opposed to any action taken by the pregnant woman which proves harmful to the fetus (Mariner 1990; Roberts 1991, 1445). Advocates of punishment believe that this serves as a deterrent to illicit drug use among pregnant women. This is highly debatable as punitive measures have historically done little to prevent drug addiction (AMA 1990). Also, questions have been raised whether the criminal prosecution of a woman for harming her infant while a fetus meets the legal standards of criminal intent, proof of causation, and evidentiary rules for the collection and handling of specimens for criminal investigations (Mariner 1990, 33-36; Nolan 1990, 19). Attempts to convict a woman who has given birth to a drug-affected infant have generally failed; however, several states are considering measures which would allow for criminal prosecution based on prenatal substance abuse (Larson 1991; Marshall 1991).

The third purpose for testing an infant for the presence of maternally ingested drugs is to provide treatment for the addicted woman in order to prevent the subsequent birth of another drug-affected newborn. Here, the birth of a drug-affected newborn simply serves as an indicator for the need to provide services to the addicted woman. Clearly the only way to prevent the birth of a drug-affected infant is to prevent drug addiction in women of child-bearing age.

"Protective" incarceration of a drug-addicted pregnant woman has been used to restrict her access to illicit drugs and thus to prevent the birth of a drug-affected infant (AMA 1990; Roberts 1991). This approach is not an issue for neonatal screening unless a positive neonatal drug screen is used to justify mandated prenatal testing of a woman during future pregnancies. Though there may be punitive and eugenic undertones (Roberts 1991, 1475; Nolan 1990, 20), measures to restrict maternal lifestyle should be judged by their efficacy and feasibility as a mode of prevention. The lack of drug treatment programs designed for drug-addicted women, whether pregnant or non-pregnant, and the failure to provide adequate prenatal care to women at risk for poor neonatal outcomes reveals the shallowness of a societal commitment to the health of these women and their infants (Chavkin 1990). Selective "protective" incarceration simply adds insult to injury. Advocates of women's reproductive freedom (Roberts 1991) who support the right of a drug-addicted woman to become pregnant do not argue in favor of a right of the drug-addicted woman, once pregnant, to abuse her fetus (Johnson 1990). Rather they argue for a societal obligation to ensure that a drug-addicted woman can exercise her right of self-determination in becoming pregnant by providing adequate drug treatment facilities (Roberts 1991, 1478). Adequate prenatal care and drug treatment facilities as opposed to incarceration is the most cost-effective approach to preventing neonatal morbidity and mortality (AMA 1990; Calhoun 1991; MacGregor 1989; Phibbs 1991).

Finally, the fourth purpose of testing is to provide therapy for the drug-affected infant. A recent report suggests the value of early intervention in improving the developmental outcome of these infants (Chasnoff 1992; Zuckerman 1992). However, most states, including Wisconsin, generally fail to provide adequate early intervention services for infants born to drug-addicted women. Placed within Chapter 146 of the Wisconsin Statutes dealing with "Miscellaneous Health Provisions," the law on neonatal testing is thus framed as an issue of public health, not criminal sanctions. In Milwaukee County, a positive neonatal drug screen is not taken as prima facie evidence of neglect sufficient to remove an infant from the mother's custody. Nevertheless, the treatment and placement services currently being provided are inadequate to meet demand (WAPC 1992).

THE SELECTIVITY OF NEONATAL TESTING

Which infants should be tested? There are two general approaches to the identification of appropriate infants for testing, that is, selective and universal testing. Selective testing uses specific criteria to identify newborns believed to be "at risk" for having a positive test. Universal testing seeks to identify all newborns who have been exposed to maternally ingested substances by testing all newborn infants.

The usual clinical approach is selective testing, apart from specific research protocols looking at the incidence of drug use within a population. Criteria used to identify newborns for testing have included signs of neonatal withdrawal, clinical evidence of maternal drug use, personal characteristics of the mother and her newborn, or socioeconomic and racial classifications based on the alleged epidemiology of drug abuse. The intent is to target a "high risk" population, a task for which each of the above criteria can be criticized as either insensitive, non-specific or discriminatory.

For example, the observation of neonatal withdrawal symptoms is problematic. Some maternally ingested drugs which are potentially detrimental to the infant will not necessarily produce symptoms of withdrawal. Many newborns affected by maternally ingested substances are asymptomatic at birth and may only become symptomatic after hospital discharge (AAP 1990). Thus clinical evidence of neonatal withdrawal is an insensitive screen for it misses a number of drug-affected newborns, particularly those exposed in utero to cocaine or marijuana as opposed to opiates. Also, a significant percentage of newborn infants who have not been exposed to maternally-ingested substances will show non-specific evidence of jitteriness, a common symptom of neonatal withdrawal (Parker 1990).

Without objective criteria for identifying "high risk" patients, selective testing may discriminate inappropriately based on socioeconomic or racial considerations which are not relevant to the medical care of the newborn. In a study looking at the incidence of illicit drug or alcohol use during pregnancy in Pinellas County, Florida, 15% of pregnant women identified at the first prenatal visit were using either alcohol, marijuana, or cocaine. The overall incidence of drug use was independent of socioeconomic status, race and whether the care was delivered in a private or public clinic setting. Women at the public clinics used more cocaine, reflecting the fact that black women tended to use cocaine more than white women. White women used more marijuana than black women regardless of the location of their health care. Although the overall incidence of drug use was equal in the two populations, the frequency at which the women were reported for drug or alcohol use was significantly different. Whereas 12% of the black women were reported, less than 2% of the white women were reported (Chasnoff 1990). Although the symptoms of marijuana abuse are more subtle than cocaine and thus may contribute to this discrepancy in the ability of physicians to recognize and thus report drug use, the study suggests the existence of unjust discrimination based on socioeconomic status or race. Any program of selective testing must demonstrate that the criteria used do not unjustly discriminate on the basis of race or socioeconomic status (Skolnick 1990).

To avoid unjust discrimination and missing any drug-affected infants who may benefit from early identification and intervention, one may choose to advocate universal testing of all newborn infants. Universal testing such as mandatory newborn screening for hereditary disorders has been justified as cost-effective in preventing disease and disability. All asymptomatic newborns are screened and affected newborns are placed into an integrated medical and social program which prevents the development of severe disability. A neonatal drug screening program would not fit this universal testing paradigm. Once born, the infant has already been exposed to the adverse effects of the maternally ingested substance. Appropriate programs of early intervention may minimize the morbidity of prenatal drug exposure, although their efficacy remains to be established (Zuckerman 1992). Asymptomatic newborns with a positive drug screen may be unaffected and not need intervention. Affected newborns may have a negative drug screen if the woman abstained from cocaine use within one to four days of the test (Mayes 1992). Most communities do not have adequate programs to provide for the needs of drug-affected newborns (Chavkin 1990). In the absence of such programs, the therapeutic purpose of screening and especially universal screening is doubtful.

THE REQUIREMENT FOR PARENTAL CONSENT

Should an infant's parent or guardian be able to refuse testing? An argument can be made for not allowing a parent or guardian to refuse to test a newborn for illicit substances provided that testing is in the infant's "best interest." As such, parental refusal of testing would be medical neglect. However, for newborn drug testing to be in an infant's "best interest," therapeutic services must be provided to that infant. If such services are unavailable, an argument in favor of testing without parental consent would be undercut. Note that this same argument would not allow parents to refuse newborn metabolic screening or immunizations based on any reason, religious or otherwise (AAP 1988).

A second argument for testing without parental consent is that to refuse testing constitutes a presumption of guilt on the part of the woman. The argument that refusal of testing may be construed as a presumption of guilt is by analogy with "driving while intoxicated" statutes. Here, refusing an alcohol test is taken as a presumption of guilt. The rationale is that the goal of preventing future harm to others overrides the ability of a driver to hide behind a presumption of innocence by refusing to be tested. This second justification of unconsented testing of the newborn (or pregnant woman) requires (1) that the future infant as fetus is at risk for being harmed by the maternal ingestion of illicit substances and (2) that we have an effective and feasible mechanism for preventing that harm.

THE CONCEPT OF PRENATAL HARM

The concept of the prevention of prenatal harm to a future infant is both controversial and complex. Parents are protected from liability for harm brought about by transmission of a genetic disease. To date, parents are not held liable for their genetic code given that the act of conception is not viewed as a sufficient cause to constitute harm (Johnson 1986). This view of parental immunity has generally been extended to the causing of harm through the transmission of an acquired disease such as AIDS (Nolan 1989). Given that only 30-40% of newborns born to a woman with AIDS will subsequently contract the disease, such an extension of parental immunity appears to be reasonable. Ambivalence about such an approach may be related to the fact that many people impute fault to the woman for having contracted AIDS in the first place. Although the woman cannot be blamed for her genetic structure, she may be held accountable for her behavior which led to the contracting of AIDS.

In addition to harm through transmission of a genetic or acquired disease, an infant may be harmed prenatally through an accidental event. The fetal right to be born free from injury initially developed with the protection of parental rights to have a child born free from harm through the action of a third party. An example would be the ability of a woman to recover for injuries to her fetus suffered through an event such as an automobile accident. Subsequently some jurisdictions have extended the concept of a prenatal tort to include the ability of a child to recover for injuries suffered as a fetus through the negligent actions of the pregnant woman (Nelson 1986, 733-39). Court-ordered cesarean sections have been performed on women against their wishes given the alleged fact that the fetus would be harmed if the cesarean was not performed. However, with an accidental event such as placenta previa or fetal distress due to umbilical cord compression, a failure to act by the pregnant woman does not constitute negligence to the extent sufficient to justify forced surgical intervention (AMA 1990; Nelson and Milliken 1988).

Finally, the infant as fetus can be harmed by the transplacental transmission of a toxic substance. The courts have been reluctant to extend maternal liability for fetal harm to cover the ingestion of licit substances; however, there appears to be less hesitancy over restricting maternal actions in the case of illicit substances given the potential harm to the fetus (AMA 1990; Johnson 1986). Though the distinction between licit and illicit substances may allow us to establish which actions by a pregnant woman are amenable to judicial control, the distinction is misdrawn if the goal is to prevent harm to the fetus. Should decisions concerning alcohol, smoking, and exposure to environmental hazards be left up to the pregnant woman or should they be controlled in some fashion? Apart from the distinction between an unenforceable "positive" duty to come to the aid of the fetus and an enforceable "negative" duty not to harm the fetus, the fact that a pregnant woman can be exposed to many licit substances or activities which may cause fetal harm would expand potential restrictions on maternal choices.

THE STANDARD OF CONDUCT

Attempting to adjudicate these conflicts through a balancing of fetal and maternal rights is inadequate. The maternal right to bodily self-determination and privacy and the fetal right to protection from harm and bodily injury are, on the face of it, in conflict when the pregnant woman acts in a manner harmful to the fetus. Ranking maternal and fetal rights fails to capture the complex moral reasoning involved in the balancing of risk and benefit to both the pregnant woman and her future infant. As an alternative, the issue of the proper balancing of risk and benefit in raising an infant (or a fetus) can be discussed more fruitfully by analogy to issues of child abuse and neglect. In other words, the pregnant woman should be held accountable to the same moral and legal standard of conduct towards her fetus (once the decision not to abort has been made) as are the parents of a minor child (AMA 1990).

A maternal duty to prevent prenatal harm to a fetus does not undercut a woman's choice to abort, as the duty is not to the fetus per se but to a fetus who will be carried to term. Furthermore, even if a maternal duty to prevent prenatal harm appeals to the "personhood" of the fetus, this leaves unanswered whether and to what extent a fetus has a "positive" right to maternal aid. The "negative" duty not to harm our neighbor is legally enforceable. A "positive" moral obligation to aid our neighbor is usually not enforceable or mandatory. Thus, even if the fetus is a "person," this fact underdetermines the range of legally enforceable maternal obligations. For example, although a cesarean section may be in the best interest of the fetus, the pregnant woman arguably does not have a legally enforceable obligation to consent to a cesarean section in the face of an accidental threat to fetal well being (Nelson and Milliken 1988).

Based on the above standard of conduct, a pregnant woman has an enforceable moral obligation (that is, a legal duty) not to expose her fetus to a proven toxic substance. This conclusion however is simply the beginning of a discussion as to how to define and implement such a moral and legal duty. How should such an obligation be legally enforced? What is the extent to which a substance must be proven toxic to the fetus? How should the woman's obligation to the fetus be balanced against other competing personal, social and economic demands? Do we expect to reduce the risk for the fetus to zero, or simply to eliminate all reasonable hazards? Using the analogy to parental obligations for a minor child, we should allow a range of discretionary choices which balance fetal risks and benefits within the personal, social and economic context of the pregnant woman. Thus, for example, a woman's legal duty not to expose her fetus to a proven toxic substance does not justify forced exclusion of the woman of childbearing age from certain jobs (Moorman 1991).

THE PRACTICAL APPLICATION
OF THE STANDARD OF CONDUCT

Although parental obligation to a minor child may be an appropriate standard of moral and legal conduct for a drug-addicted pregnant woman towards her fetus, the practical reality of applying this standard towards the goal of preventing the birth of drug-affected newborns is more difficult. The fact remains that pregnant women do not become addicted but rather addicts become pregnant. Thus any approach to the drug screening of newborn infants, and follow-up services to these infants and families, must be directed towards preventing drug addiction and not limited simply to the care of drug-addicted women during pregnancy. In the context of drug addiction, testing of a newborn infant for the purpose of punishing the addicted woman is counterproductive. Research would best be done with a test that would determine the timing and extent of in utero drug exposure, neither requirement being met by neonatal urine testing (Volpe 1992). Preventing the birth of a drug-affected infant is only possible through screening the woman either before or early during pregnancy. Neonatal urine screening would only be useful in guiding therapy for those infants whose mothers took an illicit substance shortly before birth. As most substances are cleared rapidly, a potentially large number of drug-exposed infants will be missed (Volpe 1992).

Accordingly, the following general guidelines are proposed for the development of a rational neonatal (and prenatal) testing policy: (1) if the goal is to prevent fetal, and thus neonatal injury, the intervention must be either before or during early pregnancy; (2) accordingly, intervention must be directed at the prevention and treatment of drug addiction in non-pregnant women of child-bearing age or at the prevention of pregnancy in drug-addicted women; (3) programs which attempt to prevent pregnancy in drug-addicted women need to support a woman's own reproductive choices rather than restrict choice based on alleged unfitness to be a mother (Roberts 1991); (4) neonatal testing will only contribute to the prevention of drug-affected newborns through the identification of drug-addicted women in need of intervention; (5) civil or criminal sanctions after birth will be no more successful in preventing neonatal injury as such sanctions are in preventing drug addiction; (6) civil or criminal sanctions prior to birth may discourage pregnant drug-addicts from seeking prenatal care and thus may be counterproductive.

Based on the moral and legal standard of maternal responsibility for her fetus and future infant, parental consent for either prenatal or neonatal testing should not be required provided that such testing furthers the health and well-being of both the pregnant woman and her infant. Accordingly, adequate medical and social services need to be provided that are aimed at: (1) preventing disability in drug-affected infants; (2) preventing drug addiction in women of child bearing age; and (3) preventing further drug-affected infants from being born to a drug-addicted woman. There should be mandatory reporting of all positive maternal and newborn drug screening tests to the necessary medical and social services. The fact of a positive test should not be taken as prima facie evidence of child abuse or neglect, resulting in the removal of an infant from a drug-addicted woman. If parental consent is not required for either prenatal or neonatal drug testing, the results of such testing of either the woman or her infant should be excluded from use in any civil or criminal proceeding. Finally, there should be no distinction between licit and illicit drug use. If our goal is the prevention of prenatal harm to an infant, all services and sanctions should apply equally to pregnant women who abuse either alcohol or tobacco.

CONCLUDING REMARKS

The controversy over neonatal drug screening often fails to acknowledge that the real problem in preventing the birth of drug-affected infants is to prevent drug addiction in women of child-bearing age. Further, there is often a lack of clarity concerning the purposes of neonatal drug screening. To the extent that prevention, therapy and research (rather than punishment) guides a neonatal testing policy, the sporadic testing of an infant's urine for the presence of illicit substances clearly falls short of the desired goals.

REFERENCES

American Academy of Pediatrics (AAP) Committee on Bioethics. 1988. "Religious Exemptions from Child Abuse Statutes." *Pediatrics* 81:169-71.

American Academy of Pediatrics (AAP) Committee on Substance Abuse. 1990. "Drug-Exposed Infants." *Pediatrics* 86:639-42.

American Medical Association (AMA) Board of Trustees. 1990. "Legal Interventions During Pregnancy: Court-Ordered Medical Treatments and Legal Penalties for Potentially Harmful Behavior by Pregnant Women." *Journal of the American Medical Association* 264:2663-70.

Calhoun, Biro C., and Peter T. Wheaton. 1991. "The Cost of Maternal Cocaine Abuse: I. Perinatal Cost." *Obstetrics and Gynecology* 78:731-34.

Chasnoff, Ira J., Harvey J. Landress, and Mark E. Barrett. 1990. "The Prevalence of Illicit-Drug or Alcohol Use During Pregnancy and Discrepancies in Mandatory Reporting in Pinellas County, Florida." *The New England Journal of Medicine* 322:1202-06.

Chasnoff, Ira J., Dan R. Griffith, Catherine Freier, and James Murray. 1992. "Cocaine/Polydrug Use in Pregnancy: Two-Year Follow-up." *Pediatrics* 89:284-89.

Chavkin, Wendy, and Stephen R. Kandall. 1990. "Between a "Rock" and a Hard Place: Perinatal Drug Abuse." *Pediatrics* 85:223-25.

Frank, Deborah, Barry S. Zuckerman, Hortensia Amaro et al. 1988. "Cocaine Use During Pregnancy: Prevalence and Correlates." *Pediatrics* 82:888-95.

Frank, Deborah A., Howard Bauchner, Steven Parker et al. 1990. "Neonatal body proportionality and body composition after in utero exposure to cocaine and marijuana." *Journal of Pediatrics* 17:622-26.

George, Sherry K., Jan Price, John C. Hauth et al. 1991. "Drug abuse screening of childbearing-age women in Alabama public health clinics." *American Journal of Obstetrics and Gynecology* 165:924-27.

Gillogley, Katherine M., Arthur T. Evans, Robin L. Hansen et al. 1990. "The perinatal impact of cocaine, amphetamine, and opiate use detected by universal intrapartum screening." *American Journal of Obstetrics and Gynecology* 163:1535-42.

Johnson, Dawn. 1986. "The creation of fetal rights: conflicts with women's constitutional rights to liberty, privacy, and equal protection." *Yale Law Journal* 95:599-625.

Johnson, Phillip E. 1990. "The ACLU Philosophy and the Right to Abuse the Unborn." *Criminal Justice Ethics* 9:48-51.

King, Martha P. 1991. "Maternal and Child Health Legislation: 1991." National Conference of State Legislatures, Denver, Colorado. December, 1991: 73-78.

Larson, Carol S. 1991. "Overview of State Legislative and Judicial Responses." *The Future of Children* 1:72-84.

MacGregor, Scott N., Louis G. Keith, Jay A. Bachicha et al. 1989. "Cocaine Abuse During Pregnancy: Correlation Between Prenatal Care and Perinatal Outcome." *Obstetrics & Gynecology* 74:882-85.

Mariner, Wendy K., Leonard H. Glantz, and George J. Annas. 1990. "Pregnancy, Drugs, and the Perils of Prosecution." *Criminal Justice Ethics* 9:30-41.

Marshall, Alison B. 1991. "State-by-State Legislative Review." *Perinatal Addiction Research and Education Update* (NAPARE, Chicago, Illinois), September 1991.

Matera, Cristina, Wendy B. Warren, Maureen Moomjy et al. 1990. "Prevalence of use of cocaine and other substances in an obstetric population." *American Journal of Obstetrics and Gynecology* 163:797-801.

Mayes, Linda C., Richard H. Granger, Marc H. Bornstein et al. 1992. "The Problem of Prenatal Cocaine Exposure: A Rush to Judgment." *Journal of the American Medical Association* 267:406-08.

McCalla, Sandra, Howard L. Minkoff, Joseph Feldman et al. 1991. "The biological and social consequences of perinatal cocaine use in an inner-city population: Results of an anonymous cross-sectional study." *American Journal of Obstetrics and Gynecology* 164:625-30.

Moorman, Amy H. 1991. "Sex-specific fetal protection policies of employers are prohibited by Title VII as amended by the Pregnancy Discrimination Act." *West Virginia Law Review* 94:237-259.

Nelson, Lawrence J., Brian P. Buggy and Carol J. Weil. 1986. "Forced Medical Treatment of Pregnant Women: 'Compelling Each to Live as Seems Good to the Rest.'" *Hastings Law Journal* 37:703-63.

Nelson, Lawrence J. and Nancy Milliken. 1988. "Compelled medical treatment of pregnant women: life, liberty and law in conflict." *Journal of the American Medical Association* 259:1060-66.

Ney, Judith A., Sharon L. Dooley, Louis G. Keith et al. 1990. "The prevalence of substance abuse in patients with suspected preterm labor." *American Journal of Obstetrics and Gynecology* 162:1562-67.

Nolan, Kathleen. 1989. "Ethical issues in caring for pregnant women and newborns at risk for human immunodeficiency virus infection." *Seminars in Perinatology* 13:55-65.

Nolan, Kathleen. 1990. "Protecting Fetuses from Prenatal Hazards: Whose Crimes? What Punishment?" *Criminal Justice Ethics* 9:13-23.

Parker, Stephen, Barry Zuckerman, Howard Bauchner et al. 1990. "Jitteriness in Full-Term Neonates: Prevalence and Correlates." *Pediatrics* 85:17-23.

Phibbs, Ciaran S., David A. Bateman, and Rachel M. Schwartz. 1991. "The Neonatal Costs of Maternal Cocaine Use." *Journal of the American Medical Association* 266:1521-26.

Roberts, Dorothy E. 1991. "Punishing Drug Addicts Who Have Babies: Women of Color, Equality, and the Right of Privacy." *Harvard Law Review* 104:1419-81.

Roe, Richard L. 1991. Personal Communication from Mr. Roe, Research Analyst, Legislative Reference Bureau, The State of Wisconsin, to Ms. Cindy Christiansen, Esquire, Children's Hospital of Wisconsin. Dated April 2, 1991.

Schneider, Jane W. and Ira J. Chasnoff. 1992. "Motor assessment of cocaine/polydrug exposed infants at age 4 months." *Neurotoxicology and Teratology* 14:97-101.

Schutzman, David L., Maria Frankenfield-Chernicoff, Helen E. Clatterbaugh et al. 1991. "Incidence of Intrauterine Cocaine Exposure in a Suburban Setting." *Pediatrics* 88:825-27.

Skolnick, Andrew. 1990. "Drug Screening in Prenatal Care Demands Objective Medical Criteria, Support Services." *Journal of the American Medical Association* 264:309-10.

Volpe, Joseph J. 1992. "Effect of Cocaine Use on the Fetus." *The New England Journal of Medicine* 327:399-407.

Wisconsin Association for Perinatal Care (WAPC). 1992. "Testing of an Infant's Bodily Fluid for Controlled Substances." Proceedings of a Meeting held September 6, 1991. Medical College of Wisconsin, Milwaukee, WI.

Zuckerman, Barry, Deborah A. Frank, Ralph Hingson et al. 1989. "Effects of Maternal Marijuana and Cocaine Use on Fetal Growth." *The New England Journal of Medicine* 320:762-68.

Zuckerman, Barry, and Deborah A. Frank. 1992. " 'Crack Kids': Not Broken." *Pediatrics* 89:337-39.

The War at Home:
Positivism, Law, and the Prosecution of Pregnant Women

Thomas C. Shevory

SUMMARY. The essay explores the relationship between positivist epistemology, legal analysis, and the prosecution of pregnant women. Drawing on feminist analysis of science, the paper argues that legal thought and practice have been seriously distorted by positivist perspectives, especially in terms of narrow notions of what constitutes cause and effect. The critique of positivism provides a basis for reconceiving legal responses to drug use by pregnant women that are consistent with expanded notions of legal causation. Such an expansion provides the intellectual justification for expanding institutional interventions and encouraging a generally fairer and more satisfying politics.

INTRODUCTION

The purpose in the following essay is to examine interactions between epistemology and law in legal cases involving the prosecution of pregnant

Thomas C. Shevory is Assistant Professor of Politics at Ithaca College. Recent publications include: "Through a Glass Darkly: Law, Politics, and Frozen Human Embryos," *Issues in Reproductive Technology I: An Anthology,* ed., Helen B. Holmes, Garland Publishing, 1992; and, "Where's the Rest of Me? Biotechnology, Legal Rights, and the Case of John Moore," *Southeastern Political Review,* forthcoming.

[Haworth co-indexing entry note]: "The War at Home: Positivism, Law, and the Prosecution of Pregnant Women." Shevory, Thomas C. Co-published simultaneously in *Women & Politics* (The Haworth Press, Inc.) Vol. 13, No. 3/4, 1993, pp. 99-115; and: *The Politics of Pregnancy: Policy Dilemmas in the Maternal-Fetal Relationship* (ed: Janna C. Merrick, and Robert H. Blank) The Haworth Press, Inc., 1993, pp. 99-115. Multiple copies of this article/chapter may be purchased from The Haworth Document Delivery Center [1-800-3-HAWORTH; 9:00 a.m. - 5:00 p.m. (EST)].

99

women, specifically those cases which involve substance abuse. The thesis proposed is that legal discourse in these substance abuse cases is seriously distorted by positivist epistemology.

The essay is divided into four parts. The first part describes positivist epistemology and suggests its historical connections to American legal thinking. The second part examines feminist critiques of this epistemology. The third part discusses how positivism has influenced our understanding of substance abuse during pregnancy, legitimizing its construction as an "enforcement problem." The last part suggests that courts reconceive the issue of maternal drug abuse in terms of a broader matrix of social causes, and that they draw on traditional equity powers to develop social policies which will lead to more satisfactory solutions to maternal drug use problems than we currently have.

It is worth emphasizing at the outset that the argument here is *not* that the ingestion of drugs by pregnant women does no harm, in many cases, to children that are born to them. Rather, my argument is that cause and effect relationships have been construed too narrowly in these cases, and the ingestion/damage model misconceives the nature of the problem and distorts the potential for finding solutions to it.

POSITIVIST EPISTEMOLOGY

Abraham Kaplan provides a good working definition of positivism:

> Positivists . . . all proposed a reconstruction of knowledge on a pheno-menalistic basis. . . . What we observe are bare shapes, sounds, colors, and textures which are then organized and interpreted as the familiar objects and events of experience. The contents of observation itself are free from conceptual contamination. Nietzsche's label for this philo-sophical doctrine is not, I think, unjust: he called it *"the dogma of immaculate perception."* (1964)

Positivism, then, proposes a radical disjunction between human consciousness and the phenomenal world. The world exists in totality, free from acts of human interpretation. Thus, positivism has historically been associated with various dualisms: observer/observed, self/other, mind/body, man/woman.

The historical roots of positivist epistemology can be traced to Francis Bacon, as can its ideological role in the cultural domination of women. Bacon originated the notion of a scientific method which could access uncontaminated experience. With him we discern connections between method and politics. Bacon's scientific world-view reflected a dramatic historical change from organic, ecological consciousness, to an ethic of domination of nature and women as a part of nature (Merchant 1980,164-190; see also Fox Keller 1985).

The modern history of Western scientific thought can be viewed as variations on themes developed by Bacon. The most sophisticated contemporary defense of positivism was provided earlier in this century by logical positivists. A long but fairly direct line of philosophical development can be traced between the early rationalisms of Bacon and Descartes to the refinements of logical positivist and empiricist reconstruction of science developed by Feigl (1965), Nagel (1961), Hempel (1965), and Popper (1961; 1962), among others.

The starting point for logical positivists, as for Bacon, is the hypothesis. Hempel notes, "the doctrine of objectivity is preserved because while hypotheses may be freely invented, they are not *accepted* until they pass under critical scrutiny" (Hempel, chp. 2). Hypotheses are tested "empirically" using the scientific method as a means of falsification. Verified hypotheses, then, are connected together by using logical deduction to generate theories. These theories, in turn, create the possibility for more hypotheses, on ad infinitum. Cause and effect are narrowly construed in positivist doctrine. The cause of the occurrence of a given phenomenon is construed as the "event" which most immediately preceded it, although that event is caused by something as well. The entire phenomenal world is ultimately joined together by a complex set of causal relations. The search for causes, then, in logical positivism, moves inexorably toward prior causes, so that the investigator is encouraged to uncover ever more primary substances or forces. A narrow view of causation tends, thus, to be associated with a kind of reductionism.

Positivism has strongly influenced American legal thinking. In 1913, the legal scholar Joseph W. Bingham defined the "objective" field of the law as "concrete events and their governmental consequences and the concrete contributing causes of such consequences." Bingham wrote that the grasping of these objective realities provided the basis for a legal science (Bingham 1913, 166, 168). Bingham was simply following an earlier trail blazed by the likes of Langdell, Holmes, and Hohfeld. Morton Horwitz has shown that the concept of "objective causation" in American law grew in reaction to the philosophical idealism of Kant and Hegel and in support of ascending positivist notions of science. Oliver Wendell Holmes, he writes, " 'had come very early to [hold a] deep distrust and antagonism to the a priori categories of Kant and the conceptual dialectic of Hegel' "(Horwitz 1990, 361).

Legal theorists who acceded to the notion of objective causation divided events into two categories of causes, "proximate" and "remote," with the possibility of there existing "intervening" or "supervening" causes. Yet individual actions could always be fit into a "chain of causation," so that individual responsibility could be determined. As Horwitz notes, "it was necessary to find a single 'scientific' cause and thus a single responsible defendant, for any acknowledgement of multiple causation would open the floodgates of judicial discretion" (Horwitz 1990, 361).

A version of this principle found its way into the celebrated case of *Palsgraf v. Long Island Railroad Company* (1928). Here two men ran to catch a train leaving the Rockaway Beach, Long Island station. One bumped the other, who dropped a package containing fireworks, which exploded when it hit the tracks, causing some scales to fall from the roof of the station's platform. Mrs. Helen Palsgraf was injured by the falling scales. Judge Benjamin Cardozo constrained the boundaries of causation and ruled that Mrs. Palsgraf's injuries were not proximately caused by the railroad company, and that she was unentitled to compensation for her injuries. In Cardozo's words, "[T]he law arbitrarily declines to trace a series of events beyond a certain point. This is not logic. It is practical politics"(106).

While attempts have been made to remove the notion of cause from liability disputes (Coase 1960), the continuing importance of discerning proximate causes in criminal and tort law is beyond dispute (Epstein et al., 1984, 309-350). The positivist basis of much American law is thus evident. Such a positivist conception of reality circumscribes prosecution of pregnant drug users, and rejection of it provides a means for rethinking the scope of law and the role of legal institutions in our society. The rethinking of positivist epistemology needs to be conducted within a feminist context.

FEMINIST CRITIQUE OF POSITIVISM

Positivism has not been without its critics. Over the last decade, the critique of positivism has taken a feminist turn. Feminist critiques of positivism have been aimed at a number of aspects of the scientific enterprise. Feminists have criticized the organization of science that has traditionally excluded women, minimized their contributions, and harassed those few that have been presumptuous enough to engage in research. Feminists have challenged the positivist emphasis on objectivity, factuality, and various dualisms pitting man against nature, mind against matter, and male principles against female.

Feminists have questioned the validity of the hypothetico-deductive model of scientific theory building. Since for positivists mind is separated from body, the epistemological status of theoretical claims has always been something of a problem. Since there is no direct linguistic connection to an observation in a theoretical statement, how can it be deemed as "empirical"? And if it is not empirical, what is it? In other words, how do theories "interact" with factual data? There is no satisfactory answer to these questions. But even if the status of theories could be resolved, it is very difficult (in fact, impossible) to demonstrate that all theoretical statements are simple deductions, linked to observational statements or to one another (Longino 1980, 48-49).

Helen Longino's analysis of particle physics follows earlier critiques of positivism, like those of Kuhn (1978) and Feyerabend (1975), which conceived theory as shaping the entire observational enterprise. Theory, of course, is grounded in human history and convention, since it is a product of the human imagination. Thus, the activities of explanation reveal the historical and social nature of scientific practices. If theories of science, theories which cannot be derived solely from logic or "the scientific method" narrowly conceived, shape the findings of science, then the prize of objectivity looks increasingly elusive. Criticism of objectivity cuts to the heart of the positivist construction of the scientific enterprise. If, as the logical positivists suggest, there is a discrete method for uncovering the nature of physical realities, then the social, economic, or gender status of the observer will be irrelevant, but, if theory is imbedded in social practice, then class, race, and gender characteristics are significant for shaping scientific theories. Thus, the uniformity of the backgrounds of practicing scientists (white, male) can be seen as having skewed the processes of scientific investigation. There is, in other words, no "immaculate perception."

As objectivity, as conceived by positivists, becomes insecure, factuality itself becomes problematical. "Making facts," as Ruth Hubbard has written, "is a social enterprise" (1990, 22). Thus, at various points in history, scientific "facts" have included the assertions that women's brains were smaller than men's (demonstrating their lesser intelligence), that education would cause women to become infertile, and, more recently, that differences in hormonal production in male and female fetuses result in lifelong differences in spatial perception, mathematical aptitude, and aggressiveness between women and men (Hubbard 1990, 28).

Because the ideology of male dominance has historically been grounded in the biological and psychological sciences (including medical sciences) the feminist critique of positivism has made an invaluable contribution to exposing the political nature of these enterprises. The critique of biological sciences has included a trenchant analysis of positivistic notions of causation. In biology the search for the fundamental "causes" of life has been long and arduous. Recently, the "causes" of heredity, for example, were posited by James Watson and Francis Crick to exist in the DNA molecules. As the American geneticist Thomas Hunt Morgan stated, "In the same sense in which the chemist posits invisible atoms and the physicist electrons, the student of heredity appeals to invisible elements called genes" (Hubbard 1990, 71).

Ruth Hubbard has shown the ideological necessity of construing "genes as causes." It can be traced to the nineteenth century where "there was a strong ideological need to assume the existence of material substances, often particles, located within individuals, that transmit traits from one generation to the next" (Hubbard 1990, 71). This reductionism fits the positivist impulse to uncover fundamental causes and, not coincidentally, the political impulse to assign individual responsibility for such attributes as intelligence (or "deficiency"), laziness, drunkenness, "waywardness," and "nomadism." If genes were destiny, then the hierarchies of the nineteenth (and twentieth) century social orders could be justified on the basis of a set of undeniable and irreducible facts (Kevles 1985, 41-84). And again we see the connections between the positivist demand for determining narrow causes and the moral and legal impulse to assign individual responsibility to socially deviant behavior. Law and positivist science are tied into one large ideological bundle, and the feminist critique allows us to unwrap some of its binding threads.

LAW, SCIENCE, AND THE PROSECUTION OF PREGNANT WOMEN

A positivist epistemology underlies the prosecution of pregnant women. Conceptions of science and law interact in these cases to generate a narrow notion of cause and a strict concept of legal liability. The "objective reality" posited in these kinds of cases is that more and more pregnant women are ingesting more and more dangerous substances, the result being increasing numbers of disabled children. As a social reality, the increasing number of pregnant substance abusing women is difficult to deny (Anstett 1989; Chasnoff 1989; Davis 1988; Hagan 1989). As a result many courts have unselfconsciously accepted the positivist model in which the "cause" of fetal distress is the ingestion of illegal substances by the mother.

The proximate cause of harm is the drug, the supervening cause is the mother's action, and the "effect" is an impaired child. Preventing damage to a fetus then, so the logic goes, involves a simple act of intervening between the proximate and supervening cause. The simplest means to carry this out is through direct action on the supervening cause, i.e., the direct application of legal force on pregnant women, often jail. The purpose, in what follows, is to criticize this positivist construction from a feminist perspective and offer an alternative epistemological account, which provides the basis for a different politics.

In the past few years, there have been many cases in which charges have been brought against women for variations on the theme of "fetal abuse." In Florida, for example, Sheila Dawson received 18 months' probation after pleading no contest to delivery of cocaine in the second degree (*State of Florida v. Sheila Dawson* 1990). In Illinois, Melanie Green became the first woman to be charged with manslaughter because she allegedly killed her fetus by ingesting cocaine, although the grand jury refused to carry the indictment forward (*People of the State of Illinois v. Green* 1989). District Attorney Mike Ramsey, of Bette County, California, announced in the fall of 1988 that his office would begin prosecutions against mothers whose children were born with traces of illegal drugs in their systems (Haynes, 1988). And in North Carolina, a 24-year-old woman was charged with assault with a deadly weapon (*State of North Carolina v. Inzar* (1991)). All told, maternal abuse charges associated with substance abuse, in one form or another, have been brought in more than 40 cases, in at least 21 states (Paltrow 1990; 1991).

Not surprisingly, scholarly justifications have emerged to support the legal enforcement of fetal protection. Shaw has proposed using the tort system to prevent maternal substance abuse (1984), while Balisy and Robertson have proposed using criminal statutes to forbid women from taking even legal substances, like cigarettes and alcohol (Robertson 1983; Balisy 1987).

A narrow understanding of cause and effect, however, creates certain difficulties in terms of demonstrating the actual relationship between drug use and its effects in any given case or set of cases. The evidence of direct harm or "effect" is not always clear. Some children born to mothers who have taken drugs during pregnancy (or who have tested positive for taking drugs during pregnancy) suffer no apparent ill effects. Physicians at the Medical College of the University of Virginia, for example, report that many of the babies born from mothers who test positive for heroin or cocaine use have normal birth weights and show few signs of withdrawal (Davis 1988). Physicians at Rochester's Children's Hospital have reported that of the 25-30 babies for each year with abnormalities such as soft muscle tone, jumpiness, and jitterness, these symptoms could be attributable to a variety of effects not related to drug use (Anzalone 1988). The argument here is not that ingestion of drugs does not cause harm in many cases, but that the exact nature of that harm in a given set of cases is not always clear or demonstrable.

Much complexity is involved in determining the scope and duration of the effects of various substances on newborns. The largest study of marijuana use among pregnant women, the Ottawa Prenatal Prospective Study (OPPS), indicated difficulties for newborns, including fine tremors, nervousness, and some motor abnormalities, but all of these effects disappeared by the time the infant reached 24 months. The study concluded that "prenatal exposure to marijuana was not found to significantly contribute . . . to either mental, motor or language outcome variables." In terms of alcohol, Ernhart et al., have concluded that a "conservative" threshold for drinking earlier in pregnancy is an average of three drinks per day. (The authors note that for many of the heavier drinking women in the study this average included occasionally much heavier doses) (1989, 71). While prenatal heroin use can lead to decreased mental abilities in offspring, at least one study suggests considerable variation between subjects (Wilson 1989). And while no one would desire to have children born below their potential mental capacities, legal judgments based upon sample averages are problematic.

Based on a two-year follow-up study of cocaine-exposed children, Ira Chasnoff discovered that by 18 months of age the effects of cocaine on infant head size had declined, and that comparisons of "mean development indices" through two years indicated "relatively few significant differences among groups of children on either the mental or the psychomotor scores on the Bayley Scales of Infant Development" (Chasnoff 1992, 288).

Looking at the "cause" side of the equation also generates conceptual problems. Usually, the question of whether a given harm is created by substance abuse is resolved via reference to a drug test. Some hospitals have taken the initiative to establish testing policies on their own. In San Diego, for example, hospitals routinely run drug tests without asking consent (Dalton 1988). Washington, D.C. has considered, although not passed, legislation that would require all pregnant women to submit to drug screening (Price 1986). But tests, whether based upon physician observations or the analysis of urine samples (the usual procedure) generate both false positives and false negatives. Each has unfortunate consequences. False positives may lead to unjust accusations, while false negatives undermine the justification for utilizing drug tests in the first place. As drug tests become more routine the possibility of false positives increases.[1] False negatives are possible as well, so that some infants who might have been exposed to harmful substances are simply missed (Chasnoff 1989, 74).

Connected to both these problems is the fact that a test does not indicate the actual history of drug use. It cannot establish level and duration of abuse in an individual person. Laboratory measures, of the sort usually used in fetal abuse trials, even if an accurate "snapshot," cannot estimate a pattern of use (Day and Robles 1989, 8; Milhorn 1990). The situation with pregnancy is fundamentally different than with, say, railroad employees, who can destroy many lives with a one-time drug or alcohol "binge" on the job. Drug tests are uniquely unreliable "indicators" in pregnancy cases, because they cannot determine with any accuracy potential effects upon a fetus. Unfortunately, cause and effect are widely assumed by prosecutors and judges to have been established once any quantity of drug is present.

Again, it is important to note that the argument here is *not* that the ingestion of various legal and illegal substances during pregnancy does not in many cases cause harm to neonates. Rather, the thesis is that the interpretation of the effects of drug exposure is historical and contextual, and that determinations of the effects of drug exposure in any given case or set of cases is more problematical than is often assumed. Recognition of the contextuality of scientific findings does not mean that they are untrue or should be dismissed, rather that we should be very careful when evaluating their rhetorical use in defense of an enforcement response to drug use during pregnancy. Narrow evaluations of cause and effect are problematic in and of themselves, and have the effect of moving the debate away from the larger historical and social issues that are at stake in these sorts of cases.

Cause and effect problems have not gone entirely unnoticed by prosecutors, and attempts have been made to circumvent them by charging women with "endangerment" rather than demonstrable harm. In Wichita, Kansas, Latrena Grayson was charged with child endangerment when she refused to follow a doctor's instructions not to breast feed her child because she had tested positive for cocaine use before delivery. Her child was taken from her by local social service agencies (Finger 1991). Endangerment charges have been substituted for assault or abuse charges in cases in which there is no detectable damage to the child. Such was the case in Anchorage, for example, where Teresa Boster was charged with recklessly endangering her fetus. The D.A. stated, " 'To me, it is clear that there was a crime' " (Wohlforth 1988). The first Connecticut case in the arena also relied upon "risk of injury to a child," despite the questionable legality of the charge, given the state's abortion law (which denied the parallel of child to fetus).

The positivistic basis of liberal jurisprudence, then, rationalizes the enforcement response evidenced in so many jurisdictions. A critical feminist alternative to positivist epistemology, then, can provide the basis for reconceiving notions of cause and effect and finding a legality to match them. One important aspect of this enterprise involves expanding the notion of what causes maternal substance abuse. As the notion of cause expands, the question of individual liability correspondingly broadens and diminishes.

First, we must take into account the social and individual circumstances that lead some to engage in the ingestion of psychotropic substances that might harm them or their fetuses. Social circumstance certainly has an impact on who is *charged* with criminal activity in relation to material substance abuse. While drug and alcohol use cut across social and class lines, lower class women, who are more likely to be treated in public hospitals, are more likely to be arrested than more affluent women. Chasnoff found in his study of Pinellas County, Florida, for example, that while drug use rates by black and white women were roughly equal, black women were *more than nine times* as likely than white women to have their positive blood tests reported to authorities (Chasnoff 1990, 1204).

Social and economic considerations go directly to the question of legal liability. The positivist model adopted by many courts in the prosecution of pregnant women assumes a highly individualized and libertarian notion of choice on the part of the charged woman. Balisy states it graphically: "Alcohol, drug, and tobacco abuse constitute intentional acts that the mother has the ability to prevent" (Balisy 1987, 1237). But the question of choice is extraordinarily complex, and it does little service to the woman, fetus, or society as a whole to reduce it to such stark liberal and legalistic terms. No criminal justice system could or does assume that all criminal behaviors result from individual "choices." A variety of defenses are recognized as legitimate in criminal trials which can be exculpatory based upon restrictions of choices that defendants are capable of making. These include duress, mistake, insanity, diminished capacity, extreme emotional disturbance, and self-defense. In fact, the Supreme Court, in the case of

Robinson v. California (1962), struck down a California statute which made it a criminal offense to be addicted to narcotics.

Clearly, there are relationships between drug use and social circumstances. A comparison of addicted and non-addicted women, conducted by the Family Center of Thomas Jefferson University Hospital in Philadelphia, revealed 70% of drug dependent women experienced early sexual abuse, 83% had a chemically dependent parent and, "The families of drug dependent women had higher levels of family conflict, physical violence, and lower levels of family cohesion" (Hagan 1989, 62). It is also quite clear that in individual cases in which pregnant women were charged, they had been victimized by poverty and abuse. For example, Geraldyne Grubbs, charged with criminally negligent homicide, was abused by her boyfriend who supplied her with drugs (*State of Alaska v. Grubbs* (1989)). Josephine Pelligrini, arrested in Massachusetts (*Commonwealth of Mass. v. Pelligrini,* 1989), and Dianne Pfannenstiel, arrested in Wyoming (*State of Wyoming v. Pfannenstiel,* 1990) were both subjected to abuse by their partners (Paltrow 9, 17). And Pamela Rae Stewart has been described as "very poor," and she may have been a battered woman as well (Johnson 1989, 210).

The issue of intentionality is made even more problematical in these cases by the lack of available treatment facilities. Lack of treatment facilities is, in fact, quite well documented (see, Chavkin 1990; U.S. Senate 1989, 5). Thus, women who might choose to seek treatment once they become pregnant often have their treatment options closed. Given this context it stretches credulity to assert that these women possessed criminal culpability to "harm their fetuses."

A MODEST PROPOSAL

Recently, Richard Delgado has argued for expanding the notion of criminal exculpation beyond those traditionally accepted defenses. In doing so, he implicitly subverts the positivist notion of cause that has buttressed Anglo-Saxon notions of liability since at least the beginning of the 17th century. Delgado argues for expanding criminal defense to include consideration of "rotten social background (RSB)" (Delgado 1985). Delgado argues that there is a demonstrable relationship between poverty, chronic unemployment, substandard living conditions, inadequate schools, treatment by the police, development of an alternative value system, inadequate homes, and racism (Delgado 1985, 24-34). Delgado's analysis does not include consideration for spousal or parental abuse, but either could certainly be included in principle. The analysis is consistent with the feminist analysis of law that conceives its potential for envisioning social life as more than a set of conflicting diadic relationships. (See Eisenstein 1988, Smart 1990.)

First, such an expansion of the notion of cause would help to undercut the issues of criminal liability in cases involving the prosecution of pregnant women. And it would more accurately reflect the social realities of what is occurring. Moreover, it would help to move us beyond the severely limiting conceptions of liability that continue to haunt and cripple our entire political and legal system.

Second, such an expanded notion of objectivity would have a salutary effect upon how law is conceived and, along with that, a substantially expanded role for courts in the making of public policy could be created. If a strict positivist conception of cause provides courts with the justification for fashioning a narrow conception of liability with a concomitant enforcement remedy, then an expanded conception of cause, which takes into account historical conditions, will encourage courts to expand the types of remedies that they offer. Clearly, there are high emotional and economic costs associated with removing a child from its mother and placing it in an overburdened foster care system. This is especially true for infants who are born with mental, emotional, or physical problems.

From within the either/or perspective of liberal legalism, culpability means punishment and exoneration freedom. Thus, substance abuse prosecutions of the pregnant are drawn most often in terms of the narrow framework of "innocence" and "guilt." But, as I have attempted to show, such a perspective creates a host of conceptual difficulties, and the policy outcomes (putting women in jail) have at best a tenuous connection with creating the putative social good–healthier babies. Expanding the concept of cause and effect in all substance abuse cases, and particularly those involving the pregnant, should push courts toward an expanded role in dealing with this social problem. Thus, I would propose that judges treat the causes more broadly and utilize their historical equity powers to mandate that states and localities provide the funds for making adequate drug and alcohol treatment available on demand and, moreover, that they require states to provide adequate programs for prenatal nutrition and health care. Such actions would provide support for the vast majority of women who desire the best possible care that they can have in order to have healthy children. Much more would be accomplished for children than establishing an institutional response than can ever be achieved by attempting to blame individuals for behaviors that they would, in the vast majority of cases, like to avoid anyway.

Clearly, the climate of opinion in the federal courts would disincline them, as currently constituted, to support expansion of equity powers in the direction that I have suggested, in spite of the lip service that is often paid to "protecting the rights of the unborn." Still, there are plenty of legal precedents in the areas of civil rights, education, housing, and mental health care, that give support to the idea that federal courts have wide latitude to redress social and economic problems given the defense of an appropriately identified constitutional right (see Cooper 1988).

I believe that the changes in legal doctrine suggested are consistent with Roberto Unger's notion of "superliberalism." Unger has argued for multiplying branches of government so that, "The organization of government and of conflict over governmental power should provide a suitable institutional setting for every major practical or imaginative activity of transformation." Thus he calls for the creation of institutions that would unflinchingly practice "the more ambitious varieties of injunctive relief afforded by current American law" (Unger 1984, 31-32). "Courts," under this scheme, would be armed with the theoretical tools and institutional justifications for reconstituting social life in light of actual historical necessities. Thus, recasting the epistemological basis of criminal law in pregnancy/substance abuse cases has important political and institutional implications. Unwinding positivist constructions is consistent with reshaping legal and political life in satisfying ways.

CONCLUSION

Cases involving maternal substance abuse represent one set of cases where a critique of positivism can provide a vehicle for rethinking our current constructions of legal reality. A legal system is an ideological construct and, as such, it requires epistemological justifications. Thus, attention to the connections between epistemology and law on a variety of fronts seems warranted in the hope of creating a fairer legal system. My hope, in other words, is that reevaluation of pregnancy prosecutions can provide a point of departure for reconsidering other issues involving criminal liability from both feminist and other critical perspectives.

NOTES

1. Drug testing can be divided into two types, screening and confirmatory. Two types of screening tests are generally available, chromatographic and immunoassays. False positives result from cross-reactivity of drugs (not necessarily illegal ones). Good screening tests can have as high as 99% specificity if they are

conducted properly, but they generally yield only qualitative (yes or no) results. The number of false positives and/or false negatives depends upon the cut-off level that is set by the administering agent. A low cut-off point will yield more false positives, a higher one, more false negatives. Confirmatory tests (generally using chromatology techniques) can be extremely accurate and can yield quantitative results (Milhorn 1990, 36-37). The accuracy of tests depends upon the reliability of the labs performing them. Since drug testing is seldom, if ever used, to charge people with drug *possession,* the closest parallel to cases of women being charged with delivering drugs to their fetuses is with employment cases. Employment cases have been fraught with controversies as to the reliability of testing procedures. (See, generally, U.S. House 1987.) It is not at all clear that adequate standards have been developed for reliable testing of pregnant women, especially when we consider that there is no well-established link between drug test results (as opposed to clear evidence of long-term drug use) and harm to a fetus.

REFERENCES

State of Alaska v. Grubbs, No. 4FA S89 415 Criminal (Sup. Ct. Aug. 25, 1989).

Anstett, Patricia. 1989. "Newborns Absorb Mothers' Bad Habits," *Detroit Free Press*, 13 September.

Balisy, Sam S. 1987. "Maternal Substance Abuse: The Need to Provide Legal Protection for the Fetus." *Southern California Law Review* 60: 1209-1238.

Bingham, Joseph W. 1913. "Science and Law." *Green Bag* 25: 162-168.

State of California v. Stewart, No. M508197 (Municipal Court, County of San Diego, Feb. 26, 1987).

Chasnoff, Ira J. et al. 1987. "The Prevalence of Illicit Drug or Alcohol Use During Pregnancy and Discrepancies in Mandatory Reporting in Pinellas County, Florida." *New England Journal of Medicine.* 322: 1202-1206.

Chasnoff, Ira J. et al. 1992. "Cocaine/Polydrug Use in Pregnancy: Two Year Follow-up." *Pediatrics* 89: 284-289.

Chasnoff, Ira J. and Dan R. Griffith. 1989. "Cocaine: Clinical Studies of Pregnancy and the Newborn." In *Prenatal Abuse of Licit and Illicit Drugs: Annals of the New York Academy of Sciences: Volume 562.* ed. Donald E. Hutchings. New York: New York Academy of Sciences.

Chavkin, Wendy. 1990. "Between a Rock and a Hard Place." *Pediatrics* 85: 223-5.

State of Connecticut v. Baez, No. CR089-010-4414 (Sup. Ct. of Middletown, filed July 31, 1989).

Cooper, Phillip. 1988. *Hard Judicial Choices: Federal District Court Judges and State and Local Officials.* New York: Oxford University Press.

Davis, Ophelia. 1988. "For Some Babies in MCU Units, Drug Use Means Viscious Legacy," *Richmond Times-Dispatch*, 15 December.

Dalton, Rex. 1988. *San Diego Union*, 3 April.

Day, Nancy and Nadine Robles. "Methodological Issues in the Measurement of

Substance Use." In *Prenatal Abuse of Licit and Illicit Drugs: Annals of the New York Academy of Sciences: Volume 562.* ed. Donald E. Hutchings. New York: New York Academy of Sciences.

Delgado, Richard. 1985. "'Rotten Social Background': Should the Criminal Law Recognize a Defense of Several Environmental Deprivation?" *Law and Inequality* 3: 9-90.

Eisenstein, Zillah. *The Female Body and the Law.* Los Angeles: University of California Press, 1989.

Epstein, Richard, Charles O. Gregory, Harry Kalven, Jr. 1984. *Cases and Materials on Torts.* 4th ed. Boston: Little, Brown and Co.

Ernhart, Claire B. et al. 1989. "Alcohol-Related Birth Defects: Assessing the Risk." In *Prenatal Abuse of Licit and Illicit Drugs: Annals of the New York Academy of Sciences: Volume 562.* ed. Donald E. Hutchings. New York: New York Academy of Sciences.

Feigl, Herbert. 1965. "Some Major Issues and Developments in the Philosophy of Science of Logical Empiricism." In *Minnesota Studies in the Philosophy of Science,* ed. Herbert Feigle and Michael Scriven. Minneapolis: University of Minnesota Press.

Feyerabend, Paul. 1975. *Against Method.* London: Verso.

Finger, Stan. "Legal Quandry Awaits Mothers Who Expose Babies to Drugs," *Witchita Eagle,* 21 July.

State of Florida v. Carter, No. 90-2261 (Fla. 1st DCA, dismissal ordered July 23, 1990).

State of Florida v. Shiela Dawson, No. 90-294-CF (Cir. Ct. for Escambia County April 18, 1990).

Fried, Peter A. 1989. "Postnatal Consequences of Maternal Marijuana Use in Humans." In *Prenatal Abuse of Licit and Illicit Drugs: Annals of the New York Academy of Sciences: Volume 562.* ed. Donald E. Hutchings. New York: New York Academy of Sciences.

Hagan, Teresa. Committee on Governmental Affairs, U.S. Senate, 1989. *Missing Links: Coordinating Federal Drug Policy for Women, Infants, and Children.* July 31. (S. Hrg. 101-515).

Hempel, Carl G. 1965. *Aspects of Scientific Explanation.* New York: Harcourt, Brace, and World.

Henderson, Bruce. 1989. "Mothers of Infant Addicts: Does Prosecution Help?" *Charlotte Observer,* 26 August.

Hill-Holtzman, Nancy. 1987. "Judge Drops Case Against Mom Accused of Fetal Abuse," *Los Angeles Herald Examiner,* 27 February.

Horwitz, Morton. 1990. "The Doctrine of Objective Causation." In *The Politics of Law: A Progressive Critique,* ed. David Kairys. New York: Pantheon Books.

Hubbard, Ruth. 1990. *The Politics of Women's Biology.* New Brunswick: Rutgers University Press.

People of the State of Illinois v. Green. No. 88-CM-8256 (Cir. Ct. filed May 8, 1989).

State of Indiana v. Yurchak, No. 64D01-8901-CF-181B (Porter County Super. Court filed Oct. 2, 1989).

Johnsen, Dawn. 1989. "From Driving to Drugs: Governmental Regulation of Pregnant Women's Lives after *Webster." University of Pennsylvania Law Review.* 138: 179-215.

Kaplan, Abraham. 1964. *The Conduct of Inquiry: Methodology for Behavioral Science.* New York: Chandler Publishing.

Keller, Evelyn Fox. 1985. *Reflections on Gender and Science.* New Haven: Yale University Press.

Kennedy, John H. "Cloudy Future After Infant Cocaine Case," *Boston Globe,* 23 August 1989.

Kevles, Daniel. 1985. *In the Name of Eugenics.* New York: Alfred A. Knopf.

Kuhn, Thomas. 1970. *The Structure of Scientific Revolutions.* Chicago: University of Chicago Press.

Longino, Helen E. 1989. "Can there Be a Feminist Science?" In *Feminism and Science.* ed. Nancy Tuana. Bloomington: Indiana University Press.

Commonwealth of Mass. v. Levey, No. 89-2725-2729 (Super. Ct. of Mass. Dec. 4, 1989).

Commonwealth of Mass. v. Pelligrini, No. 87970 (Super. Ct. of Mass. filed Aug. 21, 1989).

Merchant, Carolyn. 1980. *The Death of Nature: Women, Ecology, and the Scientific Revolution.* New York: Harper & Row.

Milhorn, H. Thomas Jr. 1990. *Chemical Dependence: Diagnosis, Treatment and Prevention.* New York: Springer-Verlag.

Nagel, Ernest. 1961. *The Structure of Science.* New York: Harcourt, Brace and World.

Namenwirth, Marion. 1990. "Science Seen through a Feminist Prism." In *Feminist Approaches to Science.* ed. Ruth Bleier. Elmsford, N.Y.: Pergamon Press.

State of North Carolina v. Inzar, No. 90 CRS 6960 & 90 CRS 6961 (Sup. Ct. of Robeson County April 9, 1991).

State of Ohio v. Gray, No. CR88-7406 (Ct. C.P. of Lucas County, Ohio, July 13, 1989).

Palsgraf v. Long Island Railroad. 1928. 162 N.E. 99 (N.Y. Ct. of App., 1928).

Paltrow, Lynn. 1990. "When Becoming Pregnant is a Crime." *Criminal Justice Ethics.* 41-47.

Paltrow, Lynn. 1991. "State by State Case Summary of Criminal Prosecutions against Pregnant Woman and Appendix of Public Health and Public Interest Groups Opposed to These Prosecutions." *Memorandum,* 26 July.

Popper, Karl. 1961. *The Logic of Scientific Discovery.* New York: Science Editions.

Popper, Karl. 1962. *Conjectures and Refutations.* New York: Basic Books.

Porch, Todd. 1990. "Woman Guilty of Abusing Unborn Child by Taking Drugs," *Lexington Herald Leader,* 23 May.

Price, Joyce. 1986. "District Physicians Considering Requiring Prenatal Drug Tests," *Washington Times,* 13 November 1986.

Robertson, John. 1983. "Procreative Liberty and the Control of Conception, Pregnancy, and Childbirth." *Virginia Law Review.* 69.

Robinson v. California. 1962. 370 U.S. 660.

Sataline, Suzanne. 1989. "Drug Arrest to Focus on Threat to Fetus," *Hartford Courant,* 10 August.

Shaw, Margery W. 1984. "Conditional Prospective Rights of the Fetus." *The Journal of Legal Medicine* 5:63-115.

Smart, Carol. 1989. *Feminism and the Power of Law.* New York: Routledge.

Streissguth, Ann P. 1989. "Neurobehavioral Dose-Response Effects of Prenatal Alcohol Exposure in Humans from Infancy to Adulthood." In *Prenatal Abuse of Licit and Illicit Drugs: Annals of the New York Academy of Sciences: Volume 562.* ed. Donald E. Hutchings. New York: New York Academy of Sciences.

Wilson, Geraldine S. 1989. "Clinical Studies of Infants and Children Exposed Prenatally to Heroin." In *Prenatal Abuse of Licit and Elicit Drugs: Annals of the New York Academy of Sciences: Volume 562.* ed. Donald E. Hutchings. New York: New York Academy of Sciences.

Wohlforth, Charles P. 1988. "Mother Indicted for Endangering Baby by Drug Use," *Anchorage Alaska Daily News,* 17 December.

Unger, Roberto. 1984. *The Critical Legal Studies Movement.* Cambridge: Harvard University Press.

U.S. House of Representatives. 1987. *Drug Testing of Federal Employees.* Subcommittee on Human Resources of the Committee on Post Office and Civil Service. April 7, May 20. (Serial No. 100-17).

U.S. Senate. 1989. *Missing Links: Coordinating Federal Drug Policy for Women, Infants, and Children. Committee on Governmental Affairs.* July 31. (S. Hrg. 101-515).

Vanderveen, Ernestine. 1989. "Public Health Policy: Maternal Substance Use and Child Health." In *Prenatal Abuse of Licit and Illicit Drugs: Annals of the New York Academy of Sciences: Volume 562.* ed. Donald E. Hutchings. New York: New York Academy of Sciences.

Wilson, Geraldine S. 1989. "Clinical Studies of Infants and Children Exposed Prenatally to Heroin." In *Prenatal Abuse of Licit and Illicit Drugs: Annals of the New York Academy of Sciences: Volume 562.* ed. Donald E. Hutchings. New York: New York Academy of Sciences.

State of Wyoming v. Pfannenstiel, No. 1-90-8CR (County Ct. of Laramie, WY, complaint filed Jan 5, 1990).

At Women's Expense:
The Costs of Fetal Rights

Rachel Roth

SUMMARY. Analyses of so-called maternal-fetal conflict typically take fetal rights as given. In contrast, this paper argues that rights are socially created and do not come free. It analyzes how courts participate in the social construction of fetal rights in the areas of pregnant women's medical treatment and drug and alcohol use. Women are forced to bear the costs of making fetal rights real, burdening them without demonstrating any clear pattern of benefit to fetuses. It concludes that social policy that cares about women and empowers them will serve fetuses as well.

> I can't work; I can't smoke; I can't drink.
> This isn't a fetus–it's a parole officer.
>
> –*Susannah, "thirtysomething"*[1]

In the United States today, an extensive array of policies, practices, and ways of making decisions systematically burdens and harms women in the name of the fetus. This array often fails to achieve its goal of helping the fetus, or is simply not needed to achieve that goal. The abstract question whether the fetus is a person usually frames discussion of these measures. My discussion will bracket that debate, because it misses what is most important–the actual effects of these policies.

Rachel Roth is affiliated with Yale University Department of Political Science, P.O. Box 3532 Yale Station, New Haven, CT 06520-3532.

[Haworth co-indexing entry note]: "At Women's Expense: The Costs of Fetal Rights." Roth, Rachel. Co-published simultaneously in *Women & Politics* (The Haworth Press, Inc.) Vol. 13, No. 3/4, 1993, pp. 117-135; and: *The Politics of Pregnancy: Policy Dilemmas in the Maternal-Fetal Relationship* (ed: Janna C. Merrick, and Robert H. Blank) The Haworth Press, Inc., 1993, pp. 117-135. Multiple copies of this article/chapter may be purchased from The Haworth Document Delivery Center [1-800-3-HAWORTH; 9:00 a.m. - 5:00 p.m. (EST)].

117

Nobody knows exactly how many women have been directly affected by these policies and practices so far. Women have been subject to them in almost every state in the nation–at least 48 and the District of Columbia–during the past decade.[2] The measures gained popularity throughout the 1980s and 90s, as more and more employers, hospitals, and government jurisdictions imposed limits on fertile, and especially on pregnant, women's actions. They are part of a larger set of contemporary social and political struggles to define the parameters of women's independence. In the U.S. political system, courts are important arbiters of these struggles, and their decisions often constitute a kind of moral discourse that governs both how women should be thought of and how women can be treated.

Although she does not address fetal advocacy politics, Martha Minow offers some insights about the lure of establishing fetal rights. When someone makes rights claims, she asserts her identity as an individual entitled to equality and liberty, and emphasizes her essential sameness to others as a person and a member of the polity. Rights analysis further "treats each individual as a separate unit, related only to the state rather than to a group or to social bonds" (Minow 1990, 216). Fetal rights claims, then, present a rhetorically powerful strategy by giving the fetus an individual identity, asserting its equality with the woman, and establishing its independent relationship with the state that bypasses the pregnant woman.

Rights rhetoric is also powerful because it obscures the question of costs. When a court or other institution decides to give fetuses rights, it has to assign the costs of making those rights real to some individual or collectivity. That assignment–who should bear the costs–is a political question that has received very little direct public debate. The explicit or default answer has been to impose the costs of fetal rights on women.

Now, women always bear some of the costs of reproducing the species. They bear the physical, emotional, and time costs associated with the actual bearing of children, and a disproportionate share of these same costs in the rearing of children. But fetal rights operate to impose virtually all costs on women, instead of distributing them among fertile men, taxpayers, employers, and consumers.

Perhaps the starkest illustration is the way that employers try to allay their concerns about fetal vulnerability (i.e., tort liability) by imposing all the costs of fetal protection on women. Many industries have excluded all fertile women from workplaces deemed potentially hazardous to the development of a fetus, keeping women out of relatively high paying blue-collar jobs to protect the rights of potential, but as yet non-existent, beings. Not only do employers adopting such policies fail to consider excluding fertile men, ignoring what evidence does exist about the dangers to their reproductive health, but they do not think to exclude women from female-dominated jobs known to be hazardous, such as hospital or office work.

Since the era of *Muller v. Oregon* (1908), women have borne the burdens of safeguarding the next generation—only this time, no one explicitly pretends it's for their own benefit. Yet that assumption remains, in the way employers and courts construe women as having only maternal interests, and as being constantly pregnant or impregnable, incapable of controlling their sexuality, reproduction, or hygiene at work. Scientific research and employment restrictions have singled out women, burdening them with the blame for imperfect children, and hurting their ability to earn the money they need to support themselves, save for future children, or care for actual children.[3]

Although some may argue that the issues are less clear when a woman is pregnant, the same pattern emerges: women are made responsible for caring for fetuses, whether or not they have the resources to do so. In the process, they incur tremendous costs, to their physical, mental, and emotional security, to their confidence in social institutions, and to their liberty.

In this essay, I will show the harmful effects of two kinds of fetal protection policies, those affecting women's medical treatment and drug and alcohol use. My aim is to show how unexamined assumptions about women that are deeply embedded in American law and culture produce a pattern of imposing costs and burdens on women, so that we may begin to have better informed policy debate on the wisdom and justice of this pattern.

MEDICAL TREATMENT

Pregnant women today face increasing threats to their legally established rights to choose and refuse medical treatment. The most commonly reported example is to force women to undergo cesarean sections against their will, but women have been forcibly detained in hospitals and forcibly treated as well, and may be required to undergo fetal surgery and therapy when these become standard medical practice. In these instances, competent, law-abiding, adult women lose jurisdiction over their own bodies, and are subjected to physical violation almost never perpetrated in civil society *or* in the criminal justice system.

The legal right to refuse medical treatment that has been elaborated in the last two decades has roots at least 100 years old. The right to bodily integrity, located within the penumbral right to privacy guaranteed by the Ninth and Fourteenth Amendments to the Constitution, includes the right to accept or to refuse medical treatment, even if refusing leads to death. The Fourth Amendment also protects the right to be secure in one's person from unreasonable searches and seizures. In 1891, the U.S. Supreme Court asserted that "no right is held more sacred, or is more carefully guarded . . . than the right of every individual to the possession and control of his own person" (*Union Pacific Ry. v. Botsford,* quoted in *In re A.C.* 1987, 615). In 1985, the Supreme Court reaffirmed this principle, finding it constitutionally impermissible to perform surgery to remove a bullet from a robbery suspect's chest without his consent (*Winston v. Lee* 1985).

As always, the right is not absolute, and for women it is becoming completely relative. The state can assert a countervailing interest in "innocent third parties" who may be affected by the patient's decision, and at least one court has done this (*In re A.C.* 533 A.2d 611). However, it is both interesting and troubling to note that the court follows up its assertion with examples of decisions to override a parent's refusal of medical treatment for a child because of religious beliefs. These cases do *not* compromise the parent's bodily integrity, and so are dubious precedents. The court then goes on to say that this logic has been applied to unborn children.[4]

A second pertinent area of law evolving to lay different claims on women than on men concerns people's obligations to assist others. The law does not recognize an affirmative duty to rescue. One of the most frequent illustrations is whether a person can be compelled to donate blood, bone marrow, or organs. Courts have consistently answered no, even in cases of close relatives, even in cases of imminent death.[5] However, some want to impose on women such a duty to their fetuses.[6]

Roe v. Wade, still the touchstone for legal conceptions of the fetus, is often misinterpreted to impose such duties on pregnant women. This 1973 decision legalizing abortion established a three-part framework of "separate and distinct" competing interests. During the first trimester of pregnancy, a woman's fundamental privacy right encompasses her decision to terminate a pregnancy without state interference. During the second trimester, the state may regulate abortion in ways reasonably related to its compelling interest in protecting women's health. The court found that a woman's privacy right is not absolute, and so after viability, during the final trimester, the state may regulate and even proscribe abortion to further its compelling interest in "the potentiality of human life," *except* where abortion is necessary to preserve a woman's life or health. Fetal rights advocates consistently misconstrue this part of the framework. What it says is that attaching any weight to the fetus is constitutionally optional but attaching weight to the woman is not; that is required. The court also denied that a fetus is a person within the meaning of the Fourteenth

Amendment. Although subsequent opinions have upheld restrictions on minors' access to abortion and on Medicaid funding of poor women's abortions, and dissenting opinions have defined fetuses as "those who will be citizens if their lives are not ended in the womb," *Roe's* basic framework persists (*ACOG v. Thornburgh* 1986, 2196).[7]

The true extent of judicial involvement in pregnant women's treatment is unknown, because the court decisions are often unpublished or sealed, making them extremely difficult to identify. To correct for this, Kolder, Gallagher, and Parsons surveyed directors of maternal-fetal medicine programs, and identified 21 court orders to override a pregnant patient's refusal of therapy in 11 states between 1981 and 1985 (Kolder, Gallagher, and Parsons 1987). (Both the number of states and orders would be higher if orders sought after delivery or for maternal transfusions rather than intrauterine transfusions were included.)

Admittedly, the number 21 is statistically insignificant compared to the total number of births each year. However, Kolder et al.'s study and the cases discussed below demonstrate that judicial intervention is sought and granted in many states, not just one geographic area with particularly conservative political attitudes. Moreover, the number of successful orders cannot reflect how often the threat of intervention compels a woman to "agree" to treatment she does not want, to avoid a court dispute. Even if the actual number of incidents identified so far is small, it represents a dangerous trend, because these cases can serve to redefine the boundaries of acceptable treatment of pregnant women.

In Kolder et al.'s study, courts granted 86% of applications for permission to perform involuntary cesarean sections or intrauterine transfusions or to detain a woman who refused therapy, making the vast majority of decisions within six hours. Eighty-one percent of the women involved were Black, Asian, or Hispanic, and 24% did not speak English as their primary language. When awarding temporary custody of the fetus courts never designated a relative of the pregnant woman, but usually a hospital employee. In concrete terms, these orders mean that medical personnel can forcibly restrain struggling women, anesthetize them, and cut them open, all against their will. Cesarean sections are major abdominal surgery, as one court opinion *authorizing* the procedure recognizes: "The surgery presents a number of common complications, including infection, hemorrhage, gastric aspiration of the stomach contents, and postoperative embolism. It also produces considerable discomfort. In some cases, the surgery will result in the mother's death" (*In re A.C.* 533 A.2d 611, 617).[8]

Only two appellate courts have yet ruled on the legitimacy of ordering cesarean sections (discussed below). According to Kolder et al., "decisions made by lower-court judges do not necessarily represent the settled law of the state, and unpublished trial court decisions are not binding on other judges," leaving this a poorly developed area of law (Kolder, Gallagher, and Parsons 1987, 1194).

The only state supreme court decision comes from Georgia, in 1981, about a woman who refused cesarean delivery on religious grounds after being diagnosed with placenta previa, in which the placenta blocks the fetus from passing through the cervix, endangering both its survival and that of the pregnant woman (*Jefferson v. Griffin Spalding County Hospital Authority*). The hospital sought permission from the superior court to "administer" medical treatment to save the life of both fetus and woman. The court saw "the issue [as] whether this unborn child has any legal right to the protection of the court," and decided yes, invoking *Roe v. Wade* but departing from that opinion's holding by declaring that "a viable unborn child has the right under the Constitution" not to be terminated arbitrarily (458). This statement seriously misconstrues the Supreme Court's decision by turning the state's interest in the potentiality of human life into actual constitutional rights for fetuses.

Although the court denied the hospital's request to administer medical treatment to save Jefferson's life, in keeping with judicial reluctance to abridge a competent patient's right to refuse treatment, it did grant the Department of Human Resources temporary custody of Jefferson's "unborn child" and the authority to consent to surgical delivery on its behalf. The state supreme court denied Jefferson's motion for a stay.

How did the court reach its decision? It found that the "intrusion" involved in Jefferson's life "is outweighed by the duty of the State to protect a living unborn human being from meeting his or her death before being given the opportunity to live" (460). The two concurring opinions balance more elaborately, with one naming the rights at stake and discussing their relative weights. Very little weight is given to Jefferson's rights to bodily integrity, medical decision-making, or religious freedom. Remarkably, no weight was given to the fact that the decision effectively awarded temporary custody of Jefferson herself to the state. The court erred again by turning the state power upheld in *Roe*–to stop an invasive procedure by banning abortions of viable fetuses–into the power to compel an invasive medical procedure. On a final note, the court-ordered sonagram showed that the "impossible" had happened–the placenta had moved. Jefferson gave birth vaginally to a healthy infant.

The second case arose six years later in the District of Columbia regarding a 27-year-old woman named Angela Carder who had been fighting leukemia for 14 years. Twenty-five weeks into her pregnancy, when she complained of back pain and shortness of breath, doctors discovered an inoperable tumor in her right lung and admitted her to the hospital. Carder and her doctors decided that she would undergo a cesarean at 28 weeks, at which point the fetus would have a reasonably good chance to survive, even though she might not.

Despite the fact that patient and doctors had chosen a treatment plan, hospital administrators went over their heads and sought the guidance of the trial court when Carder's condition worsened prior to 28 weeks, asking whether to intervene to [try to] "save" the fetus. The hospital gained permission and won an appeal from a three-judge panel within a single day. On June 16, 1987, Carder underwent the court-ordered cesarean section to deliver her 26 1/2 week fetus. The infant died in two hours; Carder died in two days.

After rehearing the case, the full appellate court decided 7-to-1 that the previous decisions were wrong. The trial judge, and the three appellate judges (writing after the fact), had treated the issue as one of balancing the interests of two parties, explicitly subordinating Carder's to those they ascribed to the fetus (*In re A.C.* 1987, 617). The opinion of the entire court after the rehearing goes in a different direction, attempting to chart a clear course to resolve future disputes. It does not focus on competing interests but on patients' rights to make medical decisions. The court explains that:

> in virtually all cases the question of what is to be done is to be decided by the patient–the pregnant woman–on behalf of herself and the fetus. . . . We do not quite foreclose the possibility that a conflicting state interest may be so compelling that the patient's wishes must yield, but we anticipate that such cases will be extremely rare and truly exceptional. This is not such a case. (*In re A.C.* 1990, 1237 & 1252)

This opinion does not clearly indicate what an exceptional case of conflict would look like. It may appear to beg the question of how much weight to attribute to the fetus, but in essence it gives it virtually no weight of its own, without reference to the pregnant woman's valuation of it.

In contrast, Justice Belson, the sole dissenter, holds to the original balancing framework as the appropriate one. Belson asserts that both the "viable unborn child's interest in survival" and the "state's parallel interest in protecting human life" deserve "substantial weight" (*In re A.C.* 1990, 1254). The woman's interests in "her own life, health, bodily integrity, privacy, and religious beliefs" merit "correspondingly great weight" (1258). Rhetorically, the fetus is presented as the standard; the woman's interests merely correspond to those the court ascribes to the fetus. With the fetus assigned an interest, and the state assigned an interest in it, the balance of forces is weighted two-to-one against the woman. Moreover, Belson identifies the most important factor on the fetus's side of the scale as "life itself, because the viable unborn child that dies because of the mother's refusal to have a cesarean delivery is deprived, entirely and irrevocably, of the life on which the child was about to embark" (1258).

Belson gives no actual credence to the state's professed compelling interest in women. He invokes *Beal v. Doe* (1977) and *Roe v. Wade* as authority for interfering with a woman's constitutionally protected privacy interest. Yet *Roe*'s trimester framework and *Beal*'s denial of publicly funded abortions foreclose certain options to women; they do not authorize forcing treatment on them. In addition, the passage Belson quotes as support for state authority to regulate and proscribe abortion in the third trimester unequivocally asserts the state's interest in "preservation of the life or health of the mother" (quoted at 1254-5). Belson disagrees with the "narrow view" his colleagues take of the "state's interest in preserving life" (1253). Yet was not Angela Carder's life a human life? Belson treated Carder as if she were already dead.[9]

Despite Supreme Court opinion to the contrary, Belson says that the fetus is a person. This "person" is "held captive" within the woman's body. In order to liberate the fetus, Belson disregards the risks surgery posed to Carder, designating pregnant women carrying viable fetuses as a unique category of persons upon whom the state may impose unusual burdens, without granting them unusual entitlements.

These cases raise the question who has the right to be wrong. Judges insist that they don't want the responsibility for adjudicating these disputes, yet they don't all trust women. Neither do doctors. The survey discussed above found that only 24 percent of the program directors consistently upheld competent women's right to refuse medical advice, despite the official positions of the American Medical Association and the American College of Obstetrics and Gynecology against court-ordered medical treatment of pregnant women (ACOG 1987 and AMA 1990). Doctors err in their medical judgment; justices err in their legal judgment, especially when emergency hearings deny them time for careful research and deliberation; and pregnant women err in their judgments. But only pregnant women are denied the right to exercise their judgment because of the possibility of human error. Hence, women must bear the costs of everyone else's mistakes—whether intimidation and the emotional distress of a court challenge, or actual bodily invasion. Pregnant women are ordered to do for fetuses what no one is ordered to do for children or adults.

ALCOHOL AND DRUG USE

Pregnant women who drink alcohol or take drugs have become the targets of overwhelmingly punitive responses to the growing number of substance-exposed infants. Researchers estimate that 11% of babies (375,000) born each year have been exposed to street drugs in utero (Chasnoff 1989), and that up to 4,000 are born each year with full-blown Fetal Alcohol Syndrome, with up to 11,000 more experiencing Fetal Alcohol Effect (Abel 1984). The responses to this problem range from ad-hoc decisions to prosecute and incarcerate women, to state mandated reporting of pregnant women, to proposed national legislation *making it a crime to give birth* to a baby affected by drugs or alcohol and tying grant money for treatment programs to the imposition of three years of incarceration in a custodial rehabilitation center for convicted women (Johnsen 1989). One exception is the Connecticut legislature's decision to fund four model treatment programs for women and their children (Stoddard 1990). Even so, there will only be slots for 90 of the estimated 5,000 women in need.

The trend to prosecute and incarcerate pregnant women fails as public policy because it does not achieve its purported goal of improving birth outcomes, but imperils both fetuses and the women who carry them. The point here is not whether society can constrain the legitimate or illegitimate choices of pregnant women, but whether it is sensible or fair to impose on them the entire burden of caring for fetuses, whether or not they have the resources to do so.

Pregnant and post-partum women face two overlapping paths to prosecution: being accused of crimes unrelated to their pregnancy, or being defined *as criminal* because they are pregnant substance users. Women in the first group are often charged under laws designed for other purposes or receive atypical sentences for their crimes, because judges take into account the fact that they are pregnant and are known or suspected drug or alcohol users.

Although prosecutions of post-partum women for conduct that may have harmed the fetus date back at least to 1977, the first such case to gain wide media attention was that of a California woman named Pamela Rae Stewart in 1987. After her infant son died of massive brain damage, Stewart was charged under a 1926 statute that makes it a crime for a parent to "willfully omit" furnishing necessary medical attention to a *child*. Stewart's son had been born with traces of amphetamines in his blood, and this was sufficient to trigger prosecution even though the delivering physician determined that the drugs had not caused the brain damage or death (McNulty 1990). The judge dismissed the charges, agreeing with Stewart's attorney Richard Boesin that the statute was intended to assure that fathers pay child support and not to prosecute pregnant women. Boesin hoped then that the ruling would send a message that such prosecution is "counterproductive and will do nothing but terrorize the hearts and minds of pregnant women" (*New York Times* 1987). But the prosecutions continue. More recently, in Florida, Jennifer Johnson was convicted of "delivering drugs to a minor" via her umbilical cord after birth; similar prosecutions have taken place in Georgia, Massachusetts, Michigan, and South Carolina (Hoffman 1990).[10] A pregnant Laramie, Wyoming, woman who sought emergency room treatment after her husband beat her was arrested and charged with felony child abuse because she was intoxicated (Beck 1990).[11]

Pregnant women are also subjected to inappropriate sentencing, as was Brenda Vaughn, a 29 year-old from Temple Hills, Maryland, who was convicted of forging $722 in checks, her first offense. She received a 180-day jail sentence instead of the probation typical for first offenders (Moss 1988). The judge mentioned in his opinion that some of his colleagues have similarly sentenced pregnant drug users (*United States v. Vaughn* 1989, 447). The judge reasoned:

> It is true that the defendant has not been treated the same as if she were a man in this case. But then a man who is a convicted rapist is treated differently from a woman. She has also not been treated the same as a nonpregnant woman. But Ms. Vaughn became pregnant and chose to bear the baby who, like most criminal defendants the court sees so frequently, will start life with one other severe strike against it–no father is around. Arguably, Ms. Vaughn should have demonstrated even greater responsibility toward her child. (447)

Clearly, the judge is punishing Vaughn for more than forging checks or taking cocaine while pregnant. He punishes her for expressing her sexuality and for not having an abortion. He blames her for the fact that she will be a single parent, and more than that, for contributing to crime by rearing a child without paternal influence. The judge also presumes to know what Brenda Vaughn feels. He belittles her complaints about inadequate prison diets as "ironic," "when her real craving is for a devastating drug" (447).

One of the most troubling problems with the prosecution strategy is that it applies to women who cannot obtain alcohol or drug dependency treatment even if they try. According to the AMA, "even the most persistent pregnant woman is likely to fail to find a treatment program for her substance dependency," because, even if money were no obstacle, such programs are in short supply and most will not accept pregnant women, partly due to fear of liability, since withdrawal from opiates can harm or kill a fetus (AMA 1990, 16). Additionally, very few programs provide child care, even though the National Institute on Drug Abuse identified this as a major obstacle to treatment over a decade ago (Chavkin 1990).

The following case illustrates the point. A 27-year-old pregnant woman living in Butte County, California, was a heroin addict. She diligently sought medical treatment, but found no methadone maintenance program in her poor, rural county. Instead, she drove 140 miles each day to Sacramento for methadone treatments, for which she paid $200 per month out of her AFDC check, until her car broke down and she could no longer arrange transportation.

After failing again to secure treatment closer to home, and eight and one-half months pregnant, she did what one commentator has called the responsible thing: she started taking heroin again, to prevent fetal stress and stillbirth (*Youth Law News* 1990, 19).[12] Despite the fact that she informed the medical staff of her drug habit at delivery in order to ensure proper treatment for her baby, Child Protective Services assumed custody of her child. The District Attorney also announced that he planned to prosecute her for illegal drug use. Ultimately, negative publicity deterred the D.A. from pressing charges, but the D.A.'s office expressed interest in keeping its prosecution options open (Aronson 1989; LaCroix 1989; *Youth Law News* 1990).

As with forced medical treatment, punishment for substance use falls most heavily on poor women and women of color. Health care providers are far more likely to report pregnant women of color than pregnant white women for substance use. A study of women enrolled for prenatal care at public health clinics and private doctor's offices in Pinellas County, Florida, found that "the use of [alcohol and] illicit drugs is common among pregnant women regardless of race and socioeconomic status;" yet it also found that Black women are nearly *ten times* more likely than white women to be reported to local authorities, and women of both races who were reported were more likely to be of low socioeconomic status (Chasnoff, Landress, and Barrett 1990). The Black women in this study were more likely to use cocaine than their white counterparts, who preferred marijuana, a drug health care providers are less often required to report. However, the large discrepancy in reporting, along with the fact that only 26% of the women prosecuted across the country for substance-related "fetal abuse" have been white, suggests that race and not simply drug choice plays a key role in determining reporting (Roberts 1991, 1421).

The American Medical Association, the National Medical Association, and the American Public Health Association have all gone on record opposing the prosecution of pregnant women for substance use (AMA

1990 and NMA and APHA *amicus curiae* briefs in support of Jennifer Johnson, cited in Berrien 1990, 248-9). It is worth noting that the medical establishment's interests here dovetail with pregnant women's. Having long opposed state encroachment into its professional territory, the AMA in particular now resists the imposition of legal obligations that would in effect turn its members into agents of the state.

Some fetal rights advocates have put forth stringent programs of maternal substance abuse regulation. For instance, Sam Balisy finds the state's dual interests in protecting potential life and in preventing avoidable costs (such as medical expenditures) sufficiently compelling to justify restricting pregnant women's conduct, outweighing any state interest in women's autonomy or bodily integrity, or any interests of women's own (Balisy 1987). He would prohibit women's use of alcohol and tobacco after the second trimester, and drug use at all stages of pregnancy, insisting that the state would be justified in taking physical custody of a pregnant woman to protect the fetus during the third trimester. (He cites as precedent the *Jefferson* forced cesarean case and the involuntary commitment of a pregnant schizophrenic.) While taking controlled substances is already illegal, these consequences are new. Balisy further contends that there is no justifiable distinction between a fetus and a newborn, and that women can and should be held accountable for actions taken before they decide to carry to term.

Anticipating an equal protection challenge to his policy, Balisy promises that "similar restrictions on males would be essential, however, when and if medical evidence establishes that male substance abuse also has adverse fetal effects" (Balisy 1987, 1232). He does not discuss what these restrictions would look like or how they would be enforced: what is "similar" to being a ward of the state for three months?

Consider the conditions pregnant women in jails and prisons face. Women's correctional facilities are overcrowded, operating at up to 600% over capacity; pregnant women are deprived of nutritious diets, exercise, fresh air, accessible toilets and showers, and beds to sleep in, not to mention any privacy; are the objects of hostility and harassment from staff perceiving them as unworthy of motherhood; are exposed to such contagious diseases as measles, hepatitis, and tuberculosis; are denied drug and alcohol treatment services, forcing them to quit "cold turkey" without medical or psychological support; are denied prenatal care, and access to full-time medical staff and basic medical facilities, including those for childbirth; and are handcuffed, shackled, and chained around the belly when going to court or to the hospital, even when in active labor (Barry 1989 & mimeo 1; McHugh 1980; Stein and Mistiaen 1988). However, two things pregnant women often can get in jail are drugs and alcohol, either via friends and relatives on the outside or corrections staff on the inside (AMA 1990; Barry mimeo 1).

Consequently, women inmates experience extremely poor birth outcomes. A 1983 study of health conditions in three California women's correctional facilities documents that among *prison* inmates, only 45% of pregnancies resulted in live birth. Thirty-four percent ended in miscarriage, compared to the national average of 10-15% (*Williams Obstetrics* 1989). Investigators suggest that the miscarriage rate would be higher if it took into account women whose pregnancies spontaneously terminated while they were being held in county jails, before being transferred to prison. Among *county jail inmates* at Santa Rita County Jail, the birth rate dropped by half–only 21% of pregnancies resulted in live birth. Fifty-five percent miscarried at some point in their pregnancies, and 73% of these women had stillbirths (fetal death after 20 weeks gestation). The 40% of pregnant women having stillbirths compares to less than 1% of women nationwide (*Williams Obstetrics* 1989; results reported in Barry 1985 & 1989 and in *Youth Law News* 1985). This study was sponsored by the California Department of Health, and unfortunately, there are no federally collected data on women inmates' birth experiences with which to compare it.[13]

The prosecution and incarceration strategy combines genuine, if misguided, concern for fetuses who will presently become children with utter disregard for women. A police officer in Michigan who endorses incarceration put it this way: "If the mother wants to smoke crack and kill herself, I don't care. Let her die, but don't take that poor baby with her" (quoted in Hoffman 1990, 34). What the officer misses is that if the mother dies, the baby will, too. These advocates seek an individual solution to a set of societal problems, making women wholly and solely responsible for the work of reproduction, while ignoring their own needs. ACLU attorney Lynn Paltrow reminds us of this:

People are always talking about women's duties to others as though women were not the chief caregivers in this society. But no one talks about women's duty of care to *themselves.* A pregnant addict or alcoholic needs to get help for *herself.* She's not just potentially ruining someone else's life. She's ruining her own life.

Why isn't her own life important? Why don't we care about her? (quoted in Pollitt 1990, 418)

CONCLUSION

What all of these cases show is that making women pay for fetal rights has dangerous effects. Forced medical treatment does violence to women's bodily integrity, religious beliefs, and treatment preferences. In the face of uncertainty, only women's judgments are disregarded, needlessly harassing women and leading even to death. Incarceration totally violates women's autonomy and jeopardizes fetuses' chances of becoming children. None of these measures demonstrates a clear pattern of benefit to fetuses, providing *no* justification for the burdens imposed on women.

Catharine MacKinnon reminds us that "the question whether women should be treated unequally means simply whether women should be treated as less" (MacKinnon 1987, 43). These practices and court decisions do just that, by failing to promote women's health as a goal along with fetal health. I propose that social policy that cares about women and empowers them will serve fetuses as well.

This policy requires committing resources, because so many of pregnant women's problems stem from outright poverty, from lack of health insurance even when they are employed, and from lack of facilities in their communities. Women need prenatal care to ensure their own and their fetuses' health. Funds invested in prenatal care save money by reducing the need for expensive neonatal intensive care after birth. Public education can inform women and men of the risks associated with smoking, drinking, or taking drugs.[14] Women with acute substance problems need counseling and treatment to give them control over their own lives, whether or not they are pregnant. Incarceration is expensive, does not cure addiction, and produces dismal birth outcomes. Women planning to have children usually need and/or want to continue working, and transfers to positions without toxic exposure before conception and during pregnancy allow them to work while maintaining some continuity in the workplace. Transfer programs are no substitute for eliminating the hazards that affect all workers and the surrounding community, but are a necessary feature of safe and responsive employment.

But a policy of empowerment requires more than spending money. It means changing the way decisions are made when apparent conflicts arise. The choice is not either/or. The fetus and the woman cannot be treated as equal antagonists in practice, because under such a construction, both cannot prevail. If we really want to solve problems associated with poor infant outcomes, we need first to try educating women, providing them with resources, and then respecting them to make decisions for themselves and the fetuses they carry, who will become children they have the responsibility and authority to raise. Locking women away from the opportunity to live full social lives that necessarily involve some risk is simply not tenable–morally, legally, or practically–unless we are prepared to say that women are not full members of the polity.

These suggestions have yet to earn a serious place on local or national policy agendas. Much to judges' chagrin, legislatures have not assumed leadership in addressing so-called maternal-fetal conflicts. Comprehensive, long-term, preventive social policy has not been American governments' strength. My approach calls for restructuring some basic institutions to accommodate women's needs, and really, the needs of all parents. It calls for a social commitment to reproduction that respects the value of individual autonomy.

NOTES

1. I would like to thank my advisor, Rogers Smith, for his continued support of my work; Ian Shapiro, Alex Wendt, and the members of the "Research & Writing" class in which this paper originated for challenging me to make my argument stronger and clearer, and Eve Weinbaum for helping me do it; and Val Hartouni and Ann Snitow for long-distance encouragement.

2. There is no single source for this number. The two states for which I lack documentation are North and South Dakota. In addition to court decisions, important sources include Benton 1990; Kolder, Gallagher, and Parsons 1987; and National Conference of State Legislatures 1989 & 1991.

3. For an elaboration of this argument and of the social construction of women underpinning it, see the extended version of this paper, on file with the author. For an identification of key assumptions underlying fetal protection at work, see Sally J. Kenney's article "Who is Protected: What's Wrong with Exclusionary Policies," in this volume.

4. The cases cited are *Jefferson v. Griffin Spalding County Hospital Authority,* discussed on p. 122, and three cases ordering blood transfusions on pregnant women over their objections. However, in *Taft v. Taft* (1983) the Massachusetts state supreme court overruled a decision giving a husband the authority to force his wife to undergo a "purse string" operation to hold a nonviable fetus, because the woman's rights to religious freedom and to privacy had been established, but the state's compelling interest in overriding those rights had not (*In re A.C.* 1987, 616).

5. See Martha Field's discussion of *McFall v. Shimp* (10 Pa. D. & C. 3d 90 Allegheny Ct. Comm. Pleas, 1978), concerning a person who refused to donate bone marrow to a dying cousin. Although the case did not involve parent and child, Field notes that the court made clear that closeness or distance of relationship was not the determining factor; constitutionally guaranteed bodily integrity was (Field 1989, 127 n. 39).

6. The question of a woman's duty to her fetus raises serious questions about the priorities for taking care of *children* in this country. Historically, the state has

tolerated high levels of child neglect and abuse and low levels of child support enforcement (the latter is something Congress tried to correct in its 1988 Family Support Act). Some critics of "fetal abuse" measures argue that they are appealing because they make the government look as if it's doing something for children without having to commit any resources (see e.g., Field 1989).

7. In practice, over 90% of abortions occur within the first trimester (U.S. Census Bureau 1990, Table 101). How the "undue burden" standard set forth in the 1992 decision *Planned Parenthood of Southeastern Pennsylvania v. Casey* (60 U.S.L.W. 4795) will affect the relevance of *Roe*'s framework for fetal protection issues remains to be seen.

8. A dramatic illustration of women's imposed duty to fetuses that goes in the opposite direction is the refusal to let pregnant women die. Fully 27 of 38 states with living will statutes prohibit the directive from taking effect when the patient is pregnant, significantly compromising women's right to refuse medical treatment (Benton 1990).

9. In the earlier opinion, the judges argued that "the Caesarean section would not significantly affect A.C.'s condition because she had, at best, two days left of sedated life" (*In re A.C.* 1987, 617). But Carder's father says: "For 14 years our daughter was considered terminally ill and what right did the court have to decide that her life was over" (quoted in Field 1989, 117)?

10. Last year, a Michigan judge dismissed one such charge, against a 36-year-old white lawyer, on grounds that the drug delivery law was not intended to apply to pregnant women who take controlled substances and that the case violated the woman's rights to privacy and due process. The prosecutor plans to appeal (*Los Angeles Times* 1991). In April 1991, the Michigan Court of Appeals ruled that a 24-year-old Black factory worker should not stand trial on child abuse charges for using crack hours before giving birth, because the statutes do not apply to fetuses (Kantrowitz 1991). Michigan requires reporting of positive drug tests on newborns. At press time, the Florida Supreme Court had overturned Jennifer Johnson's conviction (Lewin 1992). This action may send a message to other states to reconsider their prosecution strategies.

11. The case was dismissed, because there was no evidence that the fetus had been harmed.

12. Medical practitioners generally recommend treating babies for withdrawal after they are born, citing the first and third trimesters as the most dangerous times for a pregnant woman to withdraw from opiates, and preferring methadone maintenance even in the second trimester (Hoegerman and Schnoll 1991).

13. We can extrapolate from the experiences of incarcerated women, who suffer from an extremely high rate of health problems, to those who would be incarcerated specifically for substance use during pregnancy, because many of the women prosecuted are like the ones already detained: poor, Black, and drug dependent (Stein and Mistiaen 1988; U.S. Census Bureau 1988, Tables 304 & 306). Moreover, the evidence should persuade anyone that even a woman who is

healthy except for her addiction will probably *not* be healthy by the time she gives birth, after living in typical correctional conditions.

Incarcerated pregnant and post-partum women do have some legal recourse, thanks to a 1976 U.S. Supreme Court decision establishing that prisoners have a constitutional right to "adequate" medical care (*Estelle v. Gamble* 429 U.S. 97). For discussions of class-action lawsuits *Estelle* helped launch, see Barry 1989 & Mimeo 2, and Stein and Mistiaen 1988.

14. The first I've seen, a New York City subway ad showing a baby in neonatal intensive care warns, "The mother didn't smoke, drink, or take drugs. The father did."

REFERENCES

In re A.C. 1987. 533 A.2d 611 (D.C. App.).

In the Matter of A.C. 1988. 539 A.2d 203 (D.C. App.).

In re A.C. 1990. 573 A.2d 1235 (D.C. App.).

Abel, Ernest L. 1984. *Fetal Alcohol Syndrome and Fetal Alcohol Effects.* New York: Plenum Press.

American College of Obstetricians and Gynecologists v. Thornburgh. 1986. 106 S.Ct. 2169.

American College of Obstetricians and Gynecologists. 1987. "Patient Choice: Maternal-Fetal Conflict," Committee Opinion No. 55. Washington, D.C.

American Medical Association. 1990. "Report of the Board of Trustees on Legal Interventions During Pregnancy: Court-Ordered Medical Treatments and Legal Penalties for Potentially Harmful Behavior by Pregnant Women." Chicago.

Aronson, Peter. "Crackdown on Use of Drugs While Pregnant: Mothers Face Charges for Addicted Babies," *Recorder,* 4 April 1989.

Balisy, Sam S. 1987. "Maternal Substance Abuse: The Need to Provide Legal Protection to the Fetus," *Southern California Law Review* 60:1209-1238.

Barry, Ellen M. 1985. "Quality of Prenatal Care for Incarcerated Women Challenged," *Youth Law News* 6(6): 1-4.

Barry, Ellen M. 1989. "Pregnant Prisoners," *Harvard Women's Law Journal* 12:189-205.

Barry, Ellen M. No Date. Mimeo 1, "Pregnant, Substance-Dependent Women: De-Bunking the Myth of Incarceration." San Francisco: Legal Services for Prisoners with Children.

Barry, Ellen M. No Date. Mimeo 2, "Pregnant Women Prisoners Win Major Victories Against Two County Jail Systems in California." San Francisco: Legal Services for Prisoners with Children.

Beal v. Doe. 1977. 97 S. Ct. 2366.

Beck, Joan. "Womb Not a Haven for the Babies of Women Who Drink," *Chicago Tribune,* 8 February 1990.

Benton, Elizabeth Carlin. 1990. "The Constitutionality of Pregnancy Clauses in Living Will Statutes," *Vanderbilt Law Review* 43:1821-1837.

Berrien, Jacqueline. 1990. "Pregnancy and Drug Use: The Dangerous and Un-
    equal Use of Punitive Measures," *Yale Journal of Law and Feminism*
    2:239-250.
Chasnoff, Ira J. 1989. "Drug Use and Women: Establishing A Standard of Care,"
    Annals of New York Academy of Science 562:208-210.
Chasnoff, I., H. Landress, and M. Barrett. 1990. "The Prevalence of Illicit-Drug or
    Alcohol Use During Pregnancy and Discrepancies in Mandatory Reporting in
    Pinellas County, Florida," *New England Journal of Medicine* 322:1202-1206.
Chavkin, Wendy. 1990. "Drug Addiction and Pregnancy: Policy Crossroads,"
    American Journal of Public Health 80:483-487.
Field, Martha A. 1989. "Controlling the Woman to Protect the Fetus," *Law,
    Medicine, and Health Care* 17:114-129.
Hoegerman, Georgeanne and Sidney Schnoll. 1991. "Narcotic Use in Pregnan-
    cy," *Clinics in Perinatology* 18:51-76.
Hoffman, Jan. "Pregnant, Addicted–and Guilty?" *New York Times Magazine,* 19
    August 1990.
Jefferson v. Griffin Spalding County Hospital Authority. 1981. Ga., 274 S.E. 2d
    457.
Johnsen, Dawn. 1989. "From Driving to Drugs: Governmental Regulation of
    Pregnant Women's Lives after *Webster,*" *University of Pennsylvania Law Re-
    view* 138:179-215.
Kantrowitz, Barbara. 1991. "The Pregnancy Police," *Newsweek,* April 29.
Kolder, Veronika, Janet Gallagher, and Michael Parsons. 1987. "Court-Ordered
    Obstetrical Interventions," *New England Journal of Medicine* 316:1192-1196.
LaCroix, Susan. 1989. "Birth of a Bad Idea: Jailing Mothers for Drug Abuse,"
    Nation, May 1.
Lewin, Tamar. "Drug Verdict over Infant is Voided," *New York Times,* 24 July
    1992, sec. B.
Los Angeles Times. "Judge Rejects Drug Case Tied to Pregnancy," 5 February
    1991.
McHugh, Gerald Austin. 1980. "Protection of the Rights of Pregnant Women in
    Prisons and Detention Facilities," *New England Journal on Prison Law*
    6:231-263.
McNulty, Molly. 1990. "Pregnancy Police: Implications of Criminalizing Fetal
    Abuse," *Youth Law News* 11(1): 33-36.
MacKinnon, Catharine. 1987. "Difference and Dominance," ch. 2 of *Feminism
    Unmodified: Discourses on Life and Law.* Cambridge: Harvard University
    Press.
Minow, Martha. 1990. *Making All the Difference: Inclusion, Exclusion, and
    American Law.* Ithica: Cornell University Press.
Moss, Debra. 1988. "Pregnant? Go Directly to Jail," *American Bar Association
    Journal,* November 1.
Muller v. Oregon. 1908. 208 U.S. 412.
National Conference of State Legislatures. 1989 & 1991. "Maternal and Child
    Health Legislation." Denver.

New York Times. "Case Against Woman in Baby Death Thrown Out," 27 February 1987, sec. A.

Pollitt, Katha. 1990. " 'Fetal Rights': A New Assault on Feminism," *Nation,* March 26.

Roberts, Dorothy. 1991. "Punishing Drug Addicts who have Babies: Women of Color, Equality, and the Right of Privacy," *Harvard Law Review* 104:1419-1482.

Roe v. Wade. 1973. 410 U.S. 113.

Stein, Loren and Veronique Mistiaen. "Mothers Behind Bars," *Boston Sunday Herald Magazine,* 30 October 1988.

Stoddard, Kathy. "Fetal Rights, Fetal Wrongs: The Courts and Legislatures Respond to the Fetal Rights Hysteria," *New Haven Advocate,* 16 July 1990.

Taft v. Taft. 1983. 466 N.E.2d 395 (Mass.).

United States v. Vaughn. Daily Washington Law Reporter, March 7, 1989, pp. 441, 446-7.

U.S. Bureau of the Census. 1988. *Statistical Abstract of the United States (108th ed.).* Washington, D.C.: U.S. Government Printing Office.

U.S. Bureau of the Census. 1990. *Statistical Abstract of the United States (110th ed.).* Washington, D.C.: U.S. Government Printing Office.

Williams Obstetrics (18th ed.). 1989. Norwalk, CT: Appleton and Lange.

Winston v. Lee. 1985. 105 S.Ct. 1611.

Youth Law News. 1985. "County Jail Miscarriage Rate 50 Times State Average," 6(6): 4.

Youth Law News. 1990. "One Drug-Using Mother's Story," 11(1): 19.

Analyzing Employer Motives: Evaluating the "Scientific Evidence" upon Which Fetal Protection Policies Were Based

Suzanne Uttaro Samuels

SUMMARY. Throughout the late 1970s and 1980s, many private sector employers adopted policies barring fertile women, usually defined as all women between the ages of 15 and 50, from any jobs that might expose them to known or suspected reproductive or fetal hazards. Employers termed these policies "fetal protection policies," and contended that excluding women from the workplace was necessary to prevent fetal exposure to occupational toxins. This article attempts to evaluate the "scientific evidence" upon which fetal protection policies were based.

After defining the relevant scientific terms, this article explores the existing federal regulations that aim at limiting both maternal and paternal exposure to reproductive hazards. It then examines the existing data on the effects of paternal and maternal exposure to occupational toxicants. This paper concludes that the "scientific evidence" upon which fetal protection policies were based does not definitively establish that excluding fertile women will eliminate the risk of fetal harm.

Suzanne Uttaro Samuels is affiliated with Seton Hall University, 347 Fahy Hall, S. Orange Avenue, South Orange, NJ 07079-2696.

[Haworth co-indexing entry note]: "Analyzing Employer Motives: Evaluating the "Scientific Evidence" upon Which Fetal Protection Policies Were Based." Samuels, Suzanne Uttaro. Co-published simultaneously in *Women & Politics* (The Haworth Press, Inc.) Vol. 13, No. 3/4, 1993, pp. 137-152; and: *The Politics of Pregnancy: Policy Dilemmas in the Maternal-Fetal Relationship* (ed: Janna C. Merrick, and Robert H. Blank) The Haworth Press, Inc., 1993, pp. 137-152. Multiple copies of this article/chapter may be purchased from The Haworth Document Delivery Center [1-800-3-HAWORTH; 9:00 a.m. - 5:00 p.m. (EST)].

137

INTRODUCTION

Throughout the 1970s and 1980s, private employers excluded fertile women, defined as all women between the ages of 15 and 50 who had not been surgically sterilized, from certain jobs out of a concern about the effects of maternal and fetal exposure to workplace toxicants. These employers contended that their "fetal protection policies" were necessary to ensure that fetuses were not harmed by maternal exposure to reproductive and developmental toxicants. It has been estimated that under these policies, between 15 and 20 million women were barred from certain workplaces (*International Union, United Auto Workers v. Johnson Controls,* 886 F. 2d 914 (1989)). Moreover, it is likely that the number of jobs from which fertile women were effectively excluded was much larger than the number from which they were formally excluded.[1]

Obviously, fetal protection policies implicate existing employment discrimination statutes. Throughout the 1980s and early 1990s, a number of courts considered whether these policies violated the prohibition against sex discrimination in employment that was embodied in Title VII of the 1964 Civil Rights Act. Most significantly, in 1991, the United States Supreme Court considered this question in *International Union, United Auto Workers v. Johnson Controls,* and found that the fetal protection policy at issue constituted sex discrimination under Title VII (111 Sup. Ct. 1196 (1991)). This paper is not intended to address the nature of adjudication in this area. While the court decisions in this area, most notably the Supreme Court's decision in *Johnson Controls,* have shaped the contours of the debate about fetal protection, this paper pursues a more limited scope. It aims at analyzing the "scientific evidence" upon which these policies are based. By understanding that the scientific evidence used to support these policies is not definitive with regard to the effects of reproductive and developmental toxicants, we will be better able to assess the employer claim that these policies were necessary to ensure fetal health.

REPRODUCTIVE HAZARDS IN THE WORKPLACE

Reproductive hazards in the workplace generally refer to those toxicants that contribute to or cause certain disorders of reproduction; among these disorders are infertility, impotence, menstrual disorders, spontaneous abortion, low birth weight, birth defects, congenital mental retardation, and various genetic disorders (NIOSH 1989, 2). These toxicants may result in impairment of an individual's procreative capacity and alteration of the normal development of an embryo or fetus. In fact, the term "reproductive hazards" encompasses both reproductive toxicants, which are toxins that interfere with the reproductive or sexual functioning of the adult, and developmental toxicants, which produce a deleterious effect on the offspring of an individual. Reproductive toxicants are those that affect an individual after puberty, while developmental toxicants produce an effect between conception and puberty (OTA 1985, 11).

Terms Defined

Reproductive toxicants are those chemical, physical or biological agents that have an adverse impact upon the sexual or reproductive performance of sexually mature persons. These agents impair reproductive capacity by "interfering with or altering normal physiologic processes, regulatory mechanisms, organ function, or the genetic integrity of sperm or egg cells" (NIOSH 1989, 3-4). When exposure to these toxins damages the sperm or egg, and this damage results in congenital defects, developmental problems, or other inheritable traits, the toxin is said to be a mutagen (Williams 1980, 656). Mutagens cause genetic damage by altering the DNA of affected germ cells.

Developmental toxicants are those chemical, physical or biological agents that impair the growth or development of an embryo, fetus or prepubertal individual (NIOSH 1989, 5). Embryonic and fetal vulnerability to certain toxins is determined by the stage of development. The embryo/fetus is at the greatest risk of harm from environmental toxins during the embryonic stage, which is usually defined as the second through eighth week of gestation. At this time, all the major organ systems are being formed and scientists believe that the organs are most susceptible to injury during the earliest stages of differentiation and development (Rothstein 1984, 64-65).

A developmental toxicant affects the embryo or fetus in much the same way as it would a child or adult (Williams 1980, 655). For example, an embryo or fetus whose mother is exposed to carbon monoxide will be affected in the same way as would a child or an adult. The one distinguishing point, however, is that an embryo or fetus may be susceptible to harm at much lower levels of exposure than would be a child or adult (Rothstein 1984, 65). In addition, the adverse effects of some embryo fetotoxins may not be apparent until after birth. For example, the effects of maternal or paternal exposure to lead may become manifest in learning disabilities when the child is of school age (Rothstein 1984, 66).

A *teratogen* is an agent that acts on the dividing cells of an embryo or fetus and causes structural or functional defects such as limb deformities or birth defects (Williams 1980, 655-6; NIOSH 1989, 5-6). Teratogens appear to have the greatest adverse impact upon the development of an embryo/fetus within the first 60 to 70 days of gestation, when the organ systems are developing. Since teratogens appear to be most harmful to the embryo or fetus during the earliest stages of development, it is critical that the mother and father limit their exposure to these agents during this period. The problem is that most women are not aware that they are pregnant until they are well into this period of heightened susceptibility. By this time, serious damage to the embryo or fetus may have already occurred (Rothstein 1984, 77).[2]

TYPES OF REPRODUCTIVE TOXICANTS

According to the National Institute for Occupational Safety and Health Registry of Toxic Effects of Chemical Substances, which has entries for over 79,000 chemicals, 15,000 of these entries, or more than 20%, cite data on reproductive effects. Over 2800 chemicals have been studied for teratogenicity and 38% of these were found to have some teratogenic potential (NIOSH 1989, 2). The National Institute for Occupational Safety and Health rank reproductive impairment as sixth among the ten leading work-related diseases and impairments. This ranking is based upon the number of workers believed to be exposed to known or suspected reproductive toxicants (OTA 1985, 10).

Furthermore, occupational reproductive hazards may have an even greater effect on reproductive outcome than had been suspected previously. The cause of 60-80% of birth defects is unknown: only 20-25% of congenital abnormalities are believed to be the result of inherited genetic traits and chromosomal abnormalities, and only 10% are attributed to environmental factors such as drugs, alcohol, maternal infections, metabolic disorders or nutritional deficiencies ("Research" 1991, 1; NIOSH 1989, 3). In addition, at least 10-15% of American couples are infertile, meaning that they cannot conceive after having unprotected intercourse for at least one year. Many scientists suspect that the occurrence of both birth defects and infertility may be the result of exposure to occupational toxins (NIOSH 1989, 2).

Despite the large number of workers potentially affected by agents that impair their procreative capability and/or the development of their offspring, only a small number of chemicals used in American industry have been tested for their reproductive effects (Rothstein 1984, 65). More significantly, an even smaller number have been determined to be reproductive or developmental toxicants in humans (NIOSH 1989, 6).

The lack of evidence about the reproductive effects of chemicals used in industry stems not only from the paucity of research in this area, but from the difficulty of detecting these effects and of establishing causation (NIOSH 1989, 6). Scientists investigating reproductive hazards often rely upon the discovery of "clusters" of certain disorders of reproduction, like spontaneous abortions, stillbirths, or birth defects, as a sign that a reproductive toxicant may be present in the workplace. Even where an etiologic agent is suspected, definitive evidence is often difficult to obtain (NIOSH 1989, 9).

At present, only 30 to 40 chemical, physical and biological substances are generally accepted as having potential reproductive and developmental effects: among these are arsenic, benzene, carbon disulfide, carbon monoxide, chloroprene, dibrormochloropropane (DBCP), ethylene oxide (EtO), fluorocarbon 22, formaldehyde, glycol ethers, lead, mercury, organic mercury, methotrexate, methylene chloride, non-ionizing radiation, tetrachloride, toluene, trichloroethane, and vinyl chloride.[3] Of these 30 to 40 substances, however, only a handful–arsenic, carbon disulfide, chloroprene, DBCP, EtO, non-ionizing radiation and lead–are regulated in part because of their danger to reproductive capacity. Furthermore, of this handful, reproductive concerns have been critically important in the regulation of only DBCP, EtO and lead.

Of those agents believed to be reproductive toxicants, only dibrormochloropropane, a pesticide found to cause decreased sperm counts and infertility in male workers who used it, has been banned. In an interesting twist, it was the Environmental Protection Agency, not the Occupational Health and Safety Administration, that barred use of this chemical.[4] Ethylene oxide and lead have been regulated by OSHA and a discussion of these regulations is included here because it sheds light upon the manner in which the government has attempted to deal with reproductive toxins.

Lead Standard

Scientists generally agree that at certain levels of exposure, lead can damage a number of organ systems. The most sensitive of these systems are the nervous, gastrointestinal, hemopoietic, reproductive and renal systems (Rempel 1989, 532). Maternal and paternal exposure to lead, both before and after birth, poses the risk of serious developmental impairment to the fetus or the child.

In 1978, the Occupational Safety and Health Administration promulgated a standard that regulated workplace exposure to lead. OSHA issued the standard to reduce occupational exposure to lead and to eliminate the risk of lead poisoning through early identification of elevated blood-lead levels (Rempel 1989, 532). The standard also aimed at eliminating, or at least reducing, the levels at which fetuses are exposed to lead through parental exposure. OSHA determined that a fetus could be harmed by either maternal or paternal exposure to lead, and that this harm could occur prior to conception. Since OSHA's mandate is to protect the health and safety of working men and women, not the fetuses or offspring of workers, OSHA justified this regulation by stating that "damage to the fetus represents impairment of the reproductive capacity of the parent and must be considered material impairment of functional capacity under the OSH Act" (Bertin 1989, 280).

The Lead Standard establishes permissible exposure levels for employees working with lead. In addition, the standard mandates that an employee must be removed from a job that exposes him/her to lead if any of these conditions exist: if his/her blood-lead level is above a permissible limit; if his/her average blood-lead level for the previous six months has been above this limit; if s/he exhibits symptoms of lead poisoning; or if s/he has a medical condition that places him/her at increased risk of material impairment (Rempel 1989, 533). It is significant that the fourth category includes employees who plan to have children. Thus, employees who notify the company's physician that they plan to conceive or father a child in the near future are entitled to medical removal and rate retention protections.

The Lead Standard provides the most sweeping medical removal and rate retention protections offered to workers exposed to reproductive toxins. Under the 1978 standard, employees who are eligible for medical removal must be removed from exposure to lead until the blood-lead level is reduced to an acceptable level or until the worker's general health improves (Rothstein 1984, 100). The rate retention protection ensures that the affected worker will retain his/her wage rate, seniority and benefits for a period of 18 months. In addition, the medical removal protection guarantees that after the worker obtains medical clearance, s/he can return to his/her original job status. These protections allow a pregnant worker to transfer out of a job in which s/he is exposed to lead, while retaining his/her rate of pay, benefits and seniority, and guaranteeing that s/he be allowed to return to this job (Bell 1979, 287).

The most controversial aspect of the 1978 Lead Standard was its use of identical blood-lead levels for men and women. In setting its permissible exposure limit (PEL), OSHA contended that male or female workers with blood-lead levels of 50 micrograms of lead per deciliter of blood or less could remain at their jobs. Prior to this, fertile women had been restricted from any jobs that involved exposure to lead. In a challenge to this aspect of the standard, the District Court for the District of Columbia upheld the standard, stating that the hazard posed by lead to male reproductive capacity warranted this single low standard (Cohen 1989, 336). In promulgating the standard, OSHA also revoked an earlier provision that would have required female workers to submit to periodic pregnancy tests (Bell 1979, 287).

The sole fetal protection case to reach the U.S. Supreme Court involved an employer policy that aimed at eliminating maternal exposure to lead, as did three of the five cases adjudicated in the federal courts of appeals.[5] In all four cases, the employers asserted that the OSHA limit of 50μ/dl was not stringent enough to eliminate the risk of fetal harm. It is widely believed that the OSHA Lead Standard should be revised to reflect recent advances in scientific knowledge, which indicate that lower levels of lead exposure can impair fetal development. In fact, as part of its plan to eliminate lead poisoning in children, the federal government has announced that it intends to reduce the blood-lead level of children to less than 10 μ/dl by the year 2000 ("Research," 1991, B20). In the near future, OSHA will be under significant pressure by both the corporate and labor sectors to revise its standard on blood-lead levels.

Ethylene Oxide Standard

Ethylene Oxide (EtO) is a sterilizing agent, fumigant, pesticide and industrial chemical additive. It is most commonly used by health care workers as a sterilant in hospitals. EtO is believed to be carcinogenic and mutagenic. Maternal and paternal exposure to EtO has been linked to adverse reproductive outcomes, including spontaneous abortions and chromosomal abnormalities (Preamble 1984, 81-87). In 1984, OSHA promulgated a new permanent ethylene oxide standard that established the permissible exposure level to be one part EtO per million parts of air (1 ppm) over an eight-hour weighted average. Prior to this, the permissible exposure level had been 50 parts EtO per million parts of air (50 ppm) (Preamble 1984, 112). In April 1988, the Ethylene Oxide Standard was amended to regulate short-term exposure.

In addition, the 1984 standard mandated that workers receive medical examinations and advice in a number of situations, most significantly where the worker "wants medical advice concerning the effects of EtO exposure on his/her ability to produce a healthy child" (Preamble 1984, 122). As part of this medical surveillance, company physicians are required to inquire about a worker's reproductive history, including information about stillbirths, miscarriages, past attempts at conception, and present reproductive status (Preamble 1984, 123). In addition, the physician must make available tests for fertility and pregnancy where the employee requests these tests and where the physician concurs with the need for this testing (Preamble 1984, 124).

Unlike the Lead Standard, the EtO Standard does not provide medical removal or rate retention protections. In explaining its decision not to mandate these protections, OSHA stated that since the effects of EtO do not appear to be reversible, there was no reason to mandate temporary removal. Thus, medical removal and rate retention protections would not be "reasonably necessary for the achievement of a safe and healthful work environment" (Preamble 1984, 126).

MATERNAL V. PATERNAL EXPOSURE

In the Lead and EtO Standards, OSHA recognized that reproductive hazards are a concern for both men and women. The Preamble for both standards establishes that either maternal or paternal exposure to these agents could result in adverse reproductive outcomes. While OSHA has steadfastly adhered to the view that a fetus may be harmed as the result of either maternal or paternal exposure to workplace toxins, there is significant disagreement about the effects of paternal exposure, especially with regard to lead. In fact, much of the debate about whether fetal protection policies constitute unlawful sex discrimination centers on this issue. The following sections outline the evidence on the effects of maternal and paternal exposure to occupational toxins.

Maternal Exposure

A survey conducted in 1980 revealed that 17% of female workers with children work in jobs that could involve exposure to teratogens, which are agents that may harm a developing fetus (Rothstein 1984, 65). In addition, scientists believe that female infertility is caused by a number of agents, including lead, mercury, cadmium, textile dyes and noise (Rothstein 1984, 64). It is difficult, however, to prove a causal connection between adverse reproductive outcome and workplace conditions. As NIOSH has noted, this assessment is "confounded by occupational exposure to mixed agents, by nonoccupational factors (like age, personal habits and hobbies), and by the need to evaluate any association relative to the background incidence of the outcomes studied" (NIOSH 1989, 6).

Despite the difficulty of proving causation, there is widespread agreement among scientists that environmental toxicants may be transmitted to the fetus through maternal exposure. Moreover, it is widely accepted that fetuses are susceptible to toxins at lower levels of exposure than are women. NIOSH warns that pregnant women who are exposed to workplace toxins are more likely to suffer spontaneous abortions or still births, or to have a child with low birth weight, birth defects, or developmental handicaps than are women who are not exposed to these toxins (Furnish 1987, 18). In collecting data on birth defects, scientists have focused almost exclusively upon maternal exposure to teratogens and have virtually ignored data on the effects of paternal exposure to toxins (Williams 1980, 661). There is a paucity of data about the mutagenic effect of many toxins; in particular, there is a lack of information about the effects of paternal exposure to known occupational toxins.

Paternal Exposure

Until recently, there was little research on the transmission of toxic agents from the father to a child, either before or after conception. Earlier research focused on the effect of occupational and environmental toxicants upon male infertility and decreased sperm counts. This research concluded that exposure to certain substances, among them DBCP, lead, chloroprene, kepone, vinyl chloride, alcohol, marijuana, tobacco, anesthetic gases, chemotherapeutic drugs, and heat, could cause a decrease or total absence of sperm (Rothstein 1984, 64).

Scientists have begun to explore the possible link between birth defects and paternal exposure to environmental and occupational toxicants only recently. There appear to have been two reasons that earlier research was not undertaken, or where it was undertaken, was not accepted. First, scientists investigating the paternal contribution to birth defects had difficulty identifying the biological mechanism by which the toxicant was transmitted. Second, scientists held what has been referred to as a "macho sperm theory of conception," which is the belief that only the fittest sperm would be capable of fertilizing an egg ("Research" 1991, 1).

Recent data suggest that a number of physical, chemical and biological agents may produce spontaneous abortion or birth defects in children fathered by exposed males; among these agents are alcohol, opiates such as heroin and methadone, waste anesthetic gases, benzene, lead, pesticides, polyvinyl chloride, and solvents (Chavkin 1979, 313; NIOSH 1989, 8; "Research" 1991, 36; Williams 1980, 657-9). Moreover, recent epidemiological studies have found a strong association between paternal exposure to occupational toxins and birth defects. These studies indicate that there is a greater incidence of birth defects among the children of welders, fire fighters, and workers exposed to radiation (Cohen 1986, 280).

Paternal exposure to occupational toxins appears to harm both the germ cells and the fetus. The most recent research suggests that birth defects may result from paternal exposure prior to conception. Scientists hypothesize that certain toxins can alter sperm morphology or cause genetic mutations, and that these alterations become manifest in birth defects and in an increased incidence of spontaneous abortions and stillbirths (Cohen 1986, 52, 62).

A more controversial theory is that paternal exposure to occupational hazards may harm a developing fetus after conception. As has been stated, it is generally accepted that hazardous toxins can be transmitted to the fetus by the mother via the placental membrane. The idea that paternal exposure places the fetus or child at risk after conception, however, is less well accepted. According to this theory, paternal transmission to a child or a fetus may occur in two possible ways: the man may transport hazardous materials from work to home on his clothing, shoes and hair and thus expose a child to these materials; or an exposed man may transmit toxic substances to a fetus through vaginal absorption of those substances that are present in his seminal fluid (Williams 1980, 657).

Paternal exposure to occupational toxins appears to place a fetus at risk of spontaneous abortion, stillbirth, or a wide variety of birth defects. For this reason, many scientists have concluded that permissible exposure levels for men and women should be the same. Many believe that the lead and ethylene oxide standards, which do not distinguish between male and female workers in setting permissible exposure levels, should be the model for dealing with reproductive toxicants.

Furthermore, these new data on the paternal contribution to birth defects undermine the validity of fetal protection policies, which exclude women from jobs where reproductive toxicants are present, while allowing men to continue to be exposed to these agents. Two governmental research gathering agencies have considered the scientific basis for these policies, and both have rejected the differential treatment of female workers. The National Institute for Occupational Safety and Health has concluded that "neither sex can be said to be more vulnerable" to occupational toxins (NIOSH 1989, 4), and the Office of Technology Assessment has stated that "scientific evidence generally fails to [either] confirm or disconfirm a need for differential exposure standards for men and women based on reproductive effects" (OTA 1985, 26). Thus, it appears that there is sufficient evidence that differential treatment is necessary to prevent fetal harm.

Although employers who instituted fetal protection policies argued that women are more sensitive to certain reproductive toxins, some epidemiologists contend that pre-conception paternal exposure may ultimately be more dangerous than post-conception maternal exposure (Rothstein 1984, 63; U.S. 1990, 7-8). First, some believe that harm produced by exposure to occupational toxins may be more readily transmitted from the male prior to conception (U.S. 1990, 7-8). For example, sperm have been shown to be more sensitive to the mutagenic effects of ionizing radiation than have ova (Rothstein 1984, 63).

Second, despite the fact that the sperm are continuously reproducing and thus the danger of cumulative exposure is small, the rapid cell division that occurs during sperm production is especially sensitive to mutagenesis (Rothstein 1984, 63). Mutagenesis is the production of genetically altered sperm. For this reason, paternal exposure to workplace toxins may have multigenerational effects.

Given the fact that a fetus or child may be harmed by workplace toxins through the exposure of either the mother or father to these toxins, it is unclear why employers chose to bar only women from working with hazardous materials. More significantly, if both men and women may transmit these toxins to their offspring, why did employers choose to regulate exposures at all?

The Use of One-Sex Exclusionary Policies

In attempting to understand why employers chose to exclude only women from jobs that might involve exposure to reproductive toxins, one could view the employer's motive from either a pessimistic or an optimistic stance. If one adopts a more optimistic view, s/he might believe that the employer was compelled to adopt a fetal protection policy because of its knowledge about maternal transmission. If one adopts a more pessimistic view, however, s/he would likely focus on other factors which indicate that the employer used these policies solely to bar women from traditionally male workplaces.

An Optimistic View of Employer Motivations

Clearly, the lack of available scientific data about the male contribution to birth defects has played a part in employers' adoption of these policies. As has been stated, until recently the paternal contribution to birth defects had not been studied as extensively as had that of the female.[6] This dearth of evidence about the effects of paternal exposure appears to stem from two factors. First, it is easier to measure reproductive success for women than it is for men (i.e., stillbirths and spontaneous abortion are easier to detect than is male infertility or poor sperm morphology), and to make the connection between maternal and fetal health (Cohen 1986, 50).

Second, and perhaps more significantly, there is a widely held belief that adverse reproductive outcomes stem from some problem with the female reproductive system (Cohen 1986, 50; NIOSH 1989, 9). This bias is evident even in recent studies of environmental toxicants. In 1989, the Environmental Protection Agency issued its Proposed Guidelines for Developmental Toxicity Risk Assessment. These guidelines outlined the procedures that the EPA will utilize in assessing the developmental toxicity of certain substances ("Environmental," 1989, 9386). These guidelines aimed at examining only the effects of maternal exposure to a given environmental toxicant; the guidelines did not address the risks of transmission through the father either before or after conception.

In addition, the general lack of data about either male or female transmission of reproductive toxicants may have also compelled employers to adopt these policies. As has been stated, most substances have not been evaluated for their potential reproductive and developmental effects. Since there are major gaps in our understanding of the effects of reproductive hazards, the OTA has stated that "the management of uncertainty is the central issue in the protection of reproductive health" (OTA 1985, 7). Thus, it is possible that employers, apprised of the risk of maternal transmission of occupational toxins to a developing fetus, chose to exclude women.

To recap, employers may have barred women, but not men, because they were unaware of the scientific evidence relating to paternal transmission of occupational toxins. Even if employers were aware of the risks of paternal exposure, they may have believed that fetuses were at greater risk from maternal transmission (Rothstein 1984, 78-9; Williams 1980, 660). The employer may have unconsciously accepted the prevailing stereotype that birth defects are transmitted only through the mother. It is possible that throughout the 1980s, as women moved into previously all-male occupations, employers felt compelled to examine the occupational risks associated with these jobs. Moreover, employers may have assumed that male workers, who have traditionally been in the work force, are unaffected by reproductive toxins (NIOSH 1989, 9).

A Pessimistic View of Employer Motivations

An alternative hypothesis is that employers were aware that certain toxins could harm a developing fetus through either maternal or paternal exposure. One commentator suggests that the employer was concerned only about the risk of tort liability. The employer excluded women because s/he believed that only the employee-mother would associate a birth defect with occupational hazards and, moreover, that the child of such a worker would be more likely to recover damages for injuries (Rothstein 1984, 78-79). Thus, even if the employer was aware that toxins could be transmitted to the fetus through paternal exposure, the employer may have been relatively unconcerned about this harm since he or she would not likely have suffered economic harm as a result of this exposure.

It is also possible that employers have utilized a kind of "selective vision" in acknowledging occupational health hazards. Some commentators contend that employers have ignored or minimized occupational hazards that relate to men (Cohen 1989, 281). Employers could have utilized this selective vision in choosing which women to exclude. The fact that women were barred from jobs only in instances where they could be replaced readily by men seems to support this contention.

CONCLUSIONS

The OTA's characterization of the issue of reproductive hazards as requiring the "management of uncertainty" appears to be accurate (OTA 1985, 7). There is little information about which industrial agents cause reproductive and developmental harm; in addition, scientists have not collected enough data to make conclusions about the nature of this harm or to determine whether men and women suffer comparable harm from exposure to these agents. Furthermore, the extent to which employers are liable for harm resulting from occupational exposure remains unsettled.

Some contend that employers adopted fetal protection policies as a means of combatting this high level of uncertainty. It is clear, however, that many more employees are at risk of occupational exposure to reproductive and developmental toxicants than are actually affected by these policies. Concern about the employer justifications for fetal protection policies and about the effects of these policies quickly sparks anxiety about occupational health hazards in general. Many commentators contend that employers should clean up the workplaces as an alternative to enacting these policies. Others assert that this argument "ignores the constraints imposed by technological feasibility" (Rothstein 1984, 79). These analysts allege that the workplace cannot be made completely safe; moreover, the costs of lowering exposure levels beyond a certain point do not yield corresponding increases in safety. If the workplace cannot be made completely hazard-free, we must determine what level of risk we as a society are willing to bear for adverse reproductive outcomes like miscarriages, stillbirths and birth defects.

This discussion about reproductive and fetal hazards has revealed that the "scientific evidence" upon which fetal protection policies have been based does not definitively establish that excluding fertile women will eliminate the risk of fetal injury. Occupational toxins may harm a fetus through paternal, as well as maternal, exposure. Employers who adopted fetal protection policies often ignored this element of risk, choosing instead to focus upon maternal risk. Thus, the available evidence on the effects of maternal and paternal exposure do not support a finding that fetal protection policies are necessary to protect fetal health.

In addition, this discussion has highlighted the assumptions that often underlay research about reproductive and fetal hazards. Until recently, nearly all research on birth defects and poor reproductive outcomes has focused on the woman's responsibility for these problems; little study had been devoted to the male-mediated contribution. This focus on the maternal contribution, and corresponding lack of research on the paternal contribution, seems to have been based on the antiquated notion that it is the woman, not the man, whose health determines that of her offspring. The health of the male germ cell was not questioned; it was assumed that any problems in fetal development were the result of maternally-transmitted defects. Thus, the woman was seen as solely responsible for the health and development of her fetus. For many years this assumption was at the heart of scientific research on birth defects. Moreover, this gender-biased research was repeatedly used throughout the 1980s and early 1990s to justify fetal protection policies. As the foregoing study has demonstrated, this approach serves neither the health and safety of the worker nor the health of the fetus or child.

NOTES

1. Because many of the affected workplaces were unionized, women were excluded not only from the hazardous jobs, but from any jobs that might lead to these positions in a line of progression under a union contract. Thus, express exclusion from one job on the basis of concerns about exposure to reproductive hazards effectively foreclosed access to many other jobs that might not have posed a danger to reproductive health.

2. The embryo/fetus may also be affected by agents that are *transplacental carcinogens*. These agents, of which the drug diethylstilbestrol (DES) is perhaps best known, are capable of crossing the placenta and causing cancer during the fetus' lifetime.

3. This list is derived from a number of sources: among them, an on-going survey conducted by the U.S. General Accounting Office which is examining the activities of four agencies charged with regulating occupational reproductive toxins; the Bureau of National Affairs Occupational Safety and Health Reporter vol. 20, no. 1, 26; OTA 1985, 8; and Williams 1980, 648.

4. It does make sense, however, that the EPA should have regulated DBCP. Although it was banned because of its adverse reproductive effects upon workers who used it, it could have been released for use by the public. Moreover, there was some question about the environmental effects of this chemical. Thus, evidence indicated that DBCP was both an occupational and an environmental hazard.

5. *U.A.W. v. Johnson Controls,* 111 Sup. Ct. Rep. 1196 (1991); *Grant v. General Motors Corp.,* 908 F.2d 1303 (1990); *Hayes v. Shelby Memorial Hospital,* 726 F.2d 1543 (1984); *Wright v. Olin Corporation,* 697 F.2d 1172 (1982).

6. Needleman and Bellinger contend that there has been much less research on the effects of paternal exposure to lead. For this reason, they conclude that "the position that a given level of paternal but not maternal exposure is acceptable is without logical foundation and insupportable on empirical grounds" (Needleman and Bellinger 1988, 190-1).

REFERENCES

Bell, Carolyn. 1979. "Implementing Safety and Health Regulations for Women in the Workplace." *Feminist Studies.* 5:286-301.

Bertin, Joan E. 1989. "Reproductive Hazards in the Workplace." Cohen, Sherill and Nadine Taub eds. *Reproductive Laws for the 1990s.* Clifton, NJ: Humana Press.

Chavkin, Wendy. 1979. "Occupational Hazards to Reproduction: A Review Essay and Annotated Bibliography." *Feminist Studies.* 5:310-325.

Cohen, Felissa. 1986. "Paternal Contributions to Birth Defects." *Nursing Clinics of North America* 21, 1:49-64.

Cohen, Sherill and Nadine Taub. 1989. *Reproductive Laws for the 1990s.* Clifton, NJ: Humana Press.

Epstein, Gregory. 1984. *Cases and Materials on Torts.* Boston: Little, Brown and Co.

Furnish, Hannah Arterian. 1987. "Beyond Protection: Relevant Difference and Equality in the Toxic Work Environment." *University of California Davis Law Review.* 21:1-43.

Grant v. General Motors Corp. 908 F.2d 1303 (Sixth Circuit 1990).

Hayes v. Shelby Memorial Hospital. 762 F.2d 1543 (Eleventh Circuit 1904).

International Union, United Autoworkers v. Johnson Controls. 886 F.2d 871 (Seventh Circuit 1989).

International Union, United Autoworkers v. Johnson Controls. 111 Sup. Ct. Rep. 1196 (US 1991).

Katz, Joni F. 1989. "Hazardous Working Conditions and Fetal Protection Policies: Women Are Going Back to the Future." *Boston College Environmental Affairs Law Review.* 17:201-230.

Needleman, Herbert L. and David Bellinger. 1988. "Commentary: Recent Developments." *Environmental Research.* 46:190-191.

Petchesky, Rosalind. 1979. "Workers, Reproductive Hazards, and the Politics of Protection: An Introduction." *Feminist Studies.* 5:233-246.

Philadelphia Area Committee on Occupational Safety and Health. 1988. *Getting Job Hazards Out of the Bedroom: The Handbook on Workplace Hazards to Reproduction*. Philadelphia: Philadelphia Area Project on Occupational Safety and Health.

Rempel, David. 1989. "The Lead-Exposed Worker." *Journal of the American Medical Association*. 262, 4:532-534.

"Research on Birth Defects Shifts to Flaws in Sperm." *New York Times*, 1 January 1991, sec. 1, p. A1, 36.

Rothstein, Mark A. 1984. *Medical Screening of Workers*. Washington, D.C.: Bureau of National Affairs, Inc.

U.S. Congress. House of Representatives. Majority Staff of the Committee on Education and Labor. *A Report on the Equal Employment Opportunity Commission, Title VII and Workplace Fetal Protection Policies in the 1980s*. 101st Cong., 2nd sess., 1990.

U.S. Department of Health and Human Services, Centers for Disease Control, National Institute for Occupational Safety and Health. *Proposed National Strategy for the Prevention of Disorders of Reproduction*. Washington, D.C.: Government Printing Office, 1989.

U.S. Office of Technology Assessment. *Reproductive Hazards in the Workplace*. Washington, D.C.: Government Printing Office, 1985.

"United States Opens a Drive to Wipe Out Lead Poisoning Among Children." *New York Times*, 20 December 1990, sec. 1., p. A1.

Williams, Wendy W. 1980-81. "Firing the Woman to Protect the Fetus: The Reconciliation of Fetal Protection with Employment Opportunity Goals Under Title VII." *The Georgetown Law Journal*. 69:641-704.

Wright, Michael J. 1979. "Reproductive Hazards and 'Protective' Discrimination." *Feminist Studies*. 5:302-309.

Wright v. Olin Corporation. 697 F.2d 1172 (Fourth Circuit 1982).

Who Is Protected?
What's Wrong with Exclusionary Policies

Sally J. Kenney

SUMMARY. Many employers have excluded women whose infertility is not medically documented from allegedly hazardous work claiming they feared if the women became pregnant, their fetuses would be harmed. In *United Auto Workers v. Johnson Controls,* the Supreme Court held in 1991 that so-called "fetal protection policies" are unlawful sex discrimination. After examining four cases challenging exclusionary policies in Britain and the United States, this article unmasks and argues against the assumptions underlying such policies. By returning to well-established sex discrimination doctrine, moving away from a male norm, and reaffirming women's right to both work and have children, the Supreme Court's decision in *UAW v. Johnson Controls* is an important victory. The decision should help to break down job segregation, prompt the EEOC to act, and clear the way for addressing questions of health and safety rather than equality and difference.

INTRODUCTION

Once federal and state sex discrimination laws began to be enforced in the mid-1970s, employers in male-dominated industries could no longer refuse to hire women solely because of gender. As the first women began

---

Sally J. Kenney is affiliated with the University of Iowa, 202 Jefferson Building, Iowa City, IA 52242.

[Haworth co-indexing entry note]: "Who Is Protected? What's Wrong with Exclusionary Policies." Kenney, Sally J. Co-published simultaneously in *Women & Politics* (The Haworth Press, Inc.) Vol. 13, No. 3/4, 1993, pp. 153-173; and: *The Politics of Pregnancy: Policy Dilemmas in the Maternal-Fetal Relationship* (ed: Janna C. Merrick, and Robert H. Blank) The Haworth Press, Inc., 1993, pp. 153-173. Multiple copies of this article/chapter may be purchased from The Haworth Document Delivery Center [1-800-3-HAWORTH; 9:00 a.m. - 5:00 p.m. (EST)].

153

to work in high-paid, skilled industrial jobs such as foundries and chemical manufacturing, employers developed policies to exclude all women whose infertility was not medically documented from allegedly hazardous work because they might become pregnant (Becker 1986; Bertin 1983; Bertin 1986; Williams 1981). Employers called these exclusionary policies "fetal protection policies," however partial their protection of future generations and however removed from an actual fetus. The courts' and the media's adoption of the employers' term, like their use of the term "pro-life," reveals that opponents lost an important rhetorical battle. Calling them fetal protection policies renders women invisible, as mere vessels for future generations who have rights or interests conflicting with yet-to-be-conceived offspring (Petchesky 1987; Pollitt 1990). The policies do not protect women. Furthermore, the term protective suggests a benign, laudable policy rather than exclusion which connotes discrimination. I call them exclusionary policies because, as I shall argue, they do not protect the unborn but discriminate against women and men.

The term "fetal protection policies" also implies that the main risk to the unborn comes from its mother's exposure to toxins in the workplace while pregnant. Yet reproductive hazards are biological, physical, or chemical agents that interfere with men's and women's ability to produce healthy offspring. Examples include radiation or pesticides that may make men and women sterile, cause mutations in the genetic material, or cause a woman to miscarry (Chavkin 1984; Chenier 1982). The important point to remember is that it "takes two to tango." A malformed child could be the result of damage to either maternal or paternal chromosomes, damage to egg or sperm cells, or damage to the fetus in the womb.

Scientific studies of reproductive hazards, however, infrequently reflect the knowledge that men and women both contribute to reproduction. Feminist scholars often begin their work by critiquing the women's and girls' exclusion from their discipline, whether in the study of moral reasoning, the Renaissance, or cardiovascular disease. For reproductive hazards, the opposite is the case. Most studies only examine the effects of toxins on women's ability to reproduce, ignoring the chance that men's exposure may produce malformations (Barlow and Sullivan 1982; Davis 1991; Fletcher 1985). The consequence of leaving men out is that when the studies discover a reproductive effect, employers assume it is confined to women, and proceed to exclude women from jobs.

The failure to explore male effects is unjustified since scientists have long known about them. For example, not only are pregnant women exposed to anesthetic gases more likely to miscarry, but so are the partners of exposed men. The problem may be in the dominant conception of reproduction itself. The so-called "macho sperm theory" posits that the fittest, strongest, most perfect sperm, like Rocky storming the steps of the Philadelphia Art Museum, streaks through to "penetrate" the egg (Martin 1991). Recent evidence suggests that the egg chemically draws sperm to it, calling into question the passive egg active sperm model. As Dr. Davis, from the National Academy of Sciences quipped, "You don't have to be Sigmund Freud to figure out there are cultural factors to say why we have paid so much attention to the female and so little to the male" (Blakeslee 1991). The following four cases show how employers simultaneously magnified the risk to offspring through women's exposure to toxins while minimizing the risk through men's exposure.

CASES

American Cyanamid

In 1973, federal investigators informed American Cyanamid that if it did not begin to hire women at its Willow Island, West Virginia, chemical-based production factory it would soon face sanctions. As "the only workplace for miles offering a living wage" applications flooded in (Faludi 1991, 441). In 1975, the corporate medical director of American Cyanamid Corporation, Dr. Robert Clyne, began drafting a policy to ban women from any jobs that exposed them to any amount of 29 substances (OTA 1985, 252). He compiled the list by scanning a computer sheet of hazardous substances in a process he described as "an educated guess." Cyanamid neither conducted animal studies nor epidemiological studies of its own workforce to see if they had experienced reproductive problems. The director did not consider substituting other products, reducing exposure, or using protective equipment.

Of the 29 substances, the medical director only had evidence that one substance, lead, was embryotoxic (injuring a fetus in the womb through maternal exposure). He quickly narrowed the range of reproductive effects of concern to encompass only effects to the fetus of the mother's exposure. Although the medical director was willing to assume that any substance that was carcinogenic to adults might harm a developing fetus, he quickly dismissed the risk of infertility or sterility to either men or women and, without looking at the evidence of reproductive hazards to men or extrapolating from evidence about carcinogens, he concluded men were not at risk.

Because the medical director believed women neither knew when they were pregnant nor planned their pregnancies, Cyanamid's policy excluded all women aged 15-50 from exposure to hazardous substances unless they were sterilized. Although the company had not yet decided to implement the policy, managers at Willow Island, West Virginia, announced it in 1978. Glen Mercer, director of industrial relations, told women that seven of them could transfer to the janitorial pool for less pay if they were not sterilized. All others would lose their jobs, even if their husbands had vasectomies or they were taking oral contraceptives or they agreed to monthly pregnancy tests. The company doctor and nurse at the meetings told the women that sterilization, described as "buttonhole surgery," was a simple procedure a local doctor could perform. The company's medical insurance would pay for the procedure and women could use their sick leave.

Between February and July of 1978, five women in the lead pigments department were sterilized and two women transferred. The men who had greeted women's entry into the plant by posting signs saying "Shoot a Woman, Save a Job," placing violent pornography in their lockers, and sexually assaulting them in the locker room laughed that the sterilized women had been "spayed," were "one of the boys now," and commented, "the veterinarian's having a special" (Faludi 1991, 443, 448). Although the women did not know it, the company had decided to delay implementation of the policy, seeking better scientific justification, and it took most of the substances off the list. The women's sacrifice was in vain. Cyanamid closed the lead pigments department in 1979 and the women lost their jobs. The women claimed that requiring women but not men to be sterilized as a condition of employment was sex discrimination. Three and a half years later Cyanamid settled out of court for $200,000 to be divided among eleven plaintiffs (*Christman v. American Cyanamid*; OTA 1985, 251).

The Occupational Safety and Health Administration had become concerned that employers were using health and safety as a justification for demanding that women workers be sterilized. In 1979, OSHA issued citations to both Cyanamid and Bunker Hill, a lead smelter that instituted a similar exclusionary policy, alleging that requiring women workers to be sterilized violated the general duty of employers to provide a safe and healthy workplace (Randall and Short 1983; Tate 1981). Cyanamid challenged the citations and won the first two rounds (*Secretary of Labor v. American Cyanamid* 1981). On appeal, Judge Robert Bork wrote the opinion for the Court of Appeals for the D.C. Circuit. He ruled that an employer's general duty to provide a safe and healthy workplace did not forbid requiring sterilization as a condition of employment for women only (*OCAW v. American Cyanamid* 1984). Judge Bork held that the women underwent the sterilizations voluntarily and not because the job required it. The only issue before the court was whether they violated health and safety law, not whether the policies were discriminatory.

When Judge Bork came before the Senate Judiciary Committee as the nominee to the Supreme Court, Senator Metzenbaum called his opinion "shocking" (Senate Hearings 1987, 467). Judge Bork replied that he had faithfully followed the legislative intent of Congress. Moreover, the company was offering women a choice: "I suppose the five women who chose to stay on that job with higher pay and chose sterilization–I suppose that they were glad to have the choice–they apparently were–that the company gave them" (Senate Hearings 1987, 470). His televised testimony stunned Betty Riggs, one of the women who was sterilized, and she sent a telegram to the committee.

Only a judge who knows nothing about women who need to work could say that. I was only 26 years old, but I had to work so I had no choice.... This was the most awful thing that happened to me. (Senate Hearings 1987, 678)

Judge Bork's ruling had legal and political consequences far beyond the parties to the case. His decision effectively shut down OSHA's ability to fight exclusionary policies, unless it wrote specific guidelines. The issue was reformulated as a matter of sex discrimination rather than one of health and safety. Once so framed, the outcome turned on whether women and men were sufficiently alike in their vulnerability to toxins to merit equal treatment rather than whether exclusionary policies were sound health and safety policies.

Page v. Freight Hire

In Britain, too, the issue was taken up as a question of sex discrimination rather than health and safety. In 1980, a British haulage company fired a woman truck driver hauling dimethylformamide (DMF) because the chemical contractor said no women could haul DMF into its plant, claiming DMF was a reproductive hazard to a developing fetus. The driver, Jacqueline Page, claimed the company's action violated the Sex Discrimination Act of 1975. The industrial tribunal did not agree, relying on a Court of Appeal's holding that held that employers could treat one sex less favorably than the other for safety or administrative convenience. The industrial tribunal took the view that treating women less favorably than men could not be illegal discrimination if it struck them as reasonable. The tribunal was also willing to assume that the exclusion was reasonable without requiring the employer to offer any evidence.

On appeal, Page's barrister, joined by the Equal Opportunities Commission as *amicus curiae,* argued that the Court of Appeal had overturned the precedent the industrial tribunal relied on. They argued that the employer carried the burden of showing that DMF was embryotoxic and that it produced no effects in males. The company had failed to demonstrate that Page was exposed to enough of the substance to put her at risk–she only drove the truck, others did the loading and unloading. If there was a spill, a reproductive injury would be the least of her worries–DMF posed other serious health risks. Nor had the company offered any evidence about the relative risk of men's versus women's exposure. Page maintained that she had no intention of becoming pregnant. She was 23-years-old and divorced, and had offered to sign an indemnity form. Her partner had had a vasectomy. The lawyer for the company immediately rejected her claim that she did not want to have children, because that, he said, was a decision for her future husband, and not Page, to make. She felt that declaring her desire to remain childless made the tribunal think she was a monster.

Rather than inventing a broad exception to sex discrimination law, as the Court of Appeal had done, and then recanted, the Employment Appeal Tribunal (EAT) turned to an exception in the statute. Section 51 permitted discrimination if a statute passed before 1975 required or allowed it. The EAT held that since Parliament passed the Health and Safety at Work Act in 1974, employers could discriminate against women if they claimed health and safety as the justification. Contrary to the protestations of Page's barrister and the EOC, the EAT would not scrutinize whether the employers' argument for health and safety had any scientific merit. Page lost her appeal (Kenney 1987).

Pregnancy and Polygraphs

The EEOC warehoused the third case, thus it never reached the U.S. courts. The EEOC's policy was to do nothing to set policy or resolve complaints in the 1980s (Cooke and Kenney 1988; House Education and Labor Committee 1990). An African-American woman applied for a job at a Mississippi bank and passed her typing test. Deciding to hire her, the bank signed her up for her mandatory pre-employment polygraph test. The polygraph operator asked her a battery of questions that included, "Are you pregnant?" When she answered that she was two months pregnant, he refused to administer the test because the results of polygraphs of pregnant women are unreliable. The bank told her to come back after she had the baby. When she filed a complaint with the EEOC claiming to be the victim of blatant pregnancy discrimination, the EEOC questioned the polygraph operator. His written replies reveal that he changed his story. Writing later that he was dependent on the bank for his business, he asserted that the problem was not that he could not ensure the accuracy of a pregnant woman's polygraph, but that the stress of the test might cause the woman to miscarry.[1]

After EEOC local office completed its investigation, it sent the file to Washington. Under Chairman Clarence Thomas,[2] the EEOC had decided that any case involving reproductive hazards was too scientifically and legally complex for the agency to resolve, although it had resolved such cases in the past, submitted *amicus curiae* briefs in litigation, and had the guidance of rulings by several federal appellate courts. In this case, as in others, the investigator's report revealed the claim of reproductive hazards to be obviously spurious. Having no lawyer, the woman turned to the EEOC to enforce the law. The EEOC did nothing, and she did not get the job.

UAW v. Johnson Controls

Litigation against Johnson Controls coupled with pressure from Congress finally goaded the EEOC into action. In 1977, a mere 13 years after Congress had outlawed sex discrimination in employment, the company hired its first women for jobs with high lead exposure. It advised women who were planning to have children not to take the jobs, and required them to sign a waiver stating the company had informed them of the risks. Between 1979 and 1982, eight employees whose blood leads exceeded 30 µg/dl (the limit OSHA recommends for pregnant women) became pregnant. In 1982, Johnson Controls began to exclude all women who did not have proof of infertility from jobs in which any employee had recorded blood lead levels higher than 30 µg/dl, or where air samples exceeded 30 µg/cubic meter, as well as jobs that fed into high lead exposure jobs. Having learned from the public relations debacle of American Cyanamid, the company officially discouraged sterilization.

In 1984, the United Autoworkers union filed a class action suit arguing that Johnson Controls's adoption of an exclusionary policy at its 14 battery manufacturing plants violated Title VII. Plaintiff Mary Craig had herself sterilized to keep her job. Plaintiff Ginny Green was 50-years-old, divorced, and supporting a nine-year-old daughter on her $9 an hour job that offered opportunities for overtime at time-and-a-half. When the company transferred her to a job as a glorified laundress, she became the butt of "fertility jokes from all the Archie Bunkers" (Kirp 1990, 1). Not all of the plaintiffs were women. In March of 1984, Donald Penney had asked for a three month leave of absence to lower the amount of lead in his blood so he could father a healthy child. Johnson Controls refused, and, according to his complaint, the personnel director told him, "If you feel this way, quit" (Kirp 1990, 7).

Johnson Controls requested the district court grant it summary judge-ment–that the court dispense with a trial because there were no contested issues of fact or law. The UAW protested that two important facts were in dispute: whether fetuses were at risk from low levels of maternal exposure to lead, and whether men's exposure endangered their reproductive capac-ity. The company and the union also disagreed about how the court should classify the exclusionary policy under the law. How the court chooses to classify the policy assigns the burden of proof between employers and workers and determines how hard it is for an employer to justify its policy. Title VII of the Civil Rights Act of 1964, as amended by the Pregnancy Discrimination Act of 1978, prohibits sex discrimination in employment. Sex discrimination includes discrimination because of pregnancy, child-birth, or related medical condition (Furnish 1980). To justify excluding all women from a job, an employer must show that sex is a bona fide occupa-tional qualification for the job (BFOQ)–that you cannot do the job if you are a woman. If, however, an employer adopts a "neutral" policy that excludes disproportionately more women than men, such as a height re-quirement, the employer must justify the policy as a business necessity.

Although the policies discriminate on their faces, three circuit courts treated them as neutral, allowing the employer to argue a business neces-sity defense (Buss, 1986; *Hayes v. Shelby Memorial Hospital* 1984; *Wright v. Olin* 1984; *Zuniga v. Kleberg County Hospital* 1982).[3] Judges in both Britain and the United States had been willing to set aside the clear man-dates of sex discrimination statutes because excluding women from haz-ardous work to protect offspring they have not yet conceived seems rea-sonable and benign rather than a sinister attempt to deny women employment opportunity (Kenney 1992).

The consequences of treating facially discriminatory exclusionary poli-cies as if they were neutral (disparate impact) became more significant as the Supreme Court lessened the standard of justification for business necessity during the 1980s (*Wards Cove Packing Co. v. Atonio* 1989). Because the Court's rulings had made it virtually impossible to challenge neutral employment policies that froze women in low paying jobs, Con-gress fought to amend the law, and eventually succeeded in passing the Civil Rights Act of 1991. As *UAW v. Johnson Controls* worked its way through the appeals process, however, the reduced standard of proof for disparate impact was in effect.

Both the district court and the court of appeals analyzed the exclusion-ary policy as if it were neutral, although it discriminated against women on its face, and applied the reduced standard of justification for business necessity. Both did so without a trial record since District Judge Robert

Warren granted Johnson Controls' motion for summary judgment. The Court of Appeals for the Seventh Circuit affirmed. Both courts accepted that lead posed a risk to a developing fetus and dismissed the evidence of the effects of lead on men's reproductive capacity.

In 1978 when OSHA developed standards of exposure for lead, it explicitly rejected permitting employers to exclude all women (29 C.F.R. §1910.1044, 1978). Because of evidence that men's reproductive capacity was also at risk from high lead exposure, OSHA set a single standard for men and women. OSHA recommended that employers permit men and women planning to conceive to transfer out of high lead exposure jobs. Because of evidence that lead might harm a developing fetus, OSHA recommended that pregnant women not have blood lead levels that exceeded 30 µg/dl. Judge Warren, however, found convincing Johnson Controls' evidence that blood lead levels far below 30 µg/dl might injure children, and extrapolated that fetuses were also at risk from very low levels of maternal levels of lead in the blood. Several of the medical experts that Johnson Controls cited objected to how the company used their evidence. They did not agree that the fetuses were at risk from low levels of lead in their mothers' blood nor that men's reproductive capacity was not at risk. Since the district judge granted summary judgment, their testimony was available only in the briefs of the parties and *amici.*

At the opening of the oral argument before the court of appeals, Judge John L. Coffey reportedly leaned over the bench and remarked: "This is the case about the women who want to hurt their fetuses" (Kirp 1991, 70). Judge Coffey wrote the opinion for a seven to four majority affirming the district court's decision to grant summary judgment to Johnson Controls. Four dissenting justices on the Court of Appeals, however, including Reagan-appointed conservatives, argued that summary judgement was inappropriate because important matters of fact and law were in dispute. Judge Easterbrook, in words perhaps intended to pique the attention of the Supreme Court, wrote, "this is the most important sex-discrimination case this circuit has ever decided. It is likely the most important sex-discrimination case in any court since 1964 when Congress enacted Title VII" (886 F.2d 871, 920).

Both Judges Easterbrook and Posner wrote opinions contesting the majority's legal analysis. Policies that explicitly discriminate on the basis of sex, they argued, could only be defended under Title VII as a bona fide occupational qualification (BFOQ)–not a business necessity. Judge Easterbrook referred to another judge's characterization of the district court's reasoning as, "this *must* be a disparate impact case because an employer couldn't win it as a disparate treatment case" (910). Judge Easterbrook thought Johnson Controls' policy was excessively broad since few women would become pregnant.

Judge Cudahy resented having to decide the case without the benefit of a trial, claiming that summary judgment was inappropriate and thought classifying the policy as disparate impact was "result-oriented gimmickry" (902). He also commented on the gender of those who had the power to decide.

> It is a matter of some interest that, of the twelve federal judges to have considered this case to date, none has been female. This may be quite significant because this case, like other controversies of great potential consequence, demands, in addition to command of the disembodied rules, some insight into social reality. What is the situation of the pregnant woman, unemployed or working for the minimum wage and unprotected by health insurance, in relation to her pregnant sister, exposed to an indeterminate lead risk but well-fed, housed and doctored? Whose fetus is at greater risk? Whose decision is this to make? We, who are unfortunately all male, must address these and other equally complex questions through the clumsy vehicle of litigation. At least let it be complete litigation focusing on the right standard (902).[4]

The Supreme Court echoed the dissenters, not the majority, on the court of appeals in its ruling. On March 20th, 1991, the United States Supreme Court unanimously held that Johnson Controls' exclusionary policy discriminated against women. Justice Blackmun declared that the policy explicitly discriminated against women on the basis of their sex. The only Title VII defense for explicit sex discrimination is that sex is a bona fide occupational qualification for the job—that you cannot do the job if you are a woman. All nine justices agreed that Johnson Controls' exclusionary policy was facially discriminatory and the lower courts erred in granting the company summary judgment. Justice Blackmun argued that the three circuits had erred in treating exclusionary policies as neutral, allowing the employer to justify them under the business necessity defense.

Justice Blackmun went on, however, to say that employers could never justify an exclusionary policy as a BFOQ. Being potentially pregnant does not render women incapable of making batteries. Nor could the threat of tort liability of injured children justify the exclusion of fertile women. Noting OSHA's lead standard, Justice Blackmun concluded that if employers met established exposure standards and informed women of the risks, courts would not consider them negligent.

In a move that angered anti-abortion groups, Blackmun, author of *Roe v. Wade*, wrote: "Decisions about the welfare of future children must be left to the parents who conceive, bear, support, and raise them rather than to the employers who hire those parents (1207)." The rights of a yet-to-be-conceived fetus do not trump all other rights. Justice Blackmun's opinion issued an unambiguous message of support for Congress's desire to prevent employers from denying women jobs because they can get pregnant.

In a concurring opinion, Justice White, joined by Chief Justice Rehnquist and Justice Kennedy, thought employers might be able to defend a more narrowly-tailored policy as a BFOQ. Justice White did, however, agree that summary judgement was inappropriate and that the policy constituted disparate treatment. The likelihood of a substantial tort liability could justify a BFOQ, but the burden would be on the employer to prove that threat existed. Justice White thought the BFOQ could include considerations of cost and safety, instead of merely whether women could perform the job. He did, however, believe that Johnson Controls had overstated the risk, and that it should have considered less discriminatory alternatives to excluding all non-sterilized women.

Justice Scalia's concurring opinion dismissed the evidence on lead as irrelevant. Even if all employed women put their fetuses at risk, and men's exposure did not jeopardize the health of their offspring, Johnson Controls' policy was facially discriminatory because "Congress has unequivocally said so [in passing the Pregnancy Discrimination Act] (1216)." Those who find that result unsatisfactory should appeal to Congress to amend the law. Although he agreed with Justice Blackmun that any action required by Title VII could not give rise to tort liability, Justice Scalia did not accept that cost could not be a defense for explicit discrimination. A prohibitive expense might justify excluding women from certain jobs, but the employer would bear the burden of proof.

CRITIQUING EXCLUSIONARY POLICIES

These four cases provide the necessary context for understanding exclusionary policies. When considered in the abstract rather than in concrete, the policies seem benign. Who does not want to protect future generations? Employed women certainly share this goal. When we look closely at the context in which exclusionary policies emerge–the history, timing, and type of workplace–when we examine how employers developed, applied, communicated, and hurriedly implemented the policies, they look more suspicious. A more careful examination of specific policies and their implementation reveals that employers who advocate for them and judges who uphold their legality make several (perhaps unexamined) assumptions.

The first assumption is that fetuses are at risk from women's exposure (even if no women are pregnant) but not at risk from men's exposure. Employers adopt a gendered posture toward the risk to future generations (Paul 1986). That is, they have a double standard about what constitutes convincing evidence of harm and how one acts in the face of uncertainty. Johnson Controls extrapolated from evidence about children to claims about fetuses while denying that the evidence that lead damaged the sperm of adult male workers had any validity. Similarly, American Cyanamid maintained that exposing men to lead did not endanger their offspring but exposing women to lead did. It presumed that women were always endangering a fetus (even women who were not pregnant) until conclusive evidence emerged to the contrary, but presumed that men were not until conclusive evidence showed otherwise.

Treating evidence differently depending on whether it reveals maternal rather than paternal effects is even more troubling when one recognizes that scientists have almost exclusively focused on harms to offspring from maternal exposure. In some cases, employers have excluded women from hazardous work when one or two studies show a possible risk to the fetus even when no studies have been done on whether men's reproductive capacities are at risk. After two women at Allied Corporation were sterilized to keep their jobs, for example, officials admitted that the fluorocarbon they worked with was not hazardous to the fetus as originally thought (Faludi 1991, 438).

The second assumption is that no risk to the fetus is acceptable, however minimal. After firing a pregnant X-ray technician in 1980, Shelby Memorial Hospital's administrator testified that a pregnant woman's sunbathing in a bikini posed an unacceptable risk that radiation would injure the fetus (*Hayes v. Shelby Memorial Hospital* 1984). Yet the hospital let male X-ray technicians assume a low risk that their exposure to radiation would affect their fertility or cause mutations in their genes. When *UAW v. Johnson Controls* reached the court of appeals, Johnson Controls' assessment of the risk to the fetus troubled judges schooled in "law and economics." Judge Easterbrook denounced its "zero-risk" strategy for pregnant, or even nonsterilized, women. He preferred to assess the risks to the fetus in the context of women's lives, questioning whether the fetus was more at risk from low-level exposure to lead than from having an unemployed mother who may lose not only her ability to secure health benefits such as pre-natal care but even the ability to maintain proper nutrition. Judge Easterbrook recognized that no life choices for pregnant women, or anyone else, are zero. Pregnant women drive cars, they breathe polluted air, they drink coffee, consume sugar and food additives, and take the subway. If the dissenting judges on the court of appeals remained unconvinced that the risk to the fetus of pregnant women's exposure to lead was excessive, they were even less convinced that the risk to the offspring of those women who were not and did not intend to be pregnant was so great that employers should ban them from work.

The third assumption is that reproductive hazards affecting women are different and more serious than other occupational hazards. Exclusionary policies remove reproductive hazards from the context of sound health and safety policies. Some men who have high levels of lead in their blood will develop high blood pressure and heart disease and die prematurely.[5] These men "choose" to assume additional risks by exposing themselves to lead. Yet employers instituting exclusionary policies would deny a 45-year-old single woman the right to assume some risk to a fetus she is determined to avoid bringing into existence. The danger is that focusing on the risks of reproductive hazards, hazards that attract a lot of media attention, such as the alleged higher incidence of miscarriage among video display terminal operators, will eclipse other occupational health issues. Focusing on miscarriages may deflect public attention from serious eye, back, and hand injuries caused by working on the machines, not to mention the revolution in the working conditions of clerical workers.

Many workers' jobs expose them to carcinogens, and they have an increased risk of developing cancer. When these carcinogens are essential to a manufacturing process, or for a health treatment, employers reduce exposure as much as possible. Is an increased risk of miscarriage, particularly for a woman who is not and does not want to be pregnant, more serious than an increased risk of developing cancer? To compare these risks is not to suggest that since our society permits workers to expose themselves to substances that cause cancer it is acceptable to let them "choose" to poison their offspring. Women should not have to work with substances that damage them or their offspring. Neither should men. Neither should men or women have to face a serious risk of occupational illness. But the reality is we all assume some risk and we should not put reproductive hazards in a class by themselves and treat them more seriously than the risks of heart disease or cancer. We must embed any policy on reproductive hazards in a sound health and safety policy. Removing women workers is a simpler and less expensive alternative to lowering exposures to all hazardous substances, but we should not permit it to be employers' chief way of minimizing reproductive hazards, or more likely, insulating themselves from an exaggerated risk of tort liability.

The fourth assumption underlying exclusionary policies is that women are always pregnant. Most women, however, plan their pregnancies. All women are not equally likely to get pregnant because they are biologically

capable of doing so–or more accurately, because they have not been sterilized or reached menopause. We should not allow employers to treat a
woman on the pill, a woman whose husband has had a vasectomy, a
45-year-old single mother, a lesbian, a woman who is celibate, as if they
were pregnant, or as if they were incapable of making choices about or
controlling their reproductive capacities.

The fifth assumption the policies rest on is that a woman's childbearing
role takes priority over her role as breadwinner. A corollary assumption is
that it is only appropriate for women to hold certain kinds of jobs (usually
low-paid, dead end). Some employers, judges, and members of industrial
tribunals continue to act on the (conscious or unconscious) assumption that
women's place is in the home. Employers and policy makers may see
women as "out of place" in traditionally male jobs[6]–certainly the male
workers at American Cyanamid did. Women work for the same reasons
men do–to earn money to feed themselves and their families, to maintain
their standard of living, and to enjoy personal satisfaction and self-esteem.
When companies are concerned about reproductive hazards only in male-
dominated, well-paid jobs, and ignore reproductive hazards in job groups
dominated by women, such as dry cleaning, semi-conductor chip manufacturing, or hospital cleaning, we should be as suspicious as when state
legislators sought to "protect" women from tending bar but not from working all night in hospitals (Baer 1978; *Goesaert v. Cleary* 1948).

Sixth, some employers have assumed that excluding women should be
the first option considered rather than the last. The policies of American
Cyanamid, Freight Hire, the Mississippi bank, Johnson Controls, and
Shelby Memorial Hospital reveal that employers have been too hasty in
excluding women rather than exploring alternatives such as lowering exposure, substituting another product, using protective clothing, removing those
with high levels of exposure, or more carefully determining who is likely to
conceive. Although practicing good industrial hygiene can often minimize
exposure, employers who adopted exclusionary policies act on the assumption that they cannot rely on women, and especially pregnant women, to act
in their own interests and in the interests of their offspring.

Seventh, employers have assumed that the threat of tort liability from a
malformed child whose mother was exposed to work place hazards threatens the financial stability of business. Experts in civil liability have shown,
for example in the thalidomide case, how difficult it is to prove causation
for any malformation, even when one knows that the mother took a specific
dosage of a drug on a specific day. Proving causation for an occupational
injury presents even more obstacles (*Coley v. Commonwealth Edison* 1989;
see *Daily Labor Report* 1992, A-1; *Dillon v. S. S. Kresge Co.* 1971; *In re*

"Agent Orange 1980; *Hughson v. St. Francis* 1983; *Jarvis v. Providence Hospital* 1989; *Security National Bank v. Chloride* 1985). While one can show a pattern of increased miscarriages or malformations, it is difficult to prove that a specific occupational exposure caused any particular adverse pregnancy outcome and not that it was one of the high number of unexplained miscarriages or malformations that occur spontaneously. Such suits are nearly impossible to win.

Companies are rightly concerned about having to bear the cost of litigating, even if they are likely to win. Furthermore, being charged with causing miscarriages or malformations damages the public image of the company. However companies assess their vulnerability to lawsuits for offspring damaged as a result of occupational exposure, they would be wrong to assume that only women who believe their exposure has injured their children would sue. In fact, men may be more likely to sue. Men workers who manufactured the pesticide DBCP and veterans exposed to the defoliant Agent Orange claimed their exposure made them sterile or caused them to produce damaged offspring and have sued their employers, although it is difficult for men to win such suits, too (Daniels 1980). Since both men and women can damage their offspring as a result of an occupational exposure, and both men and women can sue, companies who adopt exclusionary policies are trying to shield themselves from the risk of lawsuits from half, or less than half, of their workforce while ignoring the risk of lawsuits from the other half. Employers should not be able to shield themselves from tort liability by making stereotyped assumptions that are untrue: that only women reproduce, that only women may damage their offspring through exposure to toxins, and that only women bring lawsuits.

To conclude, exclusionary policies rest on a misapplication of scientific evidence, and violate sex discrimination law. The policies are underinclusive because they rest on the assumption that men are not at risk. They are overinclusive because they rest on the assumption that women are always pregnant. The policies deny women employment opportunities because of their capacity to bear children while leaving men vulnerable to injury.

THE FUTURE OF EXCLUSIONARY POLICIES

Justice Blackmun's opinion in *UAW v. Johnson Controls* exposes and rejects several of the assumptions underlying exclusionary policies. By overturning the lower courts' rulings upholding exclusionary policies, the Supreme Court restores conventional sex discrimination doctrine. Judges can no longer create an exception to the narrow requirements of the BFOQ

defense because they see employers' policies as benign–they cannot substitute their own standard of what is unreasonable for the law's definition
of discrimination. The opinion holds that employers cannot force women
to choose between jobs and children, or between jobs and sterilization,
rather than cleaning up their workplaces. Beyond sending a clear message
to employers that exclusionary policies violate Title VII, the ruling has
four principal effects.

First, Justice Scalia's concurring opinion raises an important point for
feminist legal thought. Justice Scalia argued that Title VII prohibits employers from excluding fertile women from hazardous work, not because men
face reproductive hazards from lead, too, but because the Pregnancy Discrimination Act states unambiguously that employers may not exclude
women from jobs because of their capacity to become pregnant. Justice
Blackmun also refers to the plain language of the PDA, but Justice Scalia
explicitly mentions that a comparison is not required. As feminist legal
scholars have long maintained, pointing to decisions such as *General Electric v. Gilbert* and its British equivalents (*Hayes v. Malleable Working Men's
Club* 1985; *Turley v. Allders Department Stores* 1980; *Webb v. EMO Air
Cargo* 1989), the law incorporates a male standard (MacKinnon 1987).
Women can have the right to work only if they are just like men, or can
compare their circumstances to men. Pregnant women won some rights to
protection under discrimination law because they could compare themselves to men with temporarily incapacitating disabilities. In *UAW v. Johnson Controls,* the Supreme Court says unequivocally that whether women
can compare themselves to men or not, the law forbids employers punishing
women because they can bear children. The legality of exclusionary policies
no longer turns on a careful analysis of the differences between men's and
women's vulnerability to toxins and different roles in reproduction.

UAW v. Johnson Controls is a major victory of sex discrimination law,
not because it solves the problem of reproductive hazards in the workplace,
but because it alters the terms of the debate. Rather than trying to make it
appear safe by excluding women workers and ignoring the evidence about
men, employers will have to make the workplace safe for men and women.
Focusing only on whether employers could exclude women and whether
women were different from men deflected attention, not only from the
reproductive hazards from men's exposure, but from concerns about the
effects of toxins on workers more generally. The United Auto Workers
Union and groups supporting them, such as the Women's Rights Project of
the American Civil Liberties Union, did not seek, on the same terms as men,
the right of women to poison their offspring but for all workers to have the
right to a workplace free from hazards, reproductive or non-reproductive.

The Supreme Court's decision in *UAW v. Johnson Controls* removed this impediment to focusing on the safety of the workplace, rather than the sex of the worker.

Third, the decision should help promote initiatives to break down job segregation by sex. No one wants to exclude women from low-paying hazardous jobs such as working in a dry cleaners, being a surgical nurse exposed to anaesthetic gases, working with children who get measles and chicken pox, or changing the kitty litter. Many of the jobs women do are stressful and hazardous but strangely, employers have only wanted to exclude women from the ones that pay decent wages. The real solution, of course, is to clean up the workplace. The Supreme Court's decision is a powerful statement that women do not have to give up their right to bear children if they want to work. Business groups protested that because they could no longer ban women from hazardous work, the Supreme Court was forcing them to injure fetuses and incur liability. Most of the women employed by Johnson Controls, however, had no intention of becoming pregnant: they were in their forties or fifties, they were celibate, or on the pill, or their husbands had vasectomies. Only 2% of blue collar workers older than 30 become pregnant each year (Stellman and Henifin 1982, 138). They resented not only having to be sterilized to keep their jobs, but having this fact known by their co-workers who joked about neutering, veterinarians, and the women's lost femininity.

Finally, the decision should have an impact on how the Equal Employment Opportunity Commission enforces Title VII. Since the Republicans have been in power, the EEOC's policy has been to do nothing about complaints on exclusionary policies. Now that the Supreme Court has ruled in *UAW v. Johnson Controls* that exclusionary policies are unlawful sex discrimination, the EEOC can no longer justify its inaction by claiming to be mystified by tough legal and scientific issues (*Daily Labor Report* 1991).

Winning a victory in the Supreme Court is not a panacea for employed women. It remains to be seen whether lower courts will follow the Supreme Court's ruling, whether the EEOC will faithfully enforce it, and whether employers will obey the law. It also remains to be seen whether men and women workers can work together to demand a safe and healthy workplace that does not endanger their offspring. But just as we must not overstate the significance of winning, so we must not understate it either, especially since sex discrimination victories from the Rehnquist Court are few and far between.

NOTES

1. EEOC Charge Number 131-88-0684. Filed March 31, 1988.
2. Judge Thomas's record on complaints on exclusionary policies became an issue in his confirmation hearings. See *Senate Hearings* 1991, 80-82.
3. But see also *Doerr v. B. F. Goodrich* 1979 and *Grant v. General Motors* 1990.
4. While the appeal was pending before the Supreme Court, California state courts declared Johnson Controls' policy to be in conflict with California's fair employment laws (*Department of Fair Employment and Housing v. Globe Battery* 1987, *Foster v. Johnson Controls* 1990).
5. See the briefs of the American Civil Liberties Union and the American Public Health Association in *UAW v. Johnson Controls.*
6. A British industrial tribunal was more sympathetic to a pregnant worker's concern about hazards in a female-dominated environment (Johnston 1984).

REFERENCES

Baer, Judith, A. 1978. *The Chains of Protection: The Judicial Response to Women's Labor Legislation.* Westport, Conn.: Greenwood.

Barlow, Susan M., and Frank M. Sullivan. 1982. *Reproductive Hazards of Industrial Chemicals.* London: Academic Press.

Becker, Mary E. 1986. "From *Muller v. Oregon* to Fetal Vulnerability Policies." *University of Chicago Law Review* 53 (Fall):1219-73.

Bertin, Joan E. 1986. Review of *Double Exposure: Women's Health Hazards on the Job and at Home,* ed. Wendy Chavkin. *Women's Rights Law Reporter* 09 (Winter): 89-93.

———— August 1, 1983. "Workplace Bias Takes the Form of 'Fetal Protectionism.'" *Legal Times* 6(August):18.

Blakesse, Sandra. January 1, 1991. "Research on Birth Defects Turns to Flaws in Sperm." *New York Times.*

Buss, Emily. 1986. "Getting Beyond Discrimination: A Regulatory Solution to the Problem of Fetal Hazards in the Workplace." *Yale Law Journal* 95:577-98.

Chavkin, Wendy, ed. 1984. *Double Exposure: Women's Health Hazards on the Job and at Home.* New York: Monthly Review Press.

Chenier, Nancy Miller. 1982. *Reproductive Hazards at Work: Men, Women, and the Fertility Gamble.* Ottawa: Canadian Advisory Council on the Status of Women.

Christman v. American Cyanamid, Civ. Action No. 80-0024(P) (N.D.W.Va.) (complaint filed Jan. 28, 1980).

Coley v. Commonwealth Edison Co., 703 F. Supp. 748 (1989).

Cooke, Edmund D., Jr., and Sally J. Kenney. 1988. "Commentary: The View from Capitol Hill." In *Reproductive Laws for the 1990s,* eds. Sherrill Cohen and Nadine Taub. Clifton, N.J.: Humana Press.

Daniels, Lee. January 7, 1980. "Five Makers of Agent Orange Charge U.S. Misused Chemical in Vietnam: Companies Replying to Suit, Say Federal Negligence Is Responsible For Any Harm to Veterans and Kin." *New York Times.*

Davis, Devra Lee. January 1, 1991. "Fathers and Fetuses." *New York Times.*

Department of Fair Employment and Housing v. Globe Battery, FEP 83-84 K1-0262s L-33297 87-19 (September 1, 1987), 6. *Foster v. Johnson Controls,* 267 Cal.Rpt. 158 (Cal.App. 4 Dist. 1990), *cert denied* Supreme Court of California 1990 Cal. LEXIS 2107 (May 17, 1990).

Dillon v. S. S. Kresge Co., 192 N.W. 2d 661 (1971).

Doerr v. B. F. Goodrich Co., 22 Fair Empl. Prac. Cas. (BNA) 345 (N.D. Ohio 1979).

"EEOC Issues Guidance to Staffers on Biased Fetal-Protection Policies," *Daily Labor Report,* July 10, 1991.

Faludi, Susan. 1991. *Backlash: The Undeclared War Against American Women.* New York: Crown.

"Fetal Protection Issues Remain After Ruling in *Johnson Controls,*" *Daily Labor Report* 17 (January 27, 1992): A-1.

Fletcher, A. C. 1985. *Reproductive Hazards of Work.* Manchester: Equal Opportunities Commission.

Furnish, Hannah Arterian. 1980. "Prenatal Exposure to Fetally Toxic Work Environments: The Dilemma of the 1978 Pregnancy Amendments to Title VII of the Civil Rights Act of 1964." *Iowa Law Review* 66:63-129.

General Electric Co. v. Gilbert, 429 U.S. 125 (1976).

Goesaert v. Cleary, 335 U.S. 464 (1948).

Grant v. General Motors, 743 F.Supp. 1260 (N.D. Ohio 1989), *vacated and remanded* 908 F.2d 1303 (6th Cir. 1990).

Hayes v. Malleable Working Men's Club and Institute, (1985) ICR 703 (Eat).

Hayes v. Shelby Memorial Hospital, 546 F. Supp. 259 (N.D. Ala. 1982), 726 F.2d 1543 (11th Cir. 1984), *rehearing denied,* 732 F.2d 944 (11th Cir. 1984).

Hughson v. St. Francis Hospital of Port Jervis, 459 N.Y.S.2d. 814 (N. Y. App. Div. 1983).

In re "Agent Orange" Product Liability Litigation, 506 F. Supp. 762 (E.D. N.Y. 1980).

International Union, United Automobile, Aerospace and Agricultural Implement Workers of America, UAW v. Johnson Controls, Inc., 680 F. Supp. 309 (E.D. Wis. 1988), *aff'd, en banc,* 886 F.2d 871 (7th Cir. 1989), 111 S.Ct. 1196 (1991).

Jarvis v. Providence Hospital, 444 N.W.2d 236 (Mich. Ct. App. 1989).

Johnston v. Highland Regional Council, Case no. S/1480/84 (July 31, 1984).

Kenney, Sally J. 1992. *For Whose Protection? Reproductive Hazards and Exclusionary Policies in the U.S. and Britain.* University of Michigan Press.

———— 1987. "Reproductive Hazards in the Workplace: The Law and Sexual Difference." *International Journal of the Sociology of Law.* 14:393-414.

Kirp, David L. 1991. "The Pitfalls of 'Fetal Protection.'" *Society* 28(March/April): 70-75.

_____ 1990. "Toxic Choices." University of California, Berkeley, Graduate School of Public Policy Working Paper no. 172.

MacKinnon, Catharine A. 1987. *Feminism Unmodified: Discourses on Life and Law.* Cambridge, Mass.: Harvard University Press.

Martin, Emily. 1991. "The Egg and the Sperm: How Science has Constructed a Romance Based on Stereotypical Male-Female Roles." *Signs* 16(Spring):485-501.

Oil, Chemical and Atomic Workers, International Union v. American Cyanamid Co., 741 F.2d 444 (D.C. Cir. 1984).

Page v. Freight Hire (Tank Haulage) Ltd., Case no. 1381/80 (March 26, 1980), (1981) IRLR 13 (EAT).

Paul, Maureen, Cynthia Daniels, and Robert Rosofsky. 1986. "Corporate Response to Reproductive Hazards in the Workplace: Results of the Family, Work, and Health Survey." *American Journal of Industrial Medicine* 16:267-80.

Petchesky, Rosalind. 1987. "Fetal Images: The Power of Visual Culture in the Politics of Reproduction." *Feminist Studies* 13(Summer):263-92.

Pollitt, Katha. March 26, 1990. "'Fetal Rights': A New Assault on Feminism," *Nation,* March 26, 1990.

Randall, Donna M., and James F. Short, Jr. 1983. "Women in Toxic Work Environments: A Case Study of Social Problem Development." *Social Problems* 30(April):410-24.

Secretary of Labor v. American Cyanamid Co., 9 O.S.H. Cas. (BNA) 1596 (1981).

Security National Bank v. Chloride, Inc., 602 F.Supp. 294 (S. Kansas, 1985).

Stellman, Jeanne Mager, and Mary Sue Henifin. 1982. "No Fertile Women Need Apply: Employment Discrimination and Reproductive Hazards in the Workplace." In *Biological Woman–The Convenient Myth: A Collection of Feminist Essays and a Comprehensive Bibliography,* eds. Ruth Hubbard, Mary Sue Henifin, and Barbara Fried. Cambridge, Mass.: Schenkman.

Tate, Cassandra. 1981. "American Dilemma of Jobs, Health in an Idaho Town." *Smithsonian* 12:74-83.

Turley v. Allders Department Stores Ltd., (1980) IRLR 4 (EAT).

U.S. Congress. House. Committee on Education and Labor. *A Report by the Majority Staff on the EEOC, Title VII and Workplace Fetal Protection Policies in the 1980s.* 101st Cong., 2d sess., 1990.

U.S. Congress. Office of Technology Assessment. *Reproductive Health Hazards in the Workplace.* Washington, D.C.: U.S. Government Printing Office, 1985.

U.S. Congress. Senate. Committee on the Judiciary. *Committee Report on the Nomination of Clarence Thomas to be Associate Justice of the Supreme Court of the United States.* 102d Cong., 1st sess., 1991, 80-82.

U.S. Congress. Senate. Committee on the Judiciary. *Hearings on the Nomination of Robert H. Bork to be Associate Justice of the Supreme Court of the United States.* 100th Cong., 1st sess., 1987, 466-71, 678-79, 778-90.

Wards Cove Packing Co. v. Atonio, 109 S.Ct. 2115 (1989).

Webb v. EMO Air Cargo (U.K.) Ltd., (1989) IRLR 124 (EAT).

Williams, Wendy W. 1981. "Firing the Woman to Protect the Fetus: The Reconciliation of Fetal Protection with Employment Opportunity Goals Under Title VII." *Georgetown Law Journal* 69:641-704.

Wright v. Olin, 24 Fair Empl. Prac. Cas. (BNA) 1646 (W.D. N.C. 1980), 697 F.2d 1172 (4th Cir. 1982), *on remand,* 585 F. Supp. 1447 (W.D. N.C. 1984), *vacated without opinion,* 767 F.2d 915 (4th Cir, 1984).

Zuniga v. Kleberg County Hospital, 78 E.E.O.C. Dec. (CCH) 4180 6642 (November 14, 1974), C.A. no. 77-C-62 (S.D. Texas January 23, 1981), 692 F.2d 986 (5th Cir. 1982).

Women's Rights vs. "Fetal Rights": Politics, Law and Reproductive Hazards in the Workplace

Julianna S. Gonen

SUMMARY. Policies restricting the employment opportunities of women have a long history in the U.S. The most recent manifestation has been so-called "fetal protection" policies, which exclude women of childbearing age from jobs involving exposure to toxins considered dangerous to a developing fetus. Traditional arguments that women's biology is justification to keep them from jobs have resurfaced in a new form. In the present debate the issue is framed as one of competing rights, those of the fetus versus those of the woman. An analysis of public policy on this issue from a feminist legal standpoint reveals how the law's implicit male standard hinders the attainment of equal employment opportunity for women, as they must now compete with hypothetical fetuses as well as with men.

INTRODUCTION

Judge Easterbrook of the Seventh Circuit Court of Appeals called *United Auto Workers v. Johnson Controls* "the most important sex discrimination case in any court since 1964" (*UAW v. Johnson Controls, Inc.*, 886 F2d 871

Julianna S. Gonen is affiliated with the American University. The author can be reached at 2480 16th St. N.W., Washington, DC 20009.

[Haworth co-indexing entry note]: "Women's Rights vs. "Fetal Rights": Politics, Law and Reproductive Hazards in the Workplace." Gonen, Julianna S. Co-published simultaneously in *Women & Politics* (The Haworth Press, Inc.) Vol. 13, No. 3/4, 1993, pp. 175-190; and: *The Politics of Pregnancy: Policy Dilemmas in the Maternal-Fetal Relationship* (ed: Janna C. Merrick, and Robert H. Blank) The Haworth Press, Inc., 1993, pp. 175-190. Multiple copies of this article/chapter may be purchased from The Haworth Document Delivery Center [1-800-3-HAWORTH; 9:00 a.m. - 5:00 p.m. (EST)].

(1989) at 871).[1] The case concerned so-called "fetal protection policies," which industrial firms institute to exclude women of childbearing capacity from working in jobs in which they might be exposed to substances harmful to a developing fetus. Companies with these policies state that their goal is to protect the offspring of their employees; critics assert that they are illegally discriminating against women. Evidently the U.S. Supreme Court agreed with Easterbrook's assessment of the case's significance and agreed to review the case. Although the Court struck down Johnson Controls' exclusionary policy, the decision did not lay the issue to rest.

Policies restricting the employment opportunities of women have a long history in the United States, dating from the late 1800s. Even in the laissez-faire era of the turn of the century, when the Supreme Court struck down a maximum hours law for (male) bakers on the grounds that it interfered with freedom of contract in *Lochner v. New York,* the same court three years later in *Muller v. Oregon* upheld a maximum hours law for women due to the supposed inherent weakness of the sex. *Muller* explicitly did not overrule *Lochner*–it did not need to, because women were regarded as a special class of workers due to their capacity to bear children. The language of Muller is important, for it sets forth how women were viewed at the time and still are to a large extent: as childbearers first and as wage earners only secondarily.

> That woman's physical structure and the performance of maternal functions place her at a disadvantage in the struggle for subsistence is obvious. This is especially true when the burdens of motherhood are upon her. *Even when they are not,* by abundant testimony of the medical fraternity continuance for a long time on her feet at work, repeating this from day to day, tends to injurious effects upon the body, and, as healthy mothers are essential to vigorous offspring, *the physical well-being of women becomes an object of public interest and care in order to preserve the strength and vigor of the race (Muller v. Oregon* 1908, emphasis added).

Muller provided the legal (and social) justification for restricting female employment for years to come, eliminating competition for men and perpetuating sex segregation in the workforce (Hill 1979).

The problem of reproductive hazards in the workplace is an example of an issue that has been contested primarily in the federal courts, but is very much a political matter (and one with an extensive history). It involves Congress and the executive branch, as well as labor, business and feminist interest groups. While legal analyses and court decisions focus on proper statutory interpretation and the correct standard of review to apply, the issue involves larger concerns about women's legal status, the inherent bias in our law due to an implicit male standard for equality, the evolving notion of the legal personhood of the fetus, and the conflict of rights that results from this new perception of the fetus.

This article illustrates the political complexity of the fetal hazards issue through an analysis of the relevant statutory, regulatory and case law. The analysis employs the theoretical framework of feminist jurisprudence (particularly the work of Catharine MacKinnon and Zillah Eisenstein), which attempts to reveal the existence of an implicit male standard in law and politics. The goal here is to demonstrate that the problem of reproductive hazards in the workplace is not only a women's issue, and it is not simply a legal issue; rather, it is a complex public policy issue. The prevailing view of women as reproductive entities first and economically productive entities only secondarily at best leads to the privileging of the male as the standard in law and regulation. Public policy in this area has developed as it has due to fundamental (mis)conceptions of women's "proper" roles as reproducers which lead to the privileging of the rights of the fetus (potential or actual) over those of the pregnant, or potentially pregnant, woman.

THEORETICAL APPROACH

In *Muller v. Oregon* and cases that followed its precedent, legal and social assumptions concerning women's "proper" role were explicit and affected public policy concerning women's employment opportunities. While Title VII of the 1964 Civil Rights Act technically invalidated application of such sex-based assumptions to women seeking employment, sex discrimination has not been eradicated. Laws alone cannot alter firmly-held social beliefs; indeed, the law often manifests such beliefs while appearing neutral and impartial.

Feminist jurisprudence is concerned with exposing how the law (in its many forms) purports to be neutral while in fact operating based on an implicit male standard. Scholars such as Catharine MacKinnon have argued that "equality" for women has meant being treated "like men," who are the standard (MacKinnon 1983; 1987). She states that "to know if you are equal, you have to be equal to somebody who sets the standard you compare yourself with" (MacKinnon 1987, 22). Zillah Eisenstein focuses specifically on legal treatment of women's bodies; she notes that in order to achieve equality of results, women must not be treated as different from men, but they also must not be treated as exactly the same (Eisenstein

1988). "The engendered discourse of law treats women as 'different,' as in less than men, or treats them as equal, as in the same as men. The problem is that women are neither simply one or the other in terms of their sex or gender" (Eisenstein 1988, 69).

The issue, according to Eisenstein, is that the female is viewed in terms of how she is *different from* the male, and that she is thus seen as deficient. Woman is defined by what she is not (male). This construction of male-female difference generalizes all women as the same and all men as the same, and each as fundamentally different from the "opposite" sex. It fails to consider differences within the sexes and the similarities that exist between men and women. The construction is dualistic (and thus vastly oversimplified), hierarchical, and phallocentric (privileging the male as the standard).

The dualistic conception of gender is problematic in the realm of the law. In Eisenstein's theory, trying to achieve equality of results for women by treating them equally to men will not work because the system is inherently biased to the male standard. "Equal" in this sense would mean the same as men, which is not necessarily in women's interests. The law has assumed the prevailing male referent as the standard for equality because it accepts the dualism of male/female. Women have thus been treated either as fundamentally different from (i.e., inferior to) men, leading to exclusion and special "protection" in employment, or they are treated as exactly the same, which denies their specific needs and abilities.

Rather than accept the prevailing dualistic, oppositional, and hierarchical conception of sex roles, Eisenstein proposes a notion that embraces diversity without privileging one sex over the other.

> It is important to redirect the discourse on equality toward an egalitarianism that affirms the biological particularity of the female body without endorsing the historical contingencies of its engendered form. . . . The pregnant body decenters the phallus without centering itself; instead, it allows a heterogeneous viewing of equality that recognizes the particularity of the human body and constructs a notion of diversity that is distinctly compatible with equality (Eisenstein 1988, 4).

This theoretical point of departure is particularly valuable for an analysis of the law's treatment of "fetal protection policies," as it can speak to oversights in legislation, the standard of review to be applied to cases of discrimination based on childbearing capacity, and the operation of the male standard in regulation of health and safety in the workplace. Eisenstein poses the question of how law, as the authorized language of the state, manifests the (oppositional) differences of man/woman.

This analysis extends the question further to consider how the manifestation of the male/female difference affects public policy concerning women's employment opportunities. To explore this question, treatment of reproductive hazards in the workplace by the various branches of government, all of which have had a hand in forging the still-emerging public policy on this issue, is examined. All of the institutions examined formulate law in one form or another, whether it be statutory, regulatory, or case law. As Eisenstein notes, "law operates as a political language because it establishes and curtails choices and action" (Eisenstein 1988, 46). This is why the problem of reproductive hazards in the workplace is very much a political issue.

THE MALE STANDARD IN THE LAW

Congress: The Pregnancy Discrimination Act

Title VII of the Civil Rights Act did not put a swift end to sex discrimination in employment; more subtle means of excluding women were adopted subsequent to Title VII's enactment, couched in language based on pregnancy rather than overt male-female distinctions. In 1972 the EEOC issued guidelines which stated that pregnancy should not be grounds for treating women differently. However, when women brought Title VII suits against pregnancy-based instances of discrimination, courts upheld the exclusionary policies as being gender-neutral since the policies distinguished between *some* women on the one hand, and non-pregnant women and men on the other. *General Electric v. Gilbert* (1976) was the most noted of the pregnancy discrimination cases (*General Electric v. Gilbert,* 1976).

Viewing these decisions as directly circumventing the intent of Title VII, Congress passed the Pregnancy Discrimination Act (PDA) in 1978 to amend Title VII to include all exclusions based on pregnancy, childbirth or related medical conditions as sex discrimination. While the language of this act appears to be clear, it has not been sufficient to prevent companies from adopting policies which restrict women of childbearing age from certain industrial jobs.

The PDA illustrates the problem of the legal treatment of "difference." In attempting to eliminate discrimination based on pregnancy, the Act states that pregnancy should be treated as any other temporary disability; in other words, it denies the gender specificity of pregnancy. While such a view may appear necessary to combat discrimination against women based on pregnancy, pregnancy *is* special in that it only affects women and never men. A pregnant woman will in most cases also become a mother, a circumstance which will have a profound effect on her life. The Supreme Court cases which led to enactment of the PDA were criticized because they had ruled that the classification of pregnancy was not sex-based.

The PDA, however, makes the very same claim, that pregnancy is not sex-based, by equating it with other temporary disabilities. The problem is that if pregnancy is allowed to be recognized as sex-based, it is automatically then relegated to the "lesser" status that our hierarchical gender-role system assigns to women. This leads to the *Muller* type of rationale, that women must be "protected" out of hazardous jobs due to their childbearing capacity. But denial of the gender exclusivity of pregnancy does not serve women well either, for pregnant women face obstacles that men do not. This then leads to the *Gilbert* reasoning that if women want to be treated equally, a condition which affects only them must be ignored. Since women are being held to a male standard for equality, any recognition or accommodation of pregnancy is disallowed.

In a less dualistic and oppositional legal framework, recognition of pregnancy as sex-specific would not entail assigning women a status of "different" from those who do not become pregnant (i.e., men) and limiting their employment opportunities. At present, however, the choice remains relegation to "different" (inferior) status or denial altogether. There is as yet no third alternative of difference as diversity, of pregnancy as a positive factor to be accommodated rather than merely tolerated. Thus the little statutory law that has addressed the problem of reproductive risks in the workplace manifests the covert standard and resulting dualism pointed to by feminist legal theorists.

Executive Agencies: Regulation

As the Occupational Safety and Health Administration (OSHA) is charged with ensuring safe and healthful workplaces, its standards are an important factor to consider when addressing the issue of reproductive hazards in the workplace. The general duty clause of the OSH Act states that employers must assure healthful working conditions, providing workplaces free from recognized hazards that may cause death or physical harm. With regard to toxic substances in the workplace, the Act directs the Secretary of Labor to

> set the standard which most adequately assures, to the extent feasible, on the basis of the best available evidence, that no employee will suffer material impairment of health or functional capacity even if such employee has regular exposure to the hazard dealt with by such standard for the period of *his* working life" (s. 6(b)(5)-emphasis added).

OSHA policy further illustrates the problem of the implicit male standard, not only in statutory law, but in regulation as well. The exposure levels set by the OSHA are supposed to ensure that *no employee* will suffer impairment of health or functional capacity. However companies which institute "fetal protection" policies claim that the levels deemed safe for employees by OSHA are not safe for a woman carrying a developing fetus. In other words, employers may adhere faithfully to OSHA's regulations and still have lead levels which are not safe for pregnant women. "Functional capacity," as stated in the OSH Act, evidently did not include bearing children; "employee" meant "male employee." Men were considered to be the standard in defining a worker. As Eisenstein notes, "requirements and standards are designed with men in mind" (Eisenstein 1988, 54).

The regulatory arena provides the clearest illustration of the policy problems generated by the phallocentric nature of law. When originally proposed, the OSHA lead standard was to be actually two separate standards for men and women. Since fertile women were considered more susceptible to harm from lead (or at least their potential fetuses were), a lower threshold level would be applied to female employees. Rather than lowering lead exposure in the workplace, women would simply be regulated out of certain positions where the exposure level exceeded the women's standard. Thus when women were to be treated as different from men by regulations, they would again be "protected" out of the workplace.

The alternative is hardly preferable. The dual standard was rejected in favor of a single standard for workplace lead exposure. While the medical evidence is somewhat in dispute, companies have asserted that the level deemed safe by OSHA is in fact unsafe for an employee carrying a developing fetus. They then use this as justification for "fetal protection" policies which bar women from lead exposure altogether. Rather than adopting a maximum exposure level that would protect the most vulnerable employee, OSHA adopted a standard that would presumably protect the average male employee. So when regulation treats women as the same as men, women risk working in unsafe environments because their needs have not been considered when setting the standards. Again, when women are treated as different (from men), they lose important employment opportunities; but when they are treated the same (as men), they are placed at greater health risk because their specific needs are ignored. Thus regulation, as well as legislation, manifests the harmful effects of the male standard in the law.

The Courts: The Fetal Hazards Cases

Around the time that the Pregnancy Discrimination Act was passed (1978), several companies began instituting policies barring all fertile women from certain jobs based on perceived risks to fetuses. A shift in emphasis occurred, from "protecting" the woman and her health to "protecting" the potential fetus. It is estimated that such exclusionary policies could affect the jobs of up to 20 million women (Bureau of National Affairs 1987; EEOC 1980; U.S. Congress 1990). The most notorious instance of a company's exclusionary policy was that of American Cyanamid Company, which adopted its measure in 1978. Consequently, five women workers at the company were compelled to have themselves sterilized in order to keep their jobs (Bronson 1979). This resulted in one of the first court cases to address this issue, *Oil, Chemical and Atomic Workers v. American Cyanamid Co (OCAW v. American Cyanamid,* 1984). To date there have been six major court decisions (including one Supreme Court ruling) on the legality of "fetal protection" policies, all of which involved exclusion of fertile women from jobs involving exposure to lead.

The statutory and regulatory law examined in the previous sections would seem to indicate that policies excluding women based upon their ability to bear children are prohibited. In amending Title VII, the 1978 Pregnancy Discrimination Act (PDA) stated that sex discrimination included exclusions based on pregnancy, childbirth, or related medical conditions. As the companies in question are excluding women from jobs based explicitly on their capacity to bear children, this would seem to directly violate Title VII and the PDA. Also, The Occupational Safety and Health Administration (OSHA), in its final standard for lead exposure in the workplace, stated that due to evidence of harm to both men's *and* women's reproductive systems from lead, there was no basis for excluding only women from lead-exposed jobs. However, in the first three cases involving "fetal protection" policies to reach the federal appellate level, the courts did not come to this conclusion; they substituted their own judgment in place of statutory and regulatory prohibitions on such employment policies. The interaction of the judiciary with pre-existing (albeit piecemeal and incomplete) policy on this issue is a fundamental aspect of the politics of the reproductive hazards problem.

Before discussing the "fetal protection" cases, some mention must be made of the burden of proof schemes used by courts in Title VII cases. In sex discrimination cases, the plaintiff bringing suit must prove that an employer's practice is discriminatory (that a certain class of employees would not have been treated a certain way "but for" their gender). Once a prima facie case of discrimination has been established, the case can be treated in one of two ways. If it is determined that an employer's policy is facially discriminatory (disparate treatment), the employer may defend the policy only by proving that sex is a bona fide occupational qualification (BFOQ), a very narrowly-interpreted defense.

The courts also developed the disparate impact approach to discrimination cases, which was applied to sex discrimination for the first time in *Dothard v. Rawlinson* in 1977. It has been used in cases involving policies which are facially gender-neutral but which disproportionately disadvantage one sex. In these cases, once the plaintiff has proven the existence of a seemingly discriminatory policy, the burden of proof shifts to the employer, as in disparate treatment cases. However in disparate impact cases, the defense allowed to employers to justify their policies has been much broader. Rather than proving that sex is a bona fide occupational qualification, the employer must merely show a "valid business necessity" for the practice in question.

When the Pregnancy Discrimination Act amended Title VII in 1978, it stated that any distinctions in employment practices based upon one's capacity to bear children were to be included in the definition of illegal sex discrimination. Therefore, any policy which excludes women from certain jobs because of fertility would seem to require application of the disparate treatment-BFOQ standard, as the policy facially discriminates against women on the basis of childbearing capacity. The EEOC's own guidelines state that "fetal protection" policies may only be justified using the BFOQ defense. However in two appellate level decisions which were brought under Title VII, *Wright v. Olin* (1982) and *UAW v. Johnson Controls* (1989), the courts applied only the disparate impact standard and upheld the companies' exclusionary policies. This would seem to contradict both the wording of the statutes and the guidelines of the EEOC on this issue. Indeed, following the Seventh Circuit's *Johnson Controls* decision, the EEOC issued new enforcement guidelines instructing its officers to ignore the decision and continue to apply the BFOQ standard to "fetal protection" policies (EEOC 1990). As long as disparate impact, rather than disparate treatment, is applied, the burden of proof clearly favors the defendant.

It does appear, however, that the direction of judicial treatment in this area is changing. While in *Olin* and *Johnson Controls* the courts applied the disparate impact standard, in the three most recent cases involving "fetal protection" (including the *Johnson Controls* Supreme Court decision) the courts have applied the disparate treatment-BFOQ standard instead. In *Johnson Controls v. California Fair Employment and Housing Commission* (1990) and *Grant v. General Motors* (1990), the courts found that the exclusionary policies of the companies were facially discriminatory and failed to meet the BFOQ standard of defense. The Supreme Court followed suit in its decision in *UAW v. Johnson Controls,* handed down in March of 1991.

It is evident that the burden of proof scheme employed by the courts has a direct effect on the outcome of gender discrimination cases such as these. While female plaintiffs are much more likely to prevail when the challenged practices are viewed as facially discriminatory, there are problems with both standards of review employed by the courts. When an employer policy that obviously excludes women from jobs is construed as gender-neutral and only *happening* to impact more on women, the special circumstances which cause women to be more greatly impacted are dismissed as irrelevant (and the discriminatory policy is usually legitimated). A policy that excludes persons capable of bearing children does not include every single woman; but it does not include any men at all. Therefore, such a policy will impact overwhelmingly on women. When the courts dismiss this as simply due to the fact that women happen to be the ones to bear children, they deny the specificity of women's needs and capabilities and validate practices which actually penalize them for their biological sex.

The disparate treatment framework, however, also presents a problem under the theory of phallocentrism in the law. When courts rule that policies that classify childbearing capacity (or pregnancy) are discriminatory, or instances of disparate treatment of women, they acknowledge the gender specificity of pregnancy. Once this is the case, the door is once again open to hierarchical subordination of women due to their biology (as in *Muller v. Oregon* and its progeny). When applying disparate treatment, the courts state or imply that such conditions should not be considered at all in making employment decisions. But denying that women's childbearing capacity is a special condition allows employers (or the state) to ignore their specific needs and avoid fashioning a type of equality that recognizes difference but does not subordinate it.

The Supreme Court decision in *UAW v. Johnson Controls* deserves particular attention as it marks a crucial step in public policy concerning the "fetal protection" issue. Since this issue has not been explicitly dealt with in Congress, and only indirectly in the executive branch through agency regulations, this decision stands as the primary statement of national public policy on this problem. And although many advocates of worker's and women's rights lauded the decision as a stunning victory (as the court invalidated the particular company policy in question), much of the enthusiasm has been undue. The opinion must be read with caution.

The clearest problem with the decision is the fact that four justices, in two separate concurring opinions, stated that not all such "fetal protection" policies were illegitimate.[2] They concurred in Justice Blackmun's opinion for the court that Johnson Controls' policy was overly broad, but held that considerations of potential tort liability for damage incurred by a worker's offspring were valid concerns for employers and could meet even the strict BFOQ defense.

The trouble with Justice Blackmun's opinion for the court is less overt, more complex, and more fundamental. While the reasoning is laudable insofar as he affirms the right of an individual woman to make her own employment and reproductive choices, the fact that he constructs her choices as *between* the two reflects the very problems that have been discussed throughout this chapter. Note the wording:

> It is no more appropriate for the courts than it is for individual employers to decide whether a woman's reproductive role is more important to herself and her family than her economic role. Congress has left this choice to the woman as hers to make (*UAW v. Johnson Controls*, 1991).

Why must the woman have to *choose* between her reproductive role and her economic role? The opinion posits the two as mutually exclusive; one must give way to the other. Again we see the dualistic and hierarchical formulation of the law defining women's opportunities as workers and mothers. Poet and feminist theorist Adrienne Rich stated it this way: "The twentieth century, educated young woman . . . has with good reason felt that the choice was an inescapable either/or: motherhood or individuation, motherhood or creativity, motherhood or freedom" (Rich 1976, 160).

The Politics of Reproductive Hazards

It was noted earlier that the judicial-regulatory interface was an important political aspect of the fetal hazards issue; instances of conflict between courts and the EEOC have already been mentioned. As all of the court cases to deal with "fetal protection" policies have concerned lead exposure, it would seem that consideration of the OSHA lead standard would figure strongly in the courts' decisions. However as with the EEOC, the courts have largely chosen to forge their own policies without due consideration of the authority of relevant executive agencies.

In *Wright v. Olin* (1982), no mention of OSHA standards or policy was made at all, providing the most overt example of judicial dismissal of administrative authority. However, in the *American Cyanamid* case two years later, OSHA was the central concern. Unlike the others, this case was not brought under Title VII but rather under the 1970 OSH Act itself. After the company instituted its policy giving women in lead-exposed jobs the dubious options of sterilization or termination, OSHA issued a citation charging the company with violation of the general duty clause. When the company challenged the citation and it was appealed to federal court, the court ruled against OSHA and upheld the company's exclusionary policy. Thus unlike *Olin,* in which the court simply ignored OSHA, here the court and OSHA went head to head and the court chose to impose its own policy over that of the administrative agency charged with regulating occupational health and safety.

Similarly, in *UAW v. Johnson Controls* (the appellate decision), the OSHA lead standard was dealt with directly and explicitly overruled. The threshold lead level for fertile women specified in the company's exclusionary policy was below the safe level set by OSHA, but despite the disparity the court chose to uphold the policy as a "valid business necessity." In his dissent, Judge Easterbrook recognized that the courts were substituting their own policies for those of the responsible agencies. Noting the OSHA policy statement regarding the lack of justification for excluding only fertile women from lead exposure and the lead standards set by OSHA, Easterbrook stated that his "colleagues essentially take judicial notice that OSHA is wrong, an extraordinary step. The record does not contain evidence sufficient to contradict OSHA's conclusion . . ." (*UAW v. Johnson Controls,* 1991, 917).

Thus with regard to the EEOC and OSHA, the courts have largely chosen to substitute their own judgments for those of the relevant agencies. Traditionally the judiciary has been the branch of government charged with protecting the rights of individuals. This is in contrast to the legislative and executive branches, which reflect the preferences of the popular majority. On the fetal hazards issue, however, it has been the agencies, rather than the courts, that have set out to protect the rights of individual women workers to fair employment opportunity (although with limited success because of the inherent bias in our legal system, as outlined earlier). The courts in the early reproductive hazards cases, by contrast, seem to have been siding with the business convenience of the companies involved, allowing sweeping discriminatory policies to pass judicial muster purportedly in the interest of protecting a small number of hypothetical fetuses.

More typical of judicial intervention have been decisions such as *Los Angeles Dept. of Water and Power v. Manhart* (1978), in which the Supreme Court asserted that a statute or policy must treat individuals and not classes. In *Manhart,* the court determined that even if a class generalization is valid, it may not be used to discriminate against an individual who does not match that generalization. Justice Stevens' majority opinion stated that "even a true generalization about the class is an insufficient reason for disqualifying an individual to whom the generalization does not apply." This reasoning would apply to fetal protection policies, since they cover women who are not pregnant and have no intention of becoming pregnant, obviating the motive of protecting the fetus. Thus in an unusual twist, in these cases we see administrative agencies safeguarding the individual rights of workers while the courts uphold broad policies affecting an entire class of workers on the grounds of "valid business necessity."

In the context of the "fetal protection" puzzle, the notion of individual rights takes on critical importance and complex meaning due to the gendered and dualistic basis of our law. Both law and politics are fundamentally concerned with rights, those of individuals and of groups. The clash of rights fostered by developing notions of fetal 'personhood' is at the heart of the politics of workplace reproductive hazards.

WOMEN'S RIGHTS VS. "FETAL RIGHTS"

In the era of *Muller v. Oregon,* women's health was deemed a public concern because of its bearing on the "future of the race." "Protective" laws focused on women, on ensuring *their* health. However, after policies restricting women's employment opportunities based on gender were technically invalidated by Title VII, the focus shifted. The view of a woman's role as being primarily that of childbearer did not change; the rationale employed to retain her in this role, however, did change. Rather than framing restrictive policies in terms of safeguarding the health of women themselves, the emphasis shifted to the fetus, to safeguarding *its* health. This shift has been effected by according the fetus legal rights of its own and pitting these against the rights of its host, the pregnant woman.

Historically, fetuses did not have rights under the law. The common law tradition held that attainment of rights was contingent on live birth (see Condit 1991). At present, however, we are witnessing an increasing trend toward according the fetus the status of person, complete with legal rights, prior to birth. A fundamental problem arises as a consequence of this new rights framework, for in such instances two persons with legal rights (the pregnant woman and the fetus) occupy essentially the same physical space; their existences are inextricably connected.

When the rights of two distinct rights-bearing entities come into conflict, those of one must give way to those of the other. "Resolution of conflicts between these simultaneously corporeal yet conceptually individuated entities requires hegemony by one over the other" (Condit 1991, 18). This is yet another reflection of the dualistic and hierarchical nature of our law, as discussed earlier. As Eisenstein states, "law recognizes duality rather than diversity . . . [it] constructs dichotomous oppositions that deny complexity" (Eisenstein 1988, 48). The same legal system which constructs male and female as dualistic (and hence oppositional) mandates the subordination of the rights of some to those of others. And "of late it is the rights of the pregnant woman that are sacrificed to those of the fetus within her" (Condit 1991, 18).

What we are witnessing at present is the subordination of the rights of women to those of fetuses, even when the fetus is merely hypothetical, as in the so-called "fetal protection" policies in question. Just as hierarchical legal construction construes woman as different from man, who is the standard, and therefore construes her as inferior, so it views the rights of the woman as inferior to those of the fetus she carries. This sort of "resolution" of the rights dilemma stems directly from the traditional notion that women's primary function is to bear children.[3] As stated by Adrienne Rich, "to have borne and reared a child is to have done that thing which patriarchy joins with physiology to render into the definition of femaleness" (Rich 1976, 37). Eisenstein further states that "[the] viewing of women as mothers makes them their bodies . . . they are dominated by their reproductive function" (Eisenstein 1988, 83).

Thus rights that women may pursue which are unrelated to this function, such as equal employment opportunity, are deemed less important than the rights of the fetus. "[A woman's] work, her health, her choices and needs and beliefs, can all be set aside in an instant because, next to maternity, they are all perceived as trivial" (Pollitt 1990, 418). The problem becomes constructed as one of the fetus's right to be born healthy *versus* the woman's right to her occupation, to work for a living. As soon as the issue is framed this way the woman seeking to retain her employment is viewed as selfish, sacrificing the health of "children" to her own selfish desire to pursue what has not yet been entirely accepted, a life outside the home. The economic necessity of these women working is ignored or denied (as if working in a battery factory were a luxury), as are the needs of any existing children they might already have who will suffer if wages and health benefits are lost. Also missing is any notion of institutional responsibility (on the part of companies or the state) to ensure that a woman need not sacrifice either the health of her offspring or her livelihood, that the workplace should be made safe enough to protect both.

CONCLUSION

Long-held social assumptions concerning the primacy of women's childbearing function continue to work to women's detriment in the area of employment opportunity. Even when overtly discriminatory practices are outlawed, these assumptions are still present in laws and regulations which operate on an implicit male standard. Thus attempts to achieve true equality for women in the workplace on the existing legal terrain are doomed to almost certain failure, for equality is being predefined by a male standard. As long as the standard production worker is a man, and a woman is one who bears children (and not one who produces in the economic sense), women's rights in employment will never be secure. The "rights" of any hypothetical fetus she might conceive will curtail her options. What is needed is more explicit recognition of biological diversity that does not relegate one sex to inferior status. This will in turn engender a more comprehensive understanding of equality, an equality that does not mean being treated the same as one privileged standard, but that treats both sexes as equally able to contribute to both production and reproduction.

NOTES

1. This article is a revised version of a paper presented at the 1991 Annual Meeting of the American Political Science Association. I would like to thank Cynthia Daniels, Patricia Sykes, Patricia Patterson, Samantha Durst and several anonymous reviewers for their helpful comments.
2. The concurring justices were White, Rehnquist, Kennedy, and Scalia.
3. Several writers have noted that the woman's role in childbearing has been reduced to that of a container for the fetus, a temporary space in which the fetus is housed, even as a flowerpot or potting soil in which the fetus, the truly valued entity, will grow. See Rothman 1989; Kitzinger 1978; Whitbeck 1973; Pollitt 1990.

REFERENCES

Bronson, Gail. "Bitter Reaction: Issue of Fetal Damage Stirs Women Workers at Chemical Plants." *Wall Street Journal* (Feb. 9, 1979, p. 1+).

Bureau of National Affairs, "Pregnancy and Employment," BNA Special Report (1987).

Condit, Deirdre M. 1991. "Constructing Fetal 'Personhood': An Examination of Law and Language." Paper presented at the Midwest Political Science Association meeting.

Dothard v. Rawlinson, 433 U.S. 321 (1977).

EEOC, "Interpretive Guidelines on Employment Discrimination and Reproductive Hazards" (proposed), 45 *Federal Register* 7514 (Feb. 1, 1980).

EEOC, "EEOC Policy Guidance on Seventh Circuit Decision in United Auto Workers v. Johnson Controls Inc.," 18 *Daily Labor Report* (BNA) D-1 (Jan. 26, 1990).

Eisenstein, Zillah R. 1988. *The Female Body and the Law.* Berkeley: University of California Press.

General Electric Co. v. Gilbert, 429 U.S. 125 (1976).

Grant v. General Motors, 908 F2d 1303 (1990).

Hill, Anne Corinne. 1979. "Protection of Women Workers and the Courts: A Legal Case History." *Feminist Studies* 5:247-285

International Union, UAW v. Johnson Controls, Inc., 886 F2d 871 (1989) and 111 S.Ct. 1196 (1991).

Johnson Controls v. California Fair Employment and Housing Commission, 267 Cal Rptr 158 (1990).

Kitzinger, Sheila. 1978. *Women as Mothers.* New York: Vintage Books.

Lochner v. New York, 198 U.S. 45 (1905).

Los Angeles Department of Water and Power v. Manhart, 435 U.S. 702 (1978).

MacKinnon, Catharine A. 1983. "Feminism, Marxism, Method, and the State: Toward Feminist Jurisprudence." *Signs* 8:635-658.

MacKinnon, Catharine A. 1987. *Feminism Unmodified–Discourses on Life and Law.* Cambridge: Harvard University Press.

Muller v. Oregon, 208 U.S. 412 (1908).

Oil, Chemical and Atomic Workers v. American Cyanamid Co., 741 F2d 444 (1984).

Pollitt, Katha. " 'Fetal Rights'–A New Assault on Feminism." *The Nation* (March 26, 1990).

Rich, Adrienne. 1976. *Of Woman Born–Motherhood as Experience and Institution.* New York: Norton.

Rothman, Barbara Katz. 1989. *Recreating Motherhood.* New York: W.W. Norton and Company.

U.S. Congress, Committee on Education and Labor, "A Report on the EEOC, Title VII and Workplace Fetal Protection Policies in the 1980s," (April 1990).

Whitbeck, Caroline. 1973. "Theories of Sex Difference." *The Philosophical Forum.*

Wright v. Olin, 697 F2d 1172 (1982).

In the Interest of the Fetus: Mandatory Prenatal Classes in the Workplace

Rosalind Ladd
Lynn Pasquerella
Sheri Smith

INTRODUCTION

Recent policies, adopted by companies such as Sunbeam-Oster, mandate participation by pregnant women in prenatal education classes in the workplace. These requirements raise interesting and important questions about a public policy which allows intrusion by third parties into the maternal-fetal relationship.

Employer practices like those at Sunbeam rest frankly on economic considerations, specifically the desire or need to reduce health care insurance costs. Underlying such restrictive policies is the implicit claim that it is ethically justified to require employees to do or to refrain from certain activities in order to reduce economic liability for the company. This kind of argument may be termed an argument from "liability-driven" ethics (Ladd, Pasquerella, Smith 1992). Because this type of argument opens the door to a wide range of practices which may be discriminatory or coercive, especially toward women, it is deserving of careful consideration and evaluation.

Rosalind Ladd is affiliated with Wheaton College. Lynn Pasquerella is affiliated with the University of Rhode Island. Sheri Smith is affiliated with Rhode Island College.

[Haworth co-indexing entry note]: "In the Interest of the Fetus: Mandatory Prenatal Classes in the Workplace." Ladd, Rosalind, Lynn Pasquerella, and Sheri Smith. Co-published simultaneously in *Women & Politics* (The Haworth Press, Inc.) Vol. 13, No. 3/4, 1993, pp. 191-201; and: *The Politics of Pregnancy: Policy Dilemmas in the Maternal-Fetal Relationship* (ed: Janna C. Merrick, and Robert H. Blank) The Haworth Press, Inc., 1993, pp. 191-201. Multiple copies of this article/chapter may be purchased from The Haworth Document Delivery Center [1-800-3-HAWORTH; 9:00 a.m. - 5:00 p.m. (EST)].

In the context of rapidly escalating costs for health care and health care insurance, employers have come to discover the argument from liability-driven ethics. The argument is already being used to justify a whole range of restrictive policies: pre-employment genetic testing to screen out those who may be costly in the future, monitoring health habits and life-style, such as smoking outside of the workplace, and mandating participation in wellness programs (Span 1991).

Since many of these practices will undoubtedly be challenged in the courts, it is necessary to ask whether or not federal regulations should permit employers to regulate aspects of a worker's life which are not directly related to job performance. These issues also raise philosophical questions about the principles that underlie public policy, especially questions about liberty and freedom of choice, justice and fairness, and the distinction between public and private life.

THE SUNBEAM-OSTER PROGRAM

It is well documented that prenatal education and medical care are two of the most cost-effective measures available to modern medicine. According to a recent report on a study of newborns in New Hampshire, each $1.00 spent on prenatal care saves an average of $2.57 in medical costs. Nationally, the hospital costs for low-birthweight babies, a common result of poor prenatal care, are reported to be two billion dollars per year (Schwartz and Crispell 1991).

Failure to obtain prenatal care is often assumed to be due to ignorance, lack of access, or cost (Kalmuss 1990; Oberg et al. 1990). Those who were involved in establishing the mandatory prenatal program at Sunbeam, for example, speculated that mothers of low-birthweight infants sometimes neglected good nutrition, drank alcohol, and smoked during pregnancy, "probably out of ignorance." The assumption that the behavior was due to ignorance was largely a result of the fact that when women were informed of measures they might have taken to diminish risks to their fetuses, a common response was, "If I'd only known" (Taylor 1992). Since the nearest prenatal classes were offered evenings in a community 50 miles from the rural factory, access was severely limited for most women.

There is no question that Sunbeam's mandatory prenatal classes have worked from the economic point of view. In 1984, before the program began, Sunbeam paid out over $1 million under its self-insured medical plan to provide medical care for four premature babies born to workers in a plant employing fewer than 600 people (Breese 1987). The plan was implemented in two plants in 1986 and since that time, no employee has given birth to a premature infant. In the first year of the program, the average cost per maternity case decreased by almost 90% from the cost incurred two years previously, dropping from $27,243 in 1984 to $2,893 in 1986 (Breese 1987). The total cost of the program, including employees' paid time to attend classes and the salaries of two nursing instructors, was $15,000 a year (Anonymous 1987).

Sunbeam's prenatal program is offered to spouses of male employees, but required of pregnant female employees. Free pregnancy kits are available from the company nurse who refers those who test positive to the classes. Classes are conducted by registered nurses on company time, one hour every other week (Bitowski and Thompson 1992). There is continuing individual assessment of each woman's condition and follow-up is provided by an on-site company nurse. Participants also check up on each other. According to one of the instructors of maternal child nursing for Sunbeam, "When they [participants] see one of their group smoking or eating salty potato chips, they remind her of what we discussed in class." Employees refer to this as a "support group" or "networking" (Anonymous 1987).

Other companies have introduced similar classes, but offer cash incentives for participation instead of making it mandatory (Burton 1991; Swerdlin 1989). It is the mandatory nature of the Sunbeam program that raises ethical and public policy questions.

THE COMPANY'S POSITION

Companies that impose mandatory or restrictive health-care policies in the workplace can attempt to justify these practices in one of two ways, by referring either to the economic interests of the company and its employees or to the benefit for a pregnant woman and her fetus. It is the first that constitutes a new and unique "ethical" position, the appeal to liability-driven ethics. This appeal rests on three different kinds of economic considerations. Each consideration, in turn, can be explained in terms of generally accepted goals and interests of business.

(a) A company's primary economic goal is to produce a profit. Therefore, the company has a duty to protect the business by controlling costs. Regulating specific behaviors on the part of employees is an effective way to reduce costs. Thus, the company is justified in regulating certain employee behavior.

Applying this logic to the Sunbeam program, the company might argue that since education about health is a means to limiting health care costs, the employer has the right to mandate such education. Sunbeam's prenatal classes are, therefore, justified by the company's legitimate economic interests.

(b) A company has a general interest in providing cost effective benefits to employees. In this respect, the interests of the company and the interests of its employees coincide. Controlling health care costs is in the interest of all employees, for if the expense of providing health care for some employees escalates, other members of the health plan may subsequently suffer, either through being denied expected health care benefits or through the imposition of increasingly greater charges. For example, the *Washington Post* reported that the employees of the Republican National Committee, due to the expense of treating Lee Atwater's brain tumor, face increases in their share of health insurance premiums, with the result that several lower-paid employees will no longer be able to afford insurance. Since such results harm employees, companies are justified in acting to limit health care costs through mandating healthy behavior from their employees. It follows, given the enormous costs of premature births, that Sunbeam's mandatory prenatal program is in the interest of all employees and is therefore justified.

(c) Employers bear the financial burdens of providing insurance for the employee for specified health care expenses. It would be unjust to impose economic risks on the employer because of unnecessary risks employees take with their health. Therefore, the employer is justified in imposing mandatory or restrictive policies on employees in order to control financial risks.

Recently the courts have recognized the right of a company to control financial risks. In *McGann v. H & H Music Company,* the company was allowed to reduce drastically the health care benefits previously available to employees with AIDS-related diseases. The court accepted the company's argument that its purpose in reducing AIDS benefits was to reduce costs, finding that "an employer has an absolute right to alter the terms of an employee benefits plan, barring contractual provisions to the contrary" (McGann 1991). Although McGann died in 1991, the lower court's decision was upheld in November of 1992 by the U. S. Supreme Court's refusal to hear an appeal of the case by McGann's executor.

Following this line of reasoning, it would seem that, in addition to offering specific benefits, companies are allowed to determine the conditions and methods of distribution. Sunbeam would, therefore, be justified in distributing benefits only to those who comply with its mandatory prenatal education policy.

As an alternative to supporting its restrictive or mandatory policies in terms of economic interests, a company might appeal to the benefits that will accrue to the employee or her fetus. Such paternalistic appeals attempt to justify restricting the liberty of individuals for their own good. These restrictions are most easily justified in cases where a person's acts are considered unreasonable or not fully voluntary. Since a woman's behavior is not fully voluntary if she is not fully informed, the company may be justified in imposing mandatory prenatal education.

This line of reasoning was suggested by representatives of Sunbeam-Oster when they reproached many of their pregnant employees who did not see a doctor until the fourth or fifth month of pregnancy because they believed that it was not necessary. Therefore, mandatory prenatal policies can be defended as the best means of preventing pregnant women from accepting unreasonable risks out of ignorance. Such paternalistic measures benefit the women themselves who will have healthier babies, avoid the emotional pain and burdens of delivering low-birthweight, premature babies, and enjoy better personal health.

Overall, then, restrictive and mandatory policies in the workplace might appear to be justified since the policies will further the economic interests of the company and benefit the employees. The implementation by companies of mandatory prenatal classes for their pregnant employees seems to be a natural consequence of the arguments presented above. But are such programs really justified when we consider the cost to individual liberty and principles of justice and fairness?

CRITIQUE OF THE COMPANY'S POSITION: COERCION AND DISCRIMINATION

In spite of their benefits, the mandatory nature of Sunbeam's prenatal classes must be recognized as inherently coercive on the grounds that it preempts the right of the woman to make her own informed decision concerning what constitutes an acceptable risk for her and her fetus.

Coercion can be very subtle. The paradigm of coercion that is usually invoked is the direct application of physical force. However, feminists have argued that the clearest and most compelling instances of coercion are situations in which the victim acts under her own perception and judgment (Grimshaw 1988). Those in a position of authority who have something another wants may be considered coercive if they use this power by enticing others to act or think a certain way. For the pregnant women at Sunbeam, the coercion involves the choice of either submitting to a company policy

that educates and monitors their pregnancies, or refusing and taking whatever consequences might follow, which could conceivably include termination. One company manager commented, "It's a preventive measure, like
safety shoes. It's mandatory. If someone refused and there's no legitimate
reason, disciplinary action would result" (Taylor 1992). Since workers are
not usually in a position to respond to unwelcome mandatory employment
practices by seeking work elsewhere, the right to refuse participation is
severely limited.

A company policy like Sunbeam's is coercive in another way as well.
Judgments about risk cannot be made independently of social and economic constraints. For this reason, a woman might assess risks for herself
and her fetus differently than her employer or even a physician. Suppose,
for instance, the company doctor "orders" complete bed rest for several
weeks of the pregnancy. The pregnant employee must choose whether to
comply or not. Though both the company and the woman want to avoid
premature birth, the woman must also consider any other children who are
dependent upon her income. If the company is not willing to support them
through paid leave, but does offer insurance coverage to support the costs
of delivery and premature birth, risk assessment may lead her to believe
she should continue working.

Thus, we need to use caution in deciding what would make a risk
unacceptable or unreasonable. We cannot suppose that the reasonable
pregnant woman will always act to give the fetus the best chance possible
at a healthy start.

When does a risk which is unreasonable from the company's point of
view justify restricting individual behavior? Is eating potato chips a decision a pregnant woman should be free to make for herself, without having
to face the fear of being reported by co-workers acting as "company
spies" under the guise of a support-system? A mandatory program like
Sunbeam's is coercive in that it imposes the company's concept of what is
best for the woman and fetus.

Given that all mandatory or restrictive paternalistic policies will be
open to charges of coercion on the characterization presented above, it is
important to understand why mandatory prenatal classes should be regarded as an unacceptable use of coercion.

Mandatory prenatal classes have the effect of singling out pregnant
women for differential treatment in the workplace. Other workers would
benefit from better diets, closer monitoring of blood pressure, more visits
with nurses and doctors, giving up smoking and abstaining from alcohol,
but educational programs have not been mandated for them. Absent a
basis for differential treatment, pregnant women are being required to

meet a condition of employment that does not apply to other workers. Thus the principle of justice and fairness is violated.

There is another sense in which mandatory prenatal classes are discriminatory, given that pregnant women but not prospective fathers are required to attend. Prospective fathers may not know how their behavior could threaten the well-being of the fetus. For example, a worker might be unaware of the dangers from second-hand smoke. Furthermore, attending prenatal classes can provide prospective fathers with information that would enhance efforts by both partners to achieve adequate prenatal care. Thus, the arguments that are used to justify prenatal classes for women could be applied to fathers as well.

When would mandatory health education and health practices be justified in a workplace? Such discriminatory practices would be justified if and only if these practices were relevant to performance on the job. For example, members of the police and the military can with justification be required to maintain a specified level of physical fitness, since it is necessary for successful and safe performance of the duties of the job. Similarly, specific health practices can justifiably be required for astronauts. However, since having a healthy baby is not directly related in Sunbeam's case to job performance, mandatory prenatal classes are discriminatory and cannot be justified.

CRITIQUE OF THE COMPANY'S POSITION: FETAL PROTECTION AND PRIVACY

In the past, attempts have been made to limit the activities of women in the workplace based on an identification of women with the maternal function. Thus, the U.S. Supreme Court rendered a decision in 1908 which limited the number of hours women were allowed to work citing, "as healthy mothers are essential to vigorous offspring, the physical well-being of women becomes an object of public interest and care. . . . Her physical structure and a proper discharge of her maternal functions–having in view not merely her own health, but the well-being of the race–justify legislation to protect her. . . ." (*Muller v. Oregon*). Any view which identifies a woman with the maternal function, however, precludes the possibility of conflict between maternal and fetal interests. The interests of the woman and fetus might indeed come into conflict, in which case the dilemma will be one of deciding whose interests should take precedence.

The economic success that supports the use of the Sunbeam-Oster program is bolstered by the continued identification of women with the maternal function, which justifies acting for the protection of the fetus. Yet, while the state may have an interest in good prenatal care, surely companies have no authority to act unilaterally on behalf of the state. If the state has an overriding interest in the welfare of the fetus, then this would seem to require removal of the educational programs from the workplace and suggests the bizarre notion of imposing mandatory education and prenatal monitoring on all women everywhere. Seen in this light, the mandatory nature of prenatal classes at Sunbeam clearly puts it in direct contradiction to the concept of individual liberty. Thus the argument based on protecting the fetus fails, for it goes well beyond the legitimate role of private employers.

Further objections can be raised against Sunbeam's policy based on the right to privacy. Mandating prenatal classes for pregnant employees encourages a blurring of the distinction between the aspects of our lives that should be allowed to remain private and those that may be made public (ACLU 1991; Schloerb 1991). When a woman leaves her post to attend classes, this gives a signal to those around her and draws attention to the fact that she is pregnant.

There is also a problem about sharing medical information which is usually a matter of confidentiality between patient and physician. Because of health monitoring in the workplace, the policy forces pregnant women to reveal medical information that is not relevant to job performance to a company doctor or nurse. Doctors and nurses serve as double-agents, for the medical staff works for the company and must report the risks the company is interested in, even when doing so would seem to constitute a violation of the woman's right to privacy.

In many instances, employees have failed in their legal attempts to invoke the right to privacy to limit intrusion by employers. This is because the right to privacy is seen constitutionally as guarding the individual against unwanted *governmental* intrusion. The power of the state is not regarded as akin to the power of an employer, since being bound by the latter is subject to the will of the employee. In response, many states have passed legislation to protect workers from employer's restrictions and monitoring of off-the-job behavior (ACLU 1991). For the most part, however, these laws specify a narrow range of activities, such as smoking, drinking alcohol, and over-eating.

CONCLUSION AND PUBLIC POLICY RECOMMENDATIONS

In this paper, arguments have been presented against the company's position that liability-driven ethics justifies mandatory or restrictive policies, specifically, Sunbeam's policy mandating prenatal classes for all pregnant employees. The arguments are based on the claims of the pregnant woman to be free of coercion and discrimination and to be able to exercise liberty in decision-making for herself, the inappropriateness of business enforcing the state's interest in the well-being of the fetus, and the individual's right to privacy. Although companies have a legitimate interest in their own economic well-being and it is true that health care insurance costs are becoming an ever-increasing burden, these interests do not override employees' fundamental rights. Thus, federal regulations should not allow companies to impose mandatory or restrictive policies directed at employees' lifestyles, except in those cases where the health of the employee is directly related to job performance.

Yet, the benefits of prenatal education and care are great and should not be disregarded. It would be a benefit to pregnant women, fetuses, and indirectly to all other employees if good quality, convenient prenatal classes were offered in the workplace. Further, there is reason to believe that a less restrictive alternative, namely, voluntary attendance, would achieve the same goals as a mandatory policy. If one assumes rational self-interest on the part of pregnant women employees, offering classes and care on a voluntary basis should reap the same benefits without the costs in terms of liberty and discrimination.

In other companies, a purely voluntary program has worked well. Voluntary prenatal education programs have been implemented at Fruit of the Loom, AT&T, and Pepsico, Inc. Pepsico, for example, offers a prenatal program to all of its 75,000 employees; 80% of those eligible take advantage of the program (Schwartz and Crispell 1991). The International Ladies' Garment Workers Union offers prenatal instruction in Chinese for immigrants. The three session program is conducted after work. A study of 45 participants showed the following: "Ten women who weren't receiving prenatal care began seeing a doctor as a result of the program; five quit smoking; five quit drinking; ten stopped taking nonprescription drugs; seven stopped ingesting caffeine. Among these 45 women, one miscarriage was recorded, but no low-birthweight babies" (Swerdlin 1989). The program has been expanded to all 60,000 of the union's members in New York City and now includes English/Spanish sessions (Swerdlin 1989).

An alternative plan, which seems to recognize both the company's economic interests and the employee's right to privacy, would be to make insurance coverage for the pregnancy dependent on certification of prenatal education, care, and compliance. The certification could come from a company nurse or from an approved outside practitioner, just as certification of need is required in order to collect worker's compensation for injuries. It would be understood that insurance coverage could be denied for the pregnancy and associated costs if certification were not obtained, providing incentive for the pregnant woman to receive care. Although still coercive, such programs have the advantage of preserving the employee's right to privacy by removing the employer's access to specific details of the worker's health.

A third possibility is to offer incentives for participation in prenatal classes. For example, the deductible amount for delivery may be waived if the woman has attended classes or a cash bonus may be offered for visiting the doctor. Marriott Corporation provides a financial incentive for participation by pregnant employees who complete its Healthy Expectations program. The program, which has been well-received, requires women to complete a specified number of doctor's visits and to fill out an evaluation form at the end of their pregnancies. Employees receive a $100 bonus for completion of the program (Swerdlin 1989).

The goal of any public policy regarding pregnant women in the workplace should be to allow the greatest freedom of choice compatible with no harm to others. The broader question of society's right to impose restrictions on all pregnant women for the sake of their fetuses requires separate consideration, beyond the scope of this discussion. Nevertheless, it is imperative that public policy not allow intrusion by employers into the maternal-fetal relationship. Therefore, a program of mandatory prenatal classes should be rejected on ethical grounds.

REFERENCES

Anon. 1991. "Lifestyle Discrimination." *ACLU Legislative Briefing Series,* typescript.

Anon. 1987. "Prenatal Program: Healthy Births and Bottom Lines." *Employee Benefit Plan Review,* Vol. 42, 44-48.

Bitowski, B. and P. Thompson. 1992. Unpublished manuscript.

Breese, Kevin M. 1987. "Sunbeam's Prenatal Program." *Personnel Administrator,* 40-42.

Burton, WN, D. Erickson, and J. Briones. 1991. "Women's Health Programs at the Workplace." *Journal of Occupational Medicine* 33(3):349-50.

Grimshaw, Jean. 1988. "Autonomy and Identity in Feminist Thinking." *Feminist Perspectives in Philosophy,* ed. Morwenna Griffiths and Margaret Whitford. Bloomington, Indiana: Indiana University Press.

Kalmuss, D. and K. Fennelly. 1990. "Barriers to Prenatal Care Among Low-Income Women in New York City." *Family Planning Perspectives* 22(5):215-8.

Ladd, R., L. Pasquerella, and S. Smith. 1992. "Acceptable Risks in the Workplace: The Trend Toward a Liability-Driven Ethics." Paper read at the National Conference on Ethics & the Professions, Gainesville, Florida.

McGann v. H & H Music Co. 946 F.2d 401 (5th Cir. 1991).

Muller v. Oregon. U. S. Supreme Court 1908.

Oberg, C. N., B. Lia-Hoagberg, E. Hodkinson, C. Skovholt and R. Vanman. 1990. "Prenatal Care Comparisons Among Privately Insured, Uninsured, and Medicaid-Enrolled Women." *Public Health Report* 105(5):533-5.

Schloerb, John M. 1991. "Employment Discrimination Based on Employee Lifestyles: Draft Report for the ACLU." Typescript.

Schwartz, Joe and Diane Crispell. 1991. "Prenatal Programs Pay Off." *American Demographics* 14-16.

Spann, Paula. 1991. "Smoking Workers Feeling the Heat from Employers." *Providence Journal-Bulletin* XIX(271):A8-9. Reprinted from *The Washington Post.*

Swerdlin, Marcy. 1989. "Investing in Healthy Babies Pays Off." *Business and Health.* (July, 38-41.)

Taylor, Joe. 1992. Phone interview of a Sunbeam manager.

Surrogate Motherhood: Implications for the Mother-Fetus Relationship

Cherylon Robinson

SUMMARY. The use of reproductive technology for surrogate motherhood arrangements facilitates the possibility that a child might have three mothers; a genetic, a gestational and a social mother. This possibility challenges the traditional legal definition of mother as the woman who gives birth to the child; a definition that emphasizes the mother/fetus relationship. State statutes and court cases are examined to identify what changes, if any, have occurred in the legal definition of mother. Recognition of separation of roles is occurring, thus challenging the traditional legal definition of mother and the mother/fetus relationship.

INTRODUCTION

The legal structure partially defines roles within the family through state statutes dealing with marriage, divorce and parent-child relationships.[1] The traditional legal definition of mother reflects the state's emphasis on the mother-fetus relationship. State statutes prescribe that the woman who gives birth to a child is considered to be the mother of the child. This definition was legislated partially because of the ease with

Cherylon Robinson is affiliated with the University of Texas at San Antonio.

[Haworth co-indexing entry note]: "Surrogate Motherhood: Implications for the Mother-Fetus Relationship." Robinson, Cherylon. Co-published simultaneously in *Women & Politics* (The Haworth Press, Inc.) Vol. 13, No. 3/4, 1993, pp. 203-224; and: *The Politics of Pregnancy: Policy Dilemmas in the Maternal-Fetal Relationship* (ed: Janna C. Merrick, and Robert H. Blank) The Haworth Press, Inc., 1993, pp. 203-224. Multiple copies of this article/chapter may be purchased from The Haworth Document Delivery Center [1-800-3-HAWORTH; 9:00 a.m. - 5:00 p.m. (EST)].

which the mother's relationship to the child could be established; however, it also reflected an assumption that the components of the status, "mother," i.e., genetic, gestational, and social mothering, were connected. The legal definition of father, by declaring the husband of the mother the father of the child, reflects the male's relationship to the mother, not necessarily to the child. State statutes then partially define the roles of mother and father by defining the rights and responsibilities of the parents toward the child.

However, parenting roles in the United States are changing and, with those changes, both the mother-child relationship and the father-child relationship are being redefined. State statutes prescribe situations in which these rights and responsibilities of parents may be abdicated, such as in adoption. By allowing a birth mother to relinquish her rights and responsibilities toward her child and by accepting the transferral of rights and responsibilities to an adopting mother, the legal structure recognizes that the components of mothering could be separated and accomplished by different persons. Recent medical technologies have complicated the issue of defining the mother of a child by making it possible for components of the status, mother, to be accomplished by three different people (a genetic mother, a gestational mother, and a social mother). This possibility requires that the relative importance of these three components in our notion of "who is a mother?" be examined.

Keller (1971) examined the relationship between mother and child in her analysis of the future of the family in the United States. She noted that the decline in fertility rates and the use of contraceptives to space children had allowed women more freedom to pursue education and careers and concluded that this social change had resulted in a decline in the saliency of the role of mother for women. She proposed that further technological development and diffusion, including the use of artificial insemination and the possible development of an effective artificial womb, would raise questions of social and economic responsibility that would need to be addressed by public policy. She was concerned with the potential for a division of labor through the use of this technology in which it would be possible for a child to have five parents: a genetic father, a genetic mother, a gestational mother, a social father and a social mother (Keller 1971). This possibility of a division of labor challenges our definitions of mother and father and the rights and responsibilities attached to these definitions. Keller's assessment in the early 1970s of the potential effect of utilization of reproductive technology seems farsighted in light of recent developments in reproductive technology.

Reproductive technology involves the use of medical technology to achieve asexual reproduction and has included artificial insemination, in vitro fertilization, cryopreservation of ova, sperm and embryos, embryo transfer and the use of these procedures for surrogate motherhood arrangements.[2] Surrogate motherhood arrangements involve the agreement of the surrogate to conceive through the use of reproductive technology, to gestate the fetus conceived and then give up the child at birth to his/her genetic father and/or genetic mother.[3] Artificial insemination of a surrogate with the semen of the man intended to be the father is the most common procedure utilized in surrogate motherhood; however, embryo lavage or embryo transfer may be used to achieve surrogate gestation. Surrogate gestation involves the gestation of a fetus genetically unrelated to the surrogate (see Appendix A).

These different technologies provide the possibility for infertile couples to reproduce, a possibility that sometimes gets minimized in the debate over their usage. The grief of infertile couples is real, and the attraction of being able to have a child which is genetically related to one or both parent(s) is strong. However, debate over the legitimation of different reproductive technologies has raised complex societal, legal and ethical issues related to their usage. One of those issues involves the potential for reproductive technology to redefine the concept, mother, and subsequently decrease the saliency of the gestational role in that definition, thus altering the mother-fetus relationship. This issue is especially important in the debate over legitimation of surrogate motherhood because surrogates are required to relinquish their parental rights and responsibilities.

This paper will focus on the development of public policy through legislation and adjudication dealing with surrogate motherhood and the potential impact of that policy on the definition of mother and on the relationship of mother and fetus. Questions to be addressed in this paper include: What are the compelling state interests related to the mother-fetus relationship that might override procreative liberty rights in surrogate motherhood? What is the current public policy in the form of state statutes and court cases regarding surrogate motherhood? What is the potential impact of this public policy on the definition of mother? Has our previous emphasis on the mother-fetus relationship declined in importance in this definition?

RESEARCH METHODS

Using Westlaw to search court cases and statutes dealing with surrogate motherhood, cases adjudicated in state and federal courts and listed in

Westlaw prior to August, 1992, were examined. Analysis of these cases consisted of categorization by issues of relevance to the topic of this paper and by decision of the court. Statutes listed by Westlaw prior to August, 1992, were examined and analyzed by categorization of provisions. Law journal articles identified by LegalTrac as dealing with surrogate motherhood were mined for compelling state interests related to the relationship between mother and fetus in surrogate motherhood.

COMPELLING STATE INTERESTS IN SURROGATE MOTHERHOOD

There has been considerable debate on the topic of surrogate motherhood. Scholars have been concerned with the ethics of the arrangement (Robertson 1983), with its legality (Dodd 1982; Smith 1983; Townsend 1982) and with its potential impact on women (Corea 1985; Rothman 1989; Spallone & Steinberg 1987). Central to these debates is the issue of control. It has been decided by the Supreme Court that individuals have the personal right to be free from government intervention in decisions which involve reproduction, provided that these decisions do not interfere with a societal right compelling enough to override individual rights. Personal rights in the area of reproduction have frequently been labeled "the right of procreative liberty." This right was established in a series of decisions which included *Skinner v. Oklahoma* (316 U.S. 535 [1942]), *Griswold v. Connecticut* (381 U.S. 479, 485-86 (1976) and *Roe v. Wade* (410 U.S. 113 (1973)). At present, there has not been a U.S. Supreme Court decision extending this right to the use of reproductive technology as defined in this paper. There has been speculation of compelling state interests that might be violated by the use of reproductive technology for surrogate motherhood and that might result in a failure to extend this right.

Four compelling state interests that have been discussed in law journal articles as possibly violated in surrogate motherhood arrangements are pertinent to the mother-fetus relationship. The first compelling state interest involves protection against the potential exploitation of poor women. It is possible that some poor women would be motivated to become surrogates because of the compensation involved, sometimes totalling $10,000. Women might be coerced into participation by financial necessity, and this coercion would interfere with the volition of their decision. The state would have an interest in protecting the welfare of these women under "parens patriae" (Andrews 1981; Dodd 1982; Vieth 1981). However, interviews with women who have become surrogates reveal mixed results on the issue of motivation. Parker (1983) found that money was the primary motivation for the surrogates he interviewed, while money was reported as secondary to surrogates interviewed by Hanafin (cited in Andrews 1989).

Compensation is also at the center of the debate over whether surrogate motherhood will result in commercialization of reproduction. All states have laws which ban the sale of children. Many states have statutes that prohibit transfer of money beyond appropriate fees in connection with adoption. These laws were passed to protect the best interests of the child and to prevent baby selling. To treat children as property would be to dehumanize them and depersonalize and commercialize reproduction. The state has a compelling interest in preventing individuals from being bought and sold as property, a violation of the Thirteenth Amendment prohibiting slavery (Andrews 1981; Dodd 1982; Vieth 1981). Scholars disagree on whether surrogate motherhood constitutes baby selling. Those scholars who argue that surrogate motherhood does not constitute baby selling propose that compensation in surrogate motherhood pays for the service of gestating the child not for the child (Andrews 1989).

The state also has a compelling interest in protecting the family. While the legal structure has not specifically defined "the family," some court decisions involving the use of reproductive technology have reflected the nuclear family structure by declaring that it is in the best interest of a child to have two parents, a father and a mother.[4] Surrogate motherhood may be viewed as disrupting that structure through introduction of an additional person, the surrogate, possibly resulting in a new form of extended family (Dodd 1982; Vieth 1981). Surrogate motherhood might also undermine the traditional nuclear family by allowing the creation of nontraditional families, e.g., by single men and women to create single-parent families and by gay couples. Defining the traditional nuclear family as the only acceptable form of "family" is a relatively conservative definition, in view of the variety of family forms in existence in the United States (Ahlburg & De Vita 1992).

The fourth compelling state interest involves the potential for surrogate motherhood to disrupt the mother-child bond. Surrogate motherhood could be viewed as disruptive to the mother-child bond because it separates the child from his/her gestational mother and recognizes the adoptive or social mother as the mother of the child. This argument is based on the traditional idea that women have a maternal instinct (Dodd 1982; Graham 1982; Vieth 1981). The existence of a maternal instinct is debatable, but the issue highlights the importance of defining the concept of mother and is complicated by the division of "mother" into genetic, gestational and social components.

A fifth issue, maternal-fetal conflict, is also important to any discussion of the mother-fetus relationship in surrogate motherhood. Attention has been given to the conduct of the surrogate during pregnancy and the potential of that conduct to damage the fetus. The surrogate might be held to a certain level of conduct during the pregnancy, e.g., no smoking, and sued for breach of contract if she violated the agreement. If the fetus was damaged by her conduct and the father refused to accept custody of a child with a disability, custody would revert to the biological mother. If she refused custody, the baby would be placed for adoption. These discussions are part of an overall debate in which the rights of the pregnant woman are viewed as potentially in opposition to the rights of the fetus. This conflict occurs in situations in which the conduct of the female would potentially harm the fetus and in situations where medical treatment of the fetus could potentially harm the female. For example, legal intervention has been considered and/or used when drug usage by the female would damage the fetus. Additionally, courts have ordered the enforcement of caesarian sections against the will of the female (Johnsen 1987; Robertson & Schulman 1987). Debate over legal intervention that would violate personal autonomy in pregnancy decisions is likely to continue as the Republican platform for 1992 includes a provision that calls for recognition of the fetus as having the rights of a human being. These controversial issues are reflected in state statutes and court cases discussed below.

FINDINGS

Distinction is made in the findings between commercial surrogacy arrangements for which compensation is paid and noncommercial surrogacy arrangements for which compensation is not paid. The findings discussed apply only to surrogacy arrangements that have been formalized through a contract.

Statutes

The Westlaw computer search identified 19 states that have statutes that refer to surrogate motherhood as defined in this paper (see Appendix B). Statutes in ten states have adopted a policy that prohibits commercial surrogate motherhood (Arizona Rev. Stat. Ann. 25-218, Ann. Indiana

Code 31-8-1-1 through 5, 31-8-2-1 through 3, Kentucky Rev. Stat. Ann. 199.590, Louisiana Stat. Ann. Rev. 9:2713, Michigan Comp. Laws Ann. 722.851-863, Rev. Stat. of Nebraska 25-21,200, New York [effective in 1993], North Dakota Century Code 14-18-01 through 07, Utah Code 76-7-204, and Rev. Code of Washington Ann. 26.26.210-270). Statutes in Arizona, Kentucky, Michigan, New York, Utah and Washington prohibit commercial surrogacy with the Kentucky, Michigan, New York, Utah and Washington statutes referring specifically to prohibition of compensation in surrogate motherhood. In Utah and Washington, violation of the surrogate motherhood statutes is a misdemeanor, but in New York, violation constitutes a felony. Violation in Michigan may be a felony or a misdemeanor depending on the circumstances. Statutes in Indiana, Kentucky, Louisiana, Michigan, Nebraska, New York, North Dakota, Utah and Washington declare a surrogate motherhood contract to be void and unenforceable. Statutes in Michigan, New York, Utah and Washington make provisions for custody disputes that call for court decisions based on the best interests of the child.

In three of the states–Arizona, North Dakota and Utah–the statutes specifically declare the surrogate to be the mother of the child with her husband presumed to be the father. Arizona and North Dakota make this provision regardless of whether artificial insemination or embryo transfer is utilized as a procedure. The Utah statute presumably makes the same provision as it specifies artificial insemination or other procedures. In North Dakota, donors of egg and/or sperm are relieved of parental responsibilities. In these states, the genetic mother who contributes her ovum in embryo transfer to a surrogate would not be considered the mother of the child. The Michigan and New York statutes also specifically divide maternal components. The Michigan statute distinguishes between surrogate mothers who are genetically related to the child and a surrogate carrier who is not genetically related to the child. The New York statute distinguishes between the birth mother and the genetic mother.

Three states, Florida Stat. Ann. (63.212), New Hampshire Rev. Stat. Ann. (168-B:1-32) and Code of Virginia (20-156 through 165), have passed laws that prohibit commercial surrogate motherhood but would legitimate noncommercial surrogate motherhood. Noncompensated pre-planned adoptions achieved through assisted conception are permitted in Florida. While fees and costs are permitted, contracts for compensation are void and unenforceable. The "volunteer mother" is required to undergo medical tests and to follow "reasonable" medical instructions during pregnancy. If the volunteer mother changes her mind, she has seven days after the birth of the child to withdraw her consent to relinquish parental rights. If the biological father changes his mind, custody of the child remains with the volunteer mother.

The New Hampshire law distinguishes between birth mother, donor and intended mother. The intended mother in noncommercial surrogacy is declared the mother of the child regardless of whether or not she is the genetic mother. Decisions on health matters during pregnancy are made by the surrogate. One of the intended parents must be genetically related to the child, and the intended mother must be unable to bear a child. However, if the surrogate refuses to give up the child, the birth mother is declared the mother. The surrogate has 72 hours after the baby is born to change her mind. If she still wishes to relinquish parental rights, the names of the intended parents are placed on the birth certificate. The contract must be preauthorized by the court and must be in the best interest of the child. A psychological and medical examination of the participants, psychological counseling and an evaluation of the home of the intended parents are required. Counseling is also required in surrogate motherhood arrangements involving in vitro fertilization. Compensation is prohibited, but the surrogate may recover lost wages.

The Virginia statute becomes effective July 1, 1993, and shares some of the provisions of the New Hampshire statute but has different provisions affecting the mother-child relationship according to whether or not the contract had prior court approval. It calls for noncommercial surrogate motherhood contracts to have prior approval of the court but has provisions for recognition of those that do not. Court approval of surrogate motherhood contracts prior to conception requires physical and psychological screening of the intended parents, the surrogate and her husband as well as a home visit by a social worker and counseling on the effects of participation. The intended mother of the child must be infertile or pregnancy must be a risk to her or the child, and at least one of the intended parents must be biologically related to the child. Court approval of the contract results in recognition of the intended parents as the parents of the child and issuance of a new birth certificate per requirements of the law following the birth of the child and listing the intended parents as parents of the child. The surrogate may terminate the contract up to 180 days after the last assisted conception.

In surrogacy arrangements made without prior court approval, genetic relationships to the child determine parenting relationships. In surrogate motherhood arrangements involving embryo transfer in which the intended mother is genetically related to the child, the intended mother is recognized as the mother of the child. If the surrogate is the genetic mother of the child, she is considered the mother of the child. The surrogate files a signed surrogate consent and report naming the intended parents, and a new birth certificate will be issued if at least one of the intended parents is biologically related to the child. If the surrogate refuses to give up custody of the child and chooses to retain her parental rights, the child is considered to be the child of the surrogate and her husband. If neither of the intended parents is genetically related to the child, they must adopt the child in accordance with the adoption laws of Virginia. Provisions within the contract for compensation to the surrogate beyond "reasonable medical and ancillary costs" are void and unenforceable whether the contract has prior court approval or not.

Arkansas Code Ann. (9-10-201) does not mention compensation and might permit both commercial and noncommercial surrogate motherhood. The statute defines the parent(s) of a child born through a surrogate motherhood contract as the biological father and his wife, if married, the biological father only if he is unmarried, and the woman intended to be the mother if donor semen is used for the artificial insemination. It is clear from these findings that states have begun to distinguish between components of the concept "mother" and to incorporate these distinctions into their definitions of mother.

In states where surrogate motherhood legislation has not been passed, there has been speculation among legal scholars that laws dealing with adoption and artificial insemination might be applied to surrogate motherhood arrangements. This application might result in establishment of relationships not intended by the participants. Application of artificial insemination statutes, for example, might result in the surrogate and her husband being considered the parents of the child with the "donor" being relieved of parental responsibilities. Five states exclude surrogate motherhood from existing statutes (Code of Alabama 26-10A-33, Nevada Rev. Stat. 127.287, Tennessee Code Ann. 36-1-114 and West Virginia Code 48-4-16 from statutes that prohibit fees in adoption, Ohio Rev. Code Ann. 3111.31-38 from artificial insemination statutes). These statutes prevent prohibition of surrogate motherhood based on existing statutes but do not specifically legitimate it. Wisconsin Stat. Ann. 69-14 (g) requires that the surrogate be listed on the birth certificate, but the name of the genetic father is not listed. The court may change the names on the birth certificate if the child is given to his/her father.

Court Cases

Of the court cases identified by Westlaw, several are important to a discussion of the mother-fetus relationship in surrogate motherhood. Court cases involving surrogacy arrangements, in the absence of laws specifically dealing with surrogate motherhood, have looked for precedent to statutes dealing with adoption, artificial insemination and parent-child relationships. Courts in Kentucky and New York ruled no violation of state adoption statutes in *Surrogate Parenting v. Com. Ex Rel. Armstrong Ky* (704 S.W. 2d 209 [1986]) and *Matter of Adoption of Baby Girl L.J.* (505 N.Y.S. 2d 813 [Sur. 1986]). But courts in New Jersey (*Matter of Baby M* [537 A. 2d 1227 (N.J. 1988)]) and Michigan (*Doe v. Kelley* [Mich. App., 307 N.W. 2d 438 (1981)]) found that surrogacy violated state statutes prohibiting payment for adoption.[5] A California court (*In re Adoption of Matthew B.-M* (284 Cal. Rptr. 18 [Cal. App. 1 Dist. 1991])) refused to allow statutes dealing with artificial insemination to be utilized to refute the biological father's claim of paternity. In *Syrkowski v. Appleyard* (362 N.W. 2d 211 (Mich 1985), the court allowed the biological father in a surrogacy arrangement to assert paternity under the state paternity statutes. The court held that the statutes of the state required consent of the husband of the woman undergoing artificial insemination. Because the husband of the surrogate did not consent to the insemination, his paternity was rebuttable. Regardless of whether or not surrogate motherhood was found to violate state statutes, the gestational mother was recognized as the legal mother in these cases. Termination of her parental rights were considered necessary in order for the social mother to adopt the child.[6]

When the surrogate has refused to relinquish parental rights, the biological father has been allowed to file for custody of the child. These cases have been decided on the principle of the best interest of the child. A notable case involving custody of "Baby M" resulted in sole custody of the child granted to the biological father, William Stern, with Mary Beth Whitehead, the biological mother, granted visitation rights (*Matter of Baby M* [(537 A. 2d 1227 (N.J. 1988)]). Stern sought to have the surrogacy contract enforced and to have Whitehead ordered by the court to surrender custody of the child to him. He also sought to have her parental rights terminated by the courts so that his wife could adopt Baby M. The court ruled that enforcement of the surrogacy contract would go against state statutes that required proof of unfitness or abandonment of the child in order for the court to terminate parental rights. The court found that, while it would be in the best interests of Baby M to reside with her father, Whitehead would be granted visitation rights. In another case, *In re Adoption of Matthew B.-M.* (284 Cal. Rptr. 18 [Cal. App. 1 Dist. 1991]), after the social mother had filed for adoption, the surrogate attempted to withdraw her consent to adopt and to vacate judgment of paternity. The court denied the surrogate's motion and ruled that it was in the best interests of the child to remain with his biological father and social mother.

In one case (*In re Adoption of Reams* [557 N.E. 2d 159 (Ohio App. 1989)]), a male not genetically related to the child was allowed to file a petition of adoption of a child born through a surrogacy arrangement. Norma Lee Stotski agreed to be a surrogate for Richard and Beverly Reams; however, insemination with Ream's semen was unsuccessful. Stotski was then successfully inseminated with semen donated by a male who was not her husband, and the child, Tessa, was given to the Reams. A year later the Reams filed for divorce. During that year, neither had filed for adoption of Tessa; however, following the divorce applications, both Mr. and Mrs. Reams filed for adoption, and a legal battle over parentage and custody began. The custody dispute between Mr. and Mrs. Reams was not resolved, in part due to the death of Mr. Reams. In a subsequent proceeding (*Reams v. Reams* [1991 WL 160052 (Ohio App.)]), it was noted that Beverly Reams (now Seymour) was not able to assume custody and care of Tessa, and a motion to stay neglect and dependency proceedings was prevented.

The gestational mother in all of the above cases was also the genetic mother. Conversely, in *Anna J. v. Mark C.* (286 Cal. Rptr. 369), the gestational mother was not genetically related to the child. The surrogacy involved the transfer of an embryo fertilized "in vitro" utilizing ovum from a woman who had undergone a hysterectomy (Crispina C.) and the semen of her husband (Mark C.). Following the birth, the surrogate (Anna J.) refused to give up the child and sought to have herself declared the legal mother of the child. The courts rejected the arguments that birth is the only way to establish the "natural" mother of a child. Utilizing California evidence statutes, the court ordered blood tests to determine the genetic mother of the child. On the basis of these tests, Crispina C. was declared the legal mother of the child.[7]

DISCUSSION

Few states have passed statutes that specifically deal with surrogate motherhood. Additionally, state statutes that do exist are not consistent in their recognition of, or prohibition of, surrogate motherhood arrangements. Ten states have passed laws that would prohibit commercial surrogate motherhood arrangements. Three states have passed laws that legitimate noncommercial surrogate motherhood arrangements but would prohibit compensation in these arrangements. A third state possibly permits both commercial and noncommercial surrogacy arrangements. It is unclear whether existing laws passed to define parent-child relationships in other situations, such as adoption and artificial insemination by donor, are applicable to surrogacy. At least five states exclude surrogate motherhood from existing statutes on adoption or artificial insemination. These statutes would prevent prohibition of surrogate motherhood based on existing statutes.

In court decisions on the applicability of statutes dealing with adoption and artificial insemination to surrogate motherhood, opinions have been mixed as well. Some court cases have held that surrogate motherhood does violate state statutes, and others have ruled that it does not. In states where surrogate motherhood is prohibited or not excluded from existing statuses, the contract is probably unenforceable in most states. However, the courts have allowed the biological father to assert paternity, to adopt the child and to sue for custody of the child. Custody disputes between the surrogate and the biological father have been decided on a case-by-case basis, and decisions have been made based on the best interests of the child. Application of this principle in surrogate motherhood most often has resulted in custody granted to the biological father (see *Matter of Baby M* and *In re Adoption of Matthew B.-M.*). In at least one case, the intended father who was not biologically related to the child was allowed to file for custody (see *In re Adoption of Reams*).

The consistency in custody disputes and decisions involving other types of reproductive technological usage have prompted some scholars to propose that the legal structure has promoted the father-child relationship over the mother-child relationship (Blankenship et al. 1991). While this particular debate is not the focus of this paper, it does contain an issue of relevance to a discussion of the mother-fetus relationship. Central to this debate is the issue of the definition of mother and father. As has been noted, the traditional legal definition of mother reflects the gestational role. The traditional legal definition of father has reflected a social role, i.e., his relationship to the mother of the child. These definitions are associated with rights and responsibilities in state statutes that define mother-child and father-child relationships. These court cases show a trend in which the saliency of the genetic relationship of the father to the child in defining the status, father, has increased. This trend is strengthened by the development of medical technology that provides more accurate data on genetic links.

While the biological role, i.e., the gestational and genetic roles combined, appears to prevail over the social role in the legal definition of mother, there is increasing recognition that the roles may be separated.

Additionally, the saliency of the genetic and social roles of mother are increasing in relative significance. There is much support for the saliency of the social role of mother in adoption law. Similarly adjudication has resulted in the gestational mother being allowed to relinquish parental rights in surrogate motherhood and adoption of the child by the social mother. The relative importance of genetic, gestational and social mother in surrogate motherhood is more difficult to assess. Among statutes that distinguish between gestational mother and genetic mother in surrogate motherhood, some declare the gestational mother to be the legal mother (see Arizona and North Dakota statutes). On the other hand, the New Hampshire statute specifies that the intended or social mother in noncommercial surrogacy with prior court approval of the contract is the legal mother, regardless of whether or not she is genetically related to the child. If, however, the surrogate refuses to relinquish parental rights within a specified time period, she is considered to be the legal mother of the child. In Virginia, the social mother in noncommercial surrogacy is considered the legal mother even if the surrogate wants to keep the child provided that the contract had prior approval of the court. If the contract did not have prior court approval, the statute defines the genetic mother as the legal mother. Additionally, adjudication, such as *Anna J. v. Mark C.,* has strengthened the saliency of the genetic role over the gestational role in defining mother. Recognition of the separation of roles would seem to indicate a decline in the saliency of gestation in defining mother. By separating the genetic, gestational and social components of the mother role and the genetic and social components of the father role, reproductive technology has complicated our legal definition of the rights and responsibilities of these relationships.

The separation of the status, mother, into separate components associated with the development and diffusion of reproductive technology has been criticized by Rothman (1989) among others. Rothman perceives the social role of mothering as beginning during gestation. The relationship is formed as the fetus and the mother interact during gestation. She utilizes sleep to illustrate how mother and fetus come to adjust to one another and accommodate each other's needs. These adjustments involve social learning by both the fetus and the mother. Fetuses learn to recognize and gain pleasure from their mother's voice. And the mother, and those close to her, respond to and gain pleasure from the communicative kicks of the fetus. For this reason, among others, Rothman opposes surrogate motherhood (Rothman 1989).

If it is recognized that the social relationship between mother and child begins during gestation, it does not necessarily follow that this relationship has the same degree of importance for all women or that the relationship may not be broken. Pregnancy has different meanings for different women. This point is articulated very well by Andrews (1989). For some women, pregnancy becomes the central focus of their lives, including building careers associated with pregnancy, such as midwifery. For others, pregnancy occupies a small but important period of their lives. And for some women pregnancy represents a burden they are reluctant or unwilling to bear. Just as reproductive decisions are not made in a vacuum, neither are pregnancies experienced in a vacuum. Social influences on the maternal-fetal relationship involve economic, marital, and health related issues among others. Any discussion of the mother-fetus relationship should take these differing issues into consideration.

Frequently, reference is made to the testimony of women who have acted as surrogates that they do not perceive the fetus they are gestating as their own and that they view the woman who will be adopting the baby as the "real" mother. These statements seem to reflect a denial of the establishment of a social relationship between the gestating mother and the fetus. Presumably, this perception is important in the adjustment of the surrogate to relinquishing her parental rights and responsibilities. For example, in comparing law firms which specialize in surrogate motherhood arrangements, Andrews (1989) noted that surrogates who get to know the couple who will be the parents of the child are better able to relinquish their mother responsibilities than women in programs who do not meet the parents at all. Surrogates who did not meet the couple worried about how the child was being cared for. Law firms that facilitate surrogate motherhood contracts, however, are not consistent in their reinforcement of this perception through counseling, support groups or other practices (Andrews 1989). This evidence provides support for regulation of surrogate motherhood arrangements to protect the individuals involved.

CONCLUSIONS

A major assumption of this paper is that the legal structure plays a significant role in defining the normative structure within which the family operates. State statutes define who is to be considered the mother and who is to be considered the father of a child and what rights and responsibilities are associated with these relationships. Surrogate motherhood provides a reproductive alternative to childlessness and/or adoption that is attractive to many individuals. For this reason, surrogate motherhood arrangements will probably continue to be made whether or not they are legitimated by the legal system. If these arrangements are made without legitimation, they will be made in an unregulated manner that could have serious consequences. As evidenced by court cases, unregulated surrogate motherhood arrangements have potential for generating conflict over the rights and responsibilities of the individuals toward the child.

At present a legal lag exists between the development of reproductive technology and the response of the legal structure to its use in surrogate motherhood arrangements. This legal lag has resulted in legal ambiguity related to the parenting rights and responsibilities of involved individuals. In the process of responding to this ambiguity and conflicts related to it through legislation or adjudication, the legal structure will define, or redefine, the concept, mother. This definition, or redefinition, will potentially impact on the mother-fetus relationship by increasing or decreasing its importance. At present, it appears that the limited legal response has decreased the importance of the gestational component of the definition of mother and thus decreased the importance of the relationship between the mother and the fetus.

Legitimation of surrogate motherhood would increase the saliency of the social role in the legal definition of mother. This definition places an emphasis on the importance of the fulfillment of the rights and responsibilities of the mother in the relationship between the mother and the child. It would also take into consideration an increased social recognition that rights and responsibilities of parenting, including nurturing, may be accomplished by someone other than a biological parent, e.g., a stepparent, regardless of gender. The responsibility of nurturing, for example, is increasingly becoming part of our notion of the responsibilities of fathers. Thus, legal emphasis on the social role in the mother-child relationship as a social role reflecting intentions, rights and responsibilities but not necessarily a gestational relationship would be compatible with the social changes that have already occurred in the United States.

An increased emphasis on the genetic role in defining the mother-child relationship would also be consistent with legal and social changes. Advances in medical technology have increased our ability to define genetic links between individuals. The historical notion of defining a father-child relationship by the male's relationship to the mother has been undermined by statutes that allow rebuttal of paternity through the use of these medical advances.

If legitimation of surrogate motherhood is extended further in the legal structure, it will very likely take some form of contractual parenting exemplified by existing statutes outlined above. Further consideration of legitimation of surrogate motherhood through legislation proposals, however, should address specific questions that consider the possible conflict between personal liberties and compelling state interests.

- Should remuneration for surrogates be allowed? If so, what would be appropriate remuneration? Or does remuneration violate compelling state interests prohibiting exploitation of poor women and/or commercialization of reproduction?
- Should surrogate motherhood be utilized only by infertile couples? Would utilization by singles, homosexual couples, or other alternatives to the nuclear family violate a compelling state interest in protection of the family?
- Under what circumstances and for how long should the parties involved be allowed to void the contract? Would prohibiting a surrogate from breaching the contract by failing to terminate parental rights violate a compelling state interest in protection of the mother-child relationship?
- Who should control the conduct of the surrogate during pregnancy: the surrogate, the physician, the couple? Could the surrogate's right to autonomy in pregnancy decisions be undermined by recognition of the rights of the fetus as a full human being?

Debate on these questions, however, should include views other than those of the legal structure and should take into consideration the societal, political and economic impact of legitimation. If surrogate motherhood is legitimated and regulated, there will be a potential for societal consequences that have not been anticipated. One of the unintended consequences of legitimated surrogate motherhood could involve a decrease in the perceived importance of gestation in the definition of mother and an increased emphasis on the genetic and social roles in this definition. Contractual parenting requires that the intentions, rights and responsibilities of all parties involved be delineated in the contract. This procedure calls for the introduction of rationality into an area of social life which is laden with emotion. This extension of rationality represents a departure from traditional notions on the importance of the mother-fetus relationship. Contracting to relinquish parental rights by the gestational mother is a major part of this departure. Indeed, this may be the most disturbing aspect of surrogate motherhood for many people. Others, however, may view this aspect of surrogate motherhood as very positive. Through contractual parenting in surrogate motherhood, each child would be conceived intentionally by individuals who want that child very much and would, therefore, presumably be conscientious in their fulfillment of the responsibilities defined by the parent/child relationship.

NOTES

1. I want to thank Jency J. James, M.L.S., Bonny G. Bronson, Ph.D. and M. Carolyn Fuentes, J.D. for their assistance in the Westlaw search. I want to thank Juanita M. Firestone, Ph.D. and Mary M. Hale, D.P.A. and the anonymous reviewers for their suggestions on the text of this article.

2. In artificial insemination, fertilization occurs asexually through the injection of semen into the vagina. Embryo lavage in artificial insemination involves flushing the fertilized ovum from the uterus and transferal to another female. The in vitro fertilization process involves removal of ova from a female, fertilization "in vitro" and return of the fertilized ova to the woman for implantation. The term embryo transfer refers to the transfer of the fertilized ova to a female who did not provide the ova. In cryopreservation, liquid nitrogen is used to preserve sperm, ova, or embryos for later use in artificial insemination or in vitro fertilization (McCuen 1990).

3. Surrogacy arrangements are not a novel concept. Surrogacy is documented in the Bible (see Genesis 16:2 and 30:3) and continues in contemporary society in informal arrangements. The use of reproductive technology in surrogacy arrangements and commercial surrogacy, the formalization of surrogacy arrangements through contracts and compensation for that participation, are a contemporary phenomenon.

4. In *C.M. v. C.C.* (377 A. 2d 821), a semen donor was awarded parental rights and responsibilities for a child conceived through the use of artificial insemination by a single woman. These rights and responsibilities were awarded because the court declared that it was in the best interests of the child to have two parents. By contrast, while the semen donor in *Jhordan C. v. Mary K.* (234 Cal Rptr. 530 [Cal. App. 1 Dist. 1986]) was awarded visitation rights, the court specifically designated that the decision was not intended to make a judicial statement on a preference for the traditional family.

5. The court did not rule on whether surrogacy violated California's AID (artificial insemination by donor) laws in *Sherwyn & Handel v. Dept. of Social Services* (218 Cal. Rptr. 778 [Cal. App. 2 Dist. 1985]) due to a lack of justiciable controversy.

6. In Matter of *Anonymous v. Anonymous* (1991 WL 228555 [N.Y. Fam. Ct.]), the court dismissed a petition for entry of an order of filiation. The court declared the surrogate and her husband to be the parents of the child.

7. In a Michigan district court case, *Smith v. Jones,* the genetic mother was declared the mother of a child born to a gestational surrogate (Andrews 1989).

REFERENCES

Ahlburg, Dennis A. and Carol J. De Vita. 1992. "New Realities of the American Family." *Population Bulletin.* 47:1-44.

Andrews, Lori B. 1981. "Removing the Stigma." *Family Advocate.* 4:20-25, 44.

_____ 1989. *Between Strangers: Surrogate Mothers, Expectant Fathers, & Brave New Babies.* New York: Harper & Row.

Anna J. v. Mark C. 1991. 286 Cal. Rptr 369.

Anonymous v. Anonymous. 1991. WL 228555 (N.Y. Fam. Ct.).

Blankenship, Kim M. et al. 1991. "Reproductive Technologies and the U.S. Courts." Paper presented at the 1991 Annual Meetings of the Society for the Study of Social Problems, Cincinnati, Ohio.

C.M. v. C.C. 1977. 377 A. 2d 821.

Corea, Gena. 1985. *The Mother Machine: Reproductive Technology from Artificial Insemination to Artificial Womb.* New York: Harper.

Dodd, Betty J. 1982. "The Surrogate Mother Contract in Indiana." *Indiana Law Review.* 15:807-830.

Doe v. Kelley. 1981. Mich. App., 307 N.W. 2d 438.

Graham, M. Louise. 1982. "Surrogate Gestation and the Protection of Choice." *Santa Clara Law Review.* 22:291-322.

Griswold v. Connecticut. 1976. 381 U.S. 479, 485-86.

In re Adoption of Matthew B.-M. 1991. 284 Cal. Rptr. 18, Cal. App. 1 Dist.

In re Adoption of Reams. 1989. 557 N.E. 2d 159.

Jhordan C. v. Mary K. 1986. 234 Cal Rptr. 530 (Cal. App. 1 Dist.).

Johnsen, Dawn. 1987. "A New Threat to Pregnant Women's Autonomy." *Hastings Center Report.* (Aug.):33-40.

Keller, Suzanne. 1971 "Does the Family Have a Future?" *Journal of Comparative Family Studies.* 11:1-14.

Matter of Adoption of Baby Girl L.J. 1986. 505 N.Y.S. 2d 813.

Matter of Baby M. 1988. 537 A. 2d 1227.

McCuen, Gary E. 1990. *Hi-Tech Babies: Alternative Reproductive Technologies.* Hudson, WI: Gary E. McCuen Publications, Inc.

Parker, Philip J., M.D. 1983. "Motivation of Surrogate Mothers: Initial Findings." *American Journal of Psychiatry.* 140:114-118.

Reams v. Reams. 1991. WL 160052 (Ohio App.).

Robertson, John A. 1983. "Surrogate Mothers: Not So Novel After All." *The Hastings Center Report.* 13:28-34.

Robertson, John A. and Joseph D. Schulman. 1987. "Pregnancy and Prenatal Harm to Offspring: The Case of Mothers with PKU." *Hastings Center Report.* (August):23-33.

Robinson, Cherylon. 1987. *The Legal Structure, the Family, and Reproductive Technology: A Sociological Analysis.* Unpublished dissertation.

Roe v. Wade. 1973. 410 U.S. 113.

Rothman, Barbara Katz. 1989. *Recreating Motherhood: Ideology and Technology in a Patriarchal Society.* New York: W.W. Norton & Company.

Sherwyn & Handel v. Dept. of Social Services. 1985. 218 Cal. Rptr. 778 (Cal. App. 2 Dist.).

Skinner v. Oklahoma. 1942. 316 U.S. 535.

Smith, George P. II. 1983. "The Razor's Edge of Human Bonding: Artificial Fathers and Surrogate Mothers." *Western New England Law Review.* 5:639-666.

Spallone, Patricia and Deborah Lynn Steinberg. 1987. *Made to Order: The Myth of Reproductive and Genetic Progress.* New York: Pergamon Press.

Surrogate Parenting v. Com. Ex Rel. Armstrong Ky. 1986. 704 S.W. 2d 209.

Syrkowski v. Appleyard. 1985. 362 N.W. 2d 211.

Townsend, Margaret D. 1982. "Surrogate Mother Agreements: Contemporary Legal Aspects of a Biblical Notion." *University of Richmond Law Review.* 16:467-483.

Vieth, Perry J. 1981. "Surrogate Mothering: Medical Reality in a Legal Vacuum." *Journal of Legislation.* 8:140-159.

APPENDIX A
Procedures Used in Reproductive Technology

Situation	Medical Procedure	
	Artificial Insemination	In Vitro Fertilization
Donation Not Needed	I. The semen of the husband is used to inseminate his wife. The procedure is called homologous artificial insemination or AI by husband (AIH).	V. The ovum of the wife is retrieved by laparoscopy, fertilized "in vitro" with the husband's sperm. The embryo is then implanted in the wife.
Ova Donation	II. The ova donor is inseminated with the semen of the man who is to be the father of the child. The embryo is then flushed from her uterus through lavage and implanted into the uterus of the wife.	VI. The ovum of the donor is retrieved through laparoscopy and fertilized "in vitro" with the semen of the man who is to be the father of the child. The embryo is transferred to the uterus of his wife.
Womb Donation (Surrogate Motherhood)	IIIa. AID is used to inseminate a woman other than the donor's wife who carries the child to birth and then relinquishes custody to the couple. IIIb. AIH and embryo flushing could be combined to have a surrogate carry a child that was completely genetically related to the adopting couple.	VII. The ovum of a woman is fertilized "in vitro" with the semen of her husband. The embryo is transferred to another woman to be carried to birth and then relinquished to the couple.

Medical Procedure

Situation	Artificial Insemination	In Vitro Fertilization
Semen Donation	IVa. The semen of the donor is used to inseminate a woman. This procedure is called heterologous artificial insemination or AI by donor (AID). IVb. Semen donation may also be used in Situations II and III.* IVc. The semen of a donor may be combined with the semen of the husband to obscure paternity. This is called combined artificial insemination (AIC.).	VIIIa. Donated semen may be used to fertilize an ovum which is to be implanted in the woman from whom it was retrieved. The fertilized ovum is then implanted into the wife. VIIIb. Semen donation may also be used in Situations VI and VII.

*In situations IVb and VIIIb, the child would have five parents; a genetic father and mother, a gestational mother and a social mother and father (Robinson, 1987).

APPENDIX B
Provisions of Surrogate Motherhood Statutes

Statutes	Noncommercial Surrogate Motherhood Legitimated	Commercial Surrogate Motherhood Legitimated	Provision: Contract Declared Void and Unenforceable	Definition of Mother	Custody Disputes Decided by Court
Arizona	no	no		gestational	
Arkansas	yes	unclear	unclear	social	
Florida	yes	no	commercial only		
Indiana	no	no	yes		x
Kentucky	no	no	yes		
Louisiana	no	no	yes		
Michigan	no	no	yes		x
Nebraska	no	no	yes		
New Hampshire	yes	no	commercial only	gestational	
New York	no	no	yes	gestational	x
North Dakota	no	no	yes	gestational	
Utah	no	no	yes	gestational	x
Virginia	yes	no	compensation only	social/genetic	
Washington	no	no	yes		x

224

*The social mother is the mother of the child in court approved surrogacy arrangements. The genetic mother is the mother of the child in surrogacy arrangements that did not have court approval.

About the Contributors

ROBERT BLANK is Professor in Political Science at the University of Canterbury, Christchurch, New Zealand. Among his twelve books in biomedical policy are *Regulating Reproduction* (Columbia, 1990), *Mother and Fetus* (Greenwood, 1992), and *Women and the Workplace,* (Columbia, forthcoming).

JULIANNA S. GONEN is a doctoral candidate and adjunct lecturer in political science at American University in Washington, D.C. She is completing her dissertation which is a feminist legal analysis of reproductive hazards in the workplace and gender discrimination in employment.

JAY E. KANTOR is Adjunct Associate Professor of Psychiatry (Medical Humanities) at New York University Center. He chairs the Ethics Committee at the Veterans Hospital in Montrose, New York, and serves on other hospital ethics committees. His works include the textbook, *Medical Ethics for Physicians-in-Training.*

SALLY J. KENNEY is Assistant Professor with a joint appointment in Political Science and Women's Studies at the University of Iowa. She served as a consultant to the House Education and Labor Committee overseeing the EEOC's handling of cases on exclusionary policies. Her book, *For Whose Protection? Reproductive Hazards and Exclusionary Policies in Britain and the United States* is published by the University of Michigan Press.

ROSALIND LADD is Professor of Philosophy at Wheaton College, Norton, Massachusetts, and co-author of *Ethical Dilemmas in Pediatrics.*

EILEEN L. MCDONAGH is Associate Professor of Political Science at Northeastern University and a Visiting Scholar at the Murray Research Center, Radcliffe College. She has written in the areas of American political development, gender and the state, woman suffrage, and has a forthcoming book on abortion. She has published in political science and other social science journals.

225

JANNA C. MERRICK is Associate Dean and Professor of Political Science, University of South Florida at Sarasota, and Visiting Scholar, Center for Biomedical Ethics, University of Minnesota School of Medicine. She is a former Visiting Scholar at the Hastings Center. She collaborated with Arthur L. Caplan and Robert H. Blank in editing *Compelled Compassion: Government Intervention in the Treatment of Critically Ill Newborns* (Humana, 1992). She is currently co-authoring a book on reproductive rights.

ROBERT M. NELSON, M.D., is Assistant Professor of Pediatrics and Bioethics in the Department of Pediatrics and Center for the Study of Bioethics at the Medical College of Wisconsin in Milwaukee. Certified in Pediatrics, Neonatology and Pediatric Critical Care, Dr. Nelson is Medical Director of the Neonatal Intensive Care Unit at Children's Hospital of Wisconsin.

LYNN PASQUERELLA received her Ph.D. in philosophy from Brown University. She is currently Associate Professor of Philosophy at the University of Rhode Island, where she is a past recipient of the Excellence Award for Teaching. Her recent writing has focused on ethics and public policy and the philosophy of mind.

BAMBI ROBINSON received her Ph.D. in philosophy from the Ohio State University. Currently she is an Assistant Professor of Philosophy at Southeast Missouri State University. She also works at Southeast Missouri Hospital, both as a member of the ethics committee and an ethics consultant.

CHERYLON ROBINSON, Ph.D., is Assistant Professor of Sociology at The University of Texas at San Antonio. In the area of reproductive technology she has published the results of an attitudinal survey conducted with Gay Young. She is currently interviewing women who served with the Red Cross in Viet Nam.

RACHEL ROTH is a Ph.D. candidate in political science at Yale University, where she has helped organize the Graduate Employees and Students Organization (GESO). She has worked at the National Center for Youth Law and at the University of California's Center for Reproductive Health Policy.

SUZANNE U. SAMUELS completed her J.D. and Ph.D. degrees at the State University of New York at Buffalo. She is an Assistant Professor at Seton Hall University. Dr. Samuels is a member of the New York State Bar Association and has done pro bono work for the Legal Aid Society and the N.O.W. Legal Defense and Education Fund.

THOMAS C. SHEVORY is Assistant Professor of Politics at Ithaca College. Recent publications include: "Through a Glass Darkly: Law, Politics, and Frozen Human Embryos," *Issues in Reproductive Technology I: An Anthology,* ed., Helen B. Holmes, Garland Publishing, 1992. And, "Where's the Rest of Me? Biotechnology, Legal Rights, and the Case of John Moore," *Southeastern Political Review,* forthcoming.

SHERI SMITH received her Ph.D. in philosophy from Brown University and is professor of philosophy at Rhode Island College. Her recent work in applied ethics and moral philosophy includes articles sponsored by the Rhode Island Committee for the Humanities in conjunction with the Trinity Repertory Theater.

Index

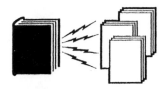

Haworth
DOCUMENT DELIVERY
SERVICE
and Local Photocopying Royalty Payment Form

This new service provides (a) a single-article order form for any article from a Haworth journal and (b) a convenient royalty payment form for local photocopying (not applicable to photocopies intended for resale).

- *Time Saving:* No running around from library to library to find a specific article.
- *Cost Effective:* All costs are kept down to a minimum.
- *Fast Delivery:* Choose from several options, including same-day FAX.
- *No Copyright Hassles:* You will be supplied by the original publisher.
- *Easy Payment:* Choose from several easy payment methods.

Open Accounts Welcome for . . .
- Library Interlibrary Loan Departments
- Library Network/Consortia Wishing to Provide Single-Article Services
- Indexing/Abstracting Services with Single Article Provision Services
- Document Provision Brokers and Freelance Information Service Providers

MAIL or *FAX* THIS ENTIRE ORDER FORM TO:

Attn: **Marianne Arnold**
Haworth Document Delivery Service
The Haworth Press, Inc.
10 Alice Street
Binghamton, NY 13904-1580

or FAX: (607) 722-1424
or CALL: 1-800-3-HAWORTH
(1-800-342-9678; 9am-5pm EST)

PLEASE SEND ME PHOTOCOPIES OF THE FOLLOWING SINGLE ARTICLES:
1) Journal Title: _____
  Vol/Issue/Year:_____Starting & Ending Pages:_____
Article Title:_____

_____

2) Journal Title: _____
  Vol/Issue/Year:_____Starting & Ending Pages:_____
Article Title:_____

_____

3) Journal Title: _____
  Vol/Issue/Year:_____Starting & Ending Pages:_____
Article Title:_____

_____

4) Journal Title: _____
  Vol/Issue/Year:_____Starting & Ending Pages:_____
Article Title:_____

_____

(See other side for Costs and Payment Information)

COSTS: Please figure your cost to order quality copies of an article.

1. Set-up charge per article: $8.00
   ($8.00 × number of separate articles)   _____

2. Photocopying charge for each article:
   1-10 pages: $1.00   _____
   11-19 pages: $3.00   _____
   20-29 pages: $5.00   _____
   30+ pages: $2.00/10 pages   _____

3. Flexicover (optional): $2.00/article   _____

4. Postage & Handling: US: $1.00 for the first article/
   $.50 each additional article   _____
   Federal Express: $25.00   _____
   Outside US: $2.00 for first article/
   $.50 each additional article _____

5. Same-day FAX service: $.35 per page   _____

6. Local Photocopying Royalty Payment: should you wish to copy the article yourself. Not intended for photocopies made for resale. $1.50 per article per copy (i.e. 10 articles x $1.50 each = $15.00)   _____

GRAND TOTAL: _____

METHOD OF PAYMENT: (please check one)

❑ Check enclosed   ❑ Please ship and bill. PO # _____
(sorry we can ship and bill to bookstores only! All others must pre-pay)

❑ Charge to my credit card: ❑ Visa; ❑ MasterCard; ❑ American Express;

Account Number:_____ Expiration date:_____

Signature: X_____ Name: _____
Institution: _____ Address: _____
City: _____ State:_____ Zip:_____
Phone Number: _____ FAX Number: _____

MAIL or *FAX* THIS ENTIRE ORDER FORM TO:

Attn: **Marianne Arnold**
Haworth Document Delivery Service
The Haworth Press, Inc.
10 Alice Street
Binghamton, NY 13904-1580

or FAX: (607) 722-1424
or CALL: 1-800-3-HAWORTH
(1-800-342-9678; 9am-5pm EST)